Popular Religion
in the Middle Ages

ROSALIND AND CHRISTOPHER BROOKE

Popular Religion in the Middle Ages

WESTERN EUROPE 1000–1300

with 44 illustrations

BARNES
&NOBLE
BOOKS
NEW YORK

Contents

Acknowledgments — 7

I Prologue — 9

II Relics and pilgrims — 14

Relics of St Bartholomew, St Alban and St Benedict 15 ·
The attitude to relics 16 · The treatise of Guibert
de Nogent 17 · The relics of Peterborough 19 ·
Pilgrimage 21 · The pilgrim guide to St James
and Compostela 22 · Conques and Sainte-Foy 26 ·
The appeal of Conques and natural beauty 29

III The saints — 31

The cult of the Blessed Virgin 31 · The Blessed Virgin
and church dedications 33 · St Nicholas 34 · St Michael 34 ·
The example of Winchester: St Peter and St Swithun 35 ·
Winchester Cathedral and the hierarchy of earth and
heaven 38 · Saints and shrines 38 · Canterbury and
St Thomas Becket 40 · Westminster Abbey and St Edward
the Confessor 41 · The saints and their miracles 42 ·
The living saint 44

IV What is popular religion? — 46

Europe 1000–1300: social structure 47 · The religious
orders 48 · Political structure: Church and kings 50 ·
The papal reform of the 11th century: papal monarchy 52 ·
The Crusading movement 56 · Popular religion 61

V   Popular and unpopular religion   **63**

Churches as evidence – their sites 63 · Style and
furnishing 83 · The example of Vézelay 91 ·
Anti-clericalism, dissent and heresy 94 · Scoffers
and blasphemers 95 · Missionaries and toleration 97
Heretics: Waldensians and Cathars 99

VI   The laity and the Church   **104**

Baptism and confirmation 104 · Burial 107 ·
Marriage 110 · The eucharist 115 · Confession 118 ·
Cathedrals and the laity 119 · Amiens 120 · Moral
teaching and the preacher 123 · Lambert le Bègue 125
Montaillou 125 · St Francis 126 · The Beguines 129

VII   The Bible   **130**

The Bible and the laity 130 · The Bible in art 133 ·
Saint-Savin and the Old Testament 134 · Zillis and the
life of Jesus 137 · The Passion, and the *Dream
of the Rood* 139 · Drama and the friars 140 · St Ailred
and *Jesus at the age of twelve* 141 · Christina of
Markyate and the compassion of Jesus 145

VIII   Judgment   **146**

Heaven, hell and purgatory 147 · The day of Judgment 150
The heaven and hell of Gislebertus 151 · The day of
wrath – *dies irae* 152 · The Jubilee of 1300 153 ·
Epilogue – The heaven and hell of Aucassin 155

Abbreviations   **156**

Bibliographical note and references   **157**

List of illustrations   **167**

Index   **171**

Acknowledgments

We take pleasure first of all in thanking the many friends and colleagues who have helped us to study the themes of this book, and particularly – since it is an essay on the borders of history and art history – the art historians, among whom special mention must be made of George Zarnecki, Neil Stratford and George Henderson. We owe valuable advice and references to Margaret Gibson, Elizabeth Hallam Smith, Paul Hodges, Robert Markus, Robert Ombres OP, Susan Ridyard and Benedicta Ward SLG; for several of the ideas used in our pages on the Crusades, we are indebted to Colin Morris and Jonathan Riley-Smith. In earlier days Hugh Sacker and Marianne Wynne helped us to understand Wolfram von Eschenbach. Barbara Hesse not only introduced us to Zillis and San Romerio but provided us with invaluable material on their history. Wim Swaan took the photographs reproduced in plates 15 and 24 especially for this book – and to him and to all others noted in the list of illustrations we make our grateful acknowledgment. We explored Wells Cathedral with Linzee Colchester, and to him and to many others who helped us to see the churches of this book we are deeply grateful. The debt we owe to Raoul Manselli and Cinzio Violante will be evident to readers of many of our pages. We have explored the libraries of London and Cambridge together and owe a particular debt to the staff of the Cambridge University Library; we pay special tribute now to the constant and devoted help of the late George Stannard. Professor Geoffrey Barraclough first suggested to RB that she write this book, and for that we shall always be grateful to him.

For permission to quote copyright material from *The Ecclesiastical History of Orderic Vitalis* (pp. 147-9) we are indebted to Dr Marjorie Chibnall and the Delegates of the Oxford University Press; and for similar permission for *The Works of Aelred of Rievaulx* (pp. 142-4) to Cistercian Publications, now of Kalama-

7

zoo, Michigan 49008, USA, and the Editorial Director, Dr E. Rozanne Elder.

Above all, for their patience, and for their help in the production of this book, we are sincerely grateful to the staff of Thames and Hudson.

It has been a true work of collaboration, and our final words must be to each other, for if we had not written it together, it would have been finished long ago, or not at all; at any rate, it would have been a very different book.

RB
CB

August 1982

I

Prologue

When we started to collect material for this book in the early 1970s, popular religion was a neglected subject: we had the idea of forming the spearhead of a revival. Like the Duke of Plazatoro, we now find ourselves leading the regiment from behind; the intervening decade has seen columns of books and articles pass by. But no general appraisal of the theme has appeared in the English-speaking world, and Professor Raoul Manselli's masterly introduction only partly overlaps with the true purpose of this book; and so we have persisted in our task.

Our first aim is to penetrate the religious aspirations, hopes and fears, and doctrines, of ordinary lay people in western Christendom.* The interest of such an enquiry is manifest, and it is evidently essential for any understanding of medieval religion. But the task bristles with difficulties. Most layfolk in these centuries were illiterate; we cannot enter their minds through their favourite literature. Buildings and artefacts are more helpful: for we can reconstruct much of the physical setting of their lives, contemplate the churches in which they worshipped, and the images of stone and glass which they looked at and valued. Even this is not always simple: the finest of medieval churches come to us altered and mutilated almost beyond recognition; we have to apply knowledge and imagination in copious draughts to see what they saw. Nor is it easy to enter the minds of lay observers, for educated clergy played the major part in issuing instructions to the architects and craftsmen who worked for them; and there is a world between the patron and the worshipper which has to be explored before we can look at medieval art with medieval eyes.

---

* There was indeed a wide spectrum of different viewpoints, from those of the educated clergy to the half-educated or downright ignorant clergy; and among the laity not only many social gradations, but many layfolk, especially in southern Europe, with a measure of learning and education. We hope that these gradations will become clearer as we proceed; and we never lose sight of them, even if for brevity we sometimes speak as if the clergy were educated, the laity unlearned.

None the less, here must be the beginning of any serious attempt to reconstruct the setting and significance of popular religion; and this book is first and foremost an attempt to reconcile the physical remains of the period, wood and stone and glass and paint, and the natural world in which they were set, with the ideas, ideals and attitudes of those who saw these works and worshipped in these buildings between 1000 and 1300.

The contemporary literature from this world was mostly the work of educated clergy, but it still has much to tell us of the activities and outlook of the laity as well. Critical insight and subtlety of interpretation are needed to discern the points of contact and the differences between lay and clerical attitudes, but the task is not impossible. A quick reading of the earliest chronicles of the First Crusade might not reveal to us that one was written by a layman, the others by clerks: their zeal and enthusiasm and sense of divinely inspired drama were almost identical. In the mid-13th century we have a marvellous spectrum of the prejudices of a 13th-century Englishman in the writings of Matthew Paris, the St Albans monk: however exaggerated and unattractive many of them may be – narrowminded, chauvinist, blinkered as they are – they are authentic of their age. They do not reflect what everybody thought; they show us something of the range of his ideas.

Sometimes the layman talks directly to us. The *Gesta Francorum* of the First Crusade is exceptional; much commoner are the surviving examples of vernacular literature. Many indeed were composed in their present form by clergy; but even these commonly revealed what a lay audience wished or was made to hear. The best take us straight to the heart of the lay world. This can seem a little paradoxical. Shakespeare's mind and attitudes were much more exceptional than those of Archbishop Whitgift or Archbishop Bancroft; by the same token must we not reckon the ideas expressed in the most sophisticated literature further away from normal minds than those of the literate clergy of lesser genius? There is some truth in this; but it is much more significant that Shakespeare reveals to us the range and limit of possible ideas, many of which would otherwise have seemed inconceivable, and illuminates dark corners we could not otherwise have hoped to penetrate. Some historians are inclined to the view that religious tolerance was unknown in the Middle Ages, others that under the surface it was common. Neither view will survive a reading of Wolfram von Eschenbach's *Willehalm*, in which tolerance is fiercely presented by a German knight of the early 13th century as an ideal not immediately apparent or accessible to his audience; but an ideal none the less (see p. 98).

The material, both physical and literary, is always of great fascination and often of great beauty too. But it is difficult to handle and requires a sustained effort of imagination if we are to use it at all. Equally difficult is its presentation, and it is this which has so long delayed the completion of the book, for each of the authors had a variety of ideas as to how some of the themes could be vividly presented, and these formed a kind of kaleidoscope in our minds and our discussions of overlapping, conflicting, bewildering impressions. Whether we have succeeded in the end, the reader will judge. We have tried in text and pictures both to let the evidence speak for itself and to interpret it and put it in some form and shape. To do this with any effect compels us to mingle themes and examples. At the outset we present a topic which is central to medieval religion – the cult of saints in all its ramifications, centred in relics, pursued by pilgrimage; we analyse its features and give examples of shrines and cults. Thus we declare our approach. Next we take a broad view of the religious history of the period and put our own theme in a historical frame, sketching the political and ecclesiastical background without which the rest makes no sense. In chapter V we look squarely at our major witnesses: the churches themselves, large and small, in their setting, in their design and function, in their ornament. But we have called this chapter 'Popular and unpopular religion' because we must also explore what they cannot tell us – the minds of those who were alienated from the official Church, anti-clericals, dissenters and heretics. Beyond that we can go confidently forward to examine a range of topics in which lay people met the Church: in contemplation of the Bible and the saints, and the Church's teaching, in pictures and sculpture; in the view of judgment, of heaven and hell.

This is a short book, and there is much we have to omit. A fascinating study could be made of medieval folklore, superstition and witchcraft; but although they were interwoven at many points with the threads we have followed, they are not the subject of this book (see p. 61). We say little too of popes and bishops, monks and friars; we say almost nothing of schools or learning, of theology and scholasticism. Since there was a constant flow of influence from clergy to laity, from the learned to the unlearned, something is lost by thus narrowing the view of the medieval

Church, even in a book on popular religion. Above all, the omission of the religious orders hides the source and inspiration of many ideas and practices, of the ascetic ideals and devotion to the Blessed Virgin, for example. We try to make this clear without straying far into the clerical, learned world.

It is possible to take the view that there was no such thing as 'popular' as opposed to 'learned' religion; it has been strongly argued by some scholars that the distinction is either meaningless or much overworked. It is clear that there were many overlaps, and many different strata among the clergy as well as among the laity; and we have emphasized how much of the evidence lies on the frontiers between the two. In a great church the work of the learned patron, and the unlearned mason, the needs of a clerical community and a throng of lay visitors and clergy of every kind, were all brought together in inextricable unity. Yet this underlines the need to study the very real distinctions which existed between the outlook of laity and clergy. Wolfram von Eschenbach was deeply influenced by theological trends in the 12th-century schools: who can say where the humaner influences in 12th-century theology ended and the proud independence of mind of the lay knight began? But both are needed to understand his great poems (see pp. 98-9, 114-15). Nor can we grasp the Crusades unless we see the different layers of doctrine which inspired them. Pope Urban II's mind worked on quite a different level from Peter the Hermit's; their doctrines were as unlike as reasonably clean water and a muddy pool covered with weeds (see pp. 58-9). Peter's doctrine horrifies us; Wolfram's is inspiring: popular religion may sometimes seem to us a dark force, sometimes like a great shaft of light. The religious climate of these centuries will never be clear unless we see that there were real differences.

Our period stretches from the year 1000, one of many when the world could be supposed to be drawing to its end, to 1300 when the Jubilee, to which the Pope was urged by popular enthusiasm, ushered in a new style of devotion. These were centuries of change in thought and art and religious inspiration; and the revival of urban life in a world whose social relations and assumptions still centred in the feudal knight and the peasant meant profound changes in the social and economic environment of religious practice. Popular religion itself heralded these changes: the growth of long-distance trade, which was one of the main causes of economic change, was made conceivable by the assumption that distant travel was possible in a thoroughly static world, and this was as much due to the adventures of pilgrims and Crusaders as to the enterprise of merchants. The famous story of St Godric of Finchale, who was a merchant turned pilgrim, nicely illustrates the link; doubtless there were many pilgrims who were inspired to become merchants too. Thus there was a unity in this world which makes the subject manageable.

The hardier pilgrims, and the Crusaders who survived the rigours of the march, visited the Byzantine Empire and Jerusalem. In Byzantium they saw a different Christian tradition with its own literature and art, and on the road to Jerusalem they passed through Moslem country and saw Islam at first hand, as many Westerners could also do in Spain and Sicily. Some Western literature breathes a deep spirit of distrust and dislike for these alien cultures – a distrust amply repaid by the writers of Byzantium and Islam. But the history of Western art in this period tells a different story: it could be said, much too simply, that the great change which came over Western painting in the 12th and 13th centuries was due primarily to the influence of Byzantine models and aspirations; and the great change in architecture was the adoption of the Islamic, Gothic arch. We shall try to make sense of this half-truth later on (pp. 83-8, 164). Meanwhile they remind us that western Europe did not live in total isolation, that it was part of a larger world, of art and culture, of thought and sentiment. Nor was it only art and architecture which were affected by movement across the frontiers of Christendom. Scientific understanding and the whole world of magic and astrology and superstition so closely linked to it were evidently transformed in this period by contact with Islam. To some, magic and witchcraft touch the very essence of popular religion. To us they must lie on the periphery, for the history of witchcraft in the central Middle Ages cannot be written; the evidence is desperately obscure. The nature of our evidence compels us to concentrate on saints and relics and other aspects of popular devotion in which clergy and laity mingled. To make this abstract statement breathe and live, we proceed at once to view the shrines and reliquaries of Western Christendom in the 11th and 12th centuries.

II
Relics and pilgrims

The chronicler Raoul Glaber described in a famous passage in his chronicle how about the year 1000 the earth was covered with a white mantle of new churches; and how subsequently relics of the saints in unwonted numbers were brought to light. Glaber was a wandering monk, an inveterate gossip; but he was genuinely observing and describing the first beginnings of a great religious revival, with a popular religious movement at its roots, at or near whose centre lay a new fervour for saints and relics and pilgrimages, whose chief memorial and witness today are the remains of countless churches. The precise year 1000 probably had little significance: then, as on many occasions in the last two thousand years, a few folk confidently expected the end of the world; but they soon found it necessary to wait a little longer. In a broader view it was a time of rapid change and of new movements, and the churches and the relics both reveal to us a society and a world on the move. What were these relics, and how connected with church-building, religious, social and economic change? It is a link which demands a real imaginative effort if we are to grasp it.

A fantastic assortment of bones, stray bits of timber, thought to be fragments of the True Cross, and the like, were reverently preserved as relics. Their possession brought to a church the protection of the saint and attracted pilgrims hoping for favours and miracles. Pilgrims brought offerings: a popular shrine could be a considerable source of revenue. There was a market for the relics: they were realizable assets. Aelfsige, abbot of the rich house of Peterborough from 1006/7 to 1042, spent three years with Queen Emma when she was in exile in Normandy, and while he was there there was a severe famine in France. The monks of Saint-Florentin de Bonneval near Chartres had sold everything they could for food; they had nothing more to sell except their patron saint, St Florentin. Aelfsige bought all of him except his head and shipped him off to Peterborough Abbey, together with many other relics and church ornaments he had been able to buy on the cheap.

Relics of St Bartholomew, St Alban and St Benedict

Famine threatened too in the south of Italy, in Apulia, and the Bishop of Benevento reckoned that the arm of St Bartholomew the Apostle had been kept in his church ready for just such an emergency. He set out with it to raise money, travelling through Italy and France and accumulating gifts, until he finally reached England, where he hoped to receive most of all, for England was wealthy and the queen benevolent to the Church. Queen Emma, indeed, now Cnut's wife and long since restored to her English throne, gave liberally, but the bishop found that he had still not raised enough. So the queen was asked if she would care to buy the arm. She said she was very ready to do so, provided it was genuine. The bishop swore an oath on the host and on other relics at Canterbury that it was indeed St Bartholomew's own arm and received in exchange for it several pounds of silver. It was fortunate for the citizens of Benevento that their bishop was so confident that his relic was genuine. Identification of holy bones could rest on strange criteria. Not every saint was recognized as such immediately. The bones of some were discovered years after death. Chance brought to light the body of a bishop buried in pontificals in Cambridgeshire in the late 10th century; a dream revealed that it was the corpse of a saintly Persian bishop called Ives who had come to convert the people of the region when they were in heathendom. A likely story, we would be inclined to say, whatever our religious convictions; but the little town is called St Ives to this day.

Even after they had been ensconced in shrines they might suffer vicissitudes of fortune. During the Danish raids on England, France and Flanders, many religious communities were scattered and their treasures also, and it was not only violence which disturbed their rest. In an emergency the guardians of relics thought it no sin to engage in subterfuge, and this further confused the issue. The multiplication of the bodies of St Alban occurred in this way. At a date unknown, Danish invaders or a Danish king stole him or a part of him and carried the relics back to Odense. But the sacrist went in secret pursuit, succeeded in

15

becoming sacrist at Odense and managed to steal him back again – or so it was alleged. Early in the reign of William the Conqueror, about 1069 or 1070, an abbot of St Albans found it necessary to flee to Ely. He asked the abbot of Ely to take the body temporarily into his keeping. It was later claimed he had sent to Ely a substitute body and hidden the real body of St Alban in a safe place. When the time came for Ely to return the body they also effected a substitution. So now three places, Odense, St Albans and Ely, each claimed to have St Alban's body and affirmed that the other two were fraudulent, and it passes the wit of man to determine the right of the matter. Such difficulties were not uncommon. St Benedict of Nursia had died at Monte Cassino, but his monastery was sacked not long after by the Lombards, and his community, after many travels, found themselves at Fleury, now generally known as Saint-Benôit-sur-Loire, in France. And there his body still is. Or is it? For since the 11th century at latest another body has been challenging that at Fleury from Monte Cassino itself. Probably most historians are more inclined to believe that the author of the *Rule* of St Benedict rests at Fleury; but the matter has not been solved, and, as they would have said in the 11th or 12th century, St Benedict knows.

The attitude to relics

For this was the key to the strange crimes and perplexities to which medieval relics were subjected. To the monks of Monte Cassino it was clear that Benedict himself would never allow his relics to be permanently housed elsewhere. Devotees of the shrines of the Welsh St Teilo resolved a similar problem by asserting that the saint, to prevent bloodshed after his death as three of the communities he had ruled battled for his remains, miraculously provided three bodies of himself by a singular, and perhaps unique, act of celestial diplomacy. To the pious thief of relics it seemed clear that if he succeeded in removing a saint, the saint himself must have found the move agreeable; it must be his wish. The only real danger – apart from secular penalties attaching to theft – was that the saint might be unwilling, and punish the thief with deadly penalties. Some of the practices show a very crude anthropomorphism in the attitude to the saint: if relics failed to perform the wonders that were desired they could be rebuked and even flogged. There was sometimes a violent element too in the treatment of relics when they were stolen. But the very frequent thefts of relics, especially in the 10th and 11th centuries, also show a very revealing mixture of motives both by the thieves and by the saints. Who can say in what proportions economic gain and pious enthusiasm mingled in these extraordinary adventures? Even more baffling to us is the element of fraud. To cheat a rival church was evidently necessary in a violent world; but often, it seems, relics were manufactured for local use. The story is told of a great painter who was shown a picture by a friend who had bought it supposing it to be his authentic work: with charming tact the painter signed the picture, though he knew it was not truly his. Many a medieval saint, contemplating his relics, might have been tempted to such an act. To us credulity and ingenious fraud seem far apart, as far as from innocence to crime; but when in the Middle Ages relics were stolen, invented, altered or multiplied, pious devotion and criminal fraud – and every shade of the spectrum between – were inextricably mingled.

From time to time, and increasingly in the 12th and 13th centuries, more sophisticated attitudes appear among the faithful. When St Hugh of Lincoln (*c.* 1140-1200) was visiting Fécamp at the end of the 12th century 'he extracted by biting two small fragments of the bone of the arm of the most blessed lover of Christ, Mary Magdalene' to the intense indignation of the abbot and monks. This Hugh partly mollified by saying: '"If, a little while ago I handled the most sacred body of the Lord of all the saints with my fingers, in spite of my unworthiness, and when I partook of it, touched it with my lips and my teeth, why should I not venture to treat in the same way the bones of the saints for my protection, and by this commemoration of them increase my reverence for them, and without profanity acquire them when I have the opportunity?"' And his biographer goes on to tell, with evident complaisance, how on another occasion he 'severed with a knife a protruding sinew' from the arm of St Oswald, the 7th-century Northumbrian king, at Peterborough Abbey.

The treatise of Guibert de Nogent

Even more sophisticated was the attitude revealed by the one serious treatise criticizing their use, 'The Relics of the Saints' by Guibert, Abbot óf Nogent, a French Benedictine house, written *c.* 1120. The occasion of it was the claim by the monks of St Médard at Soissons that they had a relic of Jesus himself, one tooth to wit. Owing to the Resurrection it was generally held that there could be no physical relics of Our Lord, and it was therefore on theological grounds that Guibert's suspicions were roused in the first instance. The monks of St Médard tried to argue that it was a milk tooth, a baby tooth, shed long before the Resurrection. But if so, asks Guibert, why was only one preserved? Why no hairs from his infant head? And thus we are embarked on a disquisition on authentic and inauthentic relics, and the doctrine of Christ's body, of faith and its merits. Guibert was no sceptic; he evidently believed fervently in true relics, as he understood them; but he saw the conflict between faith in relics as part of the divine scheme on the one hand, and the evidence of absurdity and cheating on the other. He is a fascinating case of a shrewd, intelligent observer. After disposing of Jesus's tooth he admits to an equal doubt about the Virgin's milk: superstitious nonsense, he declares; how improbable that it could have survived in an uncoagulated state; it would have gone off long ago. He tells a story against himself. A famous church sent a band of faithful with its best relics on an organized tour, a common way of raising money for a building fund, and when the leader of the band had spoken at length in Guibert's presence, extolling his relics, he said, 'I have here in this box some bread which Christ actually masticated with his teeth. If you do not believe me, here is a champion (he meant me, says Guibert), whom you know is a thoroughly learned man, and who will corroborate what I say.' Guibert admits that out of delicacy for the authorities of the church he blushed, but refrained from calling him a liar.

To Guibert's mind it was natural to assume God's grace, or the merits of faith, as the cause of miracles. He continues: with martyrs we do not inquire what kind of life preceded the all important death. Both Constantinople and Angers (he observes) claim the head of John the Baptist – what can be more ridiculous? . . . I have heard that Bishop Odo of Bayeux sought the body of St Exuperius, and was given the corpse of a peasant with the same name. Guibert disapproved of the exhumation of bodies from their tombs and their translation elsewhere. He disapproved too of the costliness of shrines. 'Who is worthy to be enclosed in gold and silver when the son of God was shut in by the vilest stone?'

The relics of Peterborough

In the mid–12th century Hugh Candidus, monk of Peterborough, listed all the treasury of relics at an abbey particularly well endowed. 'There is kept there a thing more precious than gold, even the right arm of St Oswald. . . . This we have seen with our own eyes and have kissed, and have handled with our own hands, and did wash it at the time when it was shown to Alexander bishop of Lincoln and all the convent and many other of the clergy and laity, in the time of Abbot Martin [in the 1130s]. . . . There are kept here also part of his ribs and of the soil on which he fell.' And he goes on to the other relics – of the swaddling clothes in which Our Lord was wrapped, two pieces, pieces of the manger of Our Lord, . . . a part of the five loaves with which Our Lord fed the 5,000; a piece of the raiment of St Mary . . . and of Aaron's rod. . . . Relics too of St Peter, St Paul, St Andrew (the three apostles to whom the church is dedicated), three other apostles and a shoulder-blade of one of the holy innocents. It is clear that Hugh Candidus fervently believed in the authenticity of one and all, and that it is not at all necessary for us to believe in the authenticity of most of them. But their interest is very great, not only for its revelation of Hugh and his world, and for the window it opens over a whole landscape of medieval popular religion, but also because it shows the wide links and ramifications of celestial trade in the central Middle Ages. English saints are well represented: not only Peterborough's own saints, including its 10th-century re-founder, Bishop Aethelwold of Winchester, some of whose hair is in the list, but northern saints like Aidan, and saints of southern England like Swithun, who was represented by an arm; and especially saints of the south-west, two teeth of Edward king and martyr, Ethelred the Unready's elder brother, killed in 978 and buried at Shaftesbury, St Aldhelm, St Grimbald, the monk from the Low Countries who had settled in Wessex under King Alfred, Egwin of Evesham, and many others. There was the usual collection of bits of Roman martyrs; from Germany and Bohemia relics of the founder of the German abbey of Corvey and of St Wenceslas, and numerous relics from France and the Low Countries, largely the product, no doubt, of Abbot Aelfsige's travels, and his good eye for a bargain.

But after the Norman Conquest Peterborough's fortunes declined for a time, and this gave Hugh the occasion for the most telling of his stories. In 1069 the last Old English abbot, Brand, died and William the Conqueror reckoned that he must have above all a good general on the edge of the unruly fens; so he moved Abbot Turold, who had already made a name for himself as a tough warrior at Malmesbury, to Peterborough. We tend to take it for granted that the Norman Conquest of England was a decisive event, but it did not necessarily seem so to contemporaries. William of Normandy had overthrown Harold; he might yet be overthrown himself. Among those who thought and hoped that he would be was the redoubtable Hereward the Wake, Brand's nephew, who formed an alliance with the King of Denmark. Denmark invaded England in 1070, and Hereward expected to see a Danish king once more on the English throne. He and his men came to Peterborough, stripped the abbey of all the gold, silver, precious stones and relics they could find and carried them off to the Danes. They also carried off the prior. He, poor man, was honoured by the Danes, but he was in an invidious position. The abbey had been damaged and robbed, the new Norman abbot was arriving, he himself was compromised, forced to remain with rebels against King William. His world was falling about him. Secretly he procured hammers and other tools. Then, while the Danes were feasting, he set to work to rescue Peterborough's most precious treasure. He was not after the gold and silver and jewels: indeed, he had to prize away the precious metals that encrusted a wooden chest. This chest was 'strongly banded with iron' and he had the greatest difficulty in breaking through the nails. But at last he succeeded in opening it. He took out – the arm of St Oswald, and hid it in his bed. Then he heard the Danes, merry with feasting, rising to hear Vespers. He was flushed and heated with his exertions, but he just had time to wash his face in cold water, and he was not suspected. It is significant that the relic he stole back belonged to St Oswald, the English king and martyr. The prior was upholding English tradition in a conquered and distracted land.

These examples can be paralleled in every corner of Europe. The affair of St Bartholomew starts in south Italy; but our best witness for the story is Eadmer, monk of Christ Church, a very devout Englishman, yet one whose deepest personal attachment was to St Anselm, the Italian turned Norman whom he knew and worshipped in his last years as Archbishop of Canterbury (1093–1109). Eadmer is best known for his *Life of Anselm* and his *History of Recent Events*, of which Anselm is the hero. Eadmer evidently liked his saints to be living men. Yet we owe many stories of relics to him, and in particular the observation that when he was a child before the Norman Conquest the English people considered the relics of saints the most valuable things in the world. Doubtless he had a heavenly market in mind more than an earthly; but trade in relics was also a remarkable foretaste or example of the relation between religion and the rise of capitalism. The technique and significance of a stock exchange were worked out while even in Italy joint-stock enterprise was in its infancy. For relics were not only valued and valuable; they bred money. Doubtless to pursue the analogy further would lead to superficial comparisons, even to blasphemy; but so far the similarity is clear.

To read Hugh Candidus one might suppose that the great age of prosperity of Peterborough Abbey was well before his day, in the 11th century, when it was called not only Peter's borough, but the golden borough. Yet to the modern visitor who inspects the colossal remains of the Romanesque church, to which later centuries added without profoundly remodelling the structure, and who wanders in the close where the arches of the Gothic infirmary now form a stone avenue to a street, it must seem clear that the building fund was never in such good heart as in the 12th century and in the early 13th. The great nave tells us more than this. We do not know in detail how it was financed, and the abbey had substantial landed resources. But it was not in the first rank of rich houses, and we may be sure that the saints of Peterborough played their part. They helped to provide the funds to pay for the stone and timber and the craftsmanship which adorned it; and the great nave in its turn advertised their power, gave Peterborough its one really large public building, and sheltered the devotees of abbey and saints when they came to celebrate the saints' feast days, or to visit their relics. Meanwhile the collecting boxes were as familiar a sight then as now, like the 'hollow trunk with a hole in the middle of the top' which the sacrist and sub-sacrist of Bury had made 'and fastened with an iron bar, and caused it to be set up in the great church near the door outside the choir, where the common folk pass to and fro, so that they might place their alms therein for the building of the tower.'

Pilgrimage

The success of particular saints has fluctuated with fashion. Throughout the central Middle Ages St James at Compostela in northern Spain and St Peter at Rome never lacked visitors in throngs, nor yet the greatest shrines of all in Jerusalem and Galilee. If in general esteem Peter and James had to yield second place to the Blessed Virgin, she left no relics behind save incidentals – pieces of her veil, miracle-worshipping images and the like; and her local attachments could not command universal acclaim. Her worshippers at Notre-Dame at Paris, for example, might not pay over-much attention to the Black Virgin of Chartres. Below this level extraordinary variations of fashion and sentiment obtained. The values of our earthly stock exchanges are the victims, or the servants, of sentiments as baffling to the outsider as any fashion, and commonly bear little coherent relation to economic realities or trends. In a similar way the fashion for many of the cults of the Middle Ages, at the human level, seems capricious, even inexplicable. It has indeed, all differences allowed, much similarity in its fluctuation and caprice to modern fashions; and one key element in the story of many cults was what we should call advertising. Of this perhaps the best surviving record is the pilgrim guide to the route to St James, Santiago de Compostela.

The pilgrim guide to St James and Compostela

The circumstances of medieval travel easily lead us to assume that men's vision was always more parochial, their chance to wander much less, than ours. Yet the cult of St Thomas Becket or the fame of a great teacher in Paris like Abelard spread with a speed and to a distance which we should still find very surprising today. A part of the explanation lies in the modes and meaning of travel in that age. A litigant in a Church court in England or Scandinavia came readily in the 12th century to envisage the possibility of pursuing his case to the papal Curia in Rome, which might be a month's or six weeks' journey away. In every part of Europe by the mid-12th century would be found survivors of one or other of the Crusades, and in many parts there were merchants and shipowners prepared to venture long distances in search of goods and profit. But the most significant and characteristic mode of travel was the pilgrimage. In the late 20th century we go to the sea or the hills; our medieval ancestors went to a shrine, or trail of shrines, far or near.

Anyone who has read the Prologue to Chaucer's *Canterbury Tales* will be familiar with two aspects of the medieval pilgrimage.

It was a great social occasion, into which religion did not necessarily enter very deeply, and it was a kind of entertainment and relaxation which bound together men and women from every walk of life. But it would be superficial and naive to empty the medieval pilgrimage of all its religious content. If we pause for a moment to consider those who gather in a great museum today, we will recognize that they comprise many different types of folk and motive: tramps and men of means who are seeking shelter; schoolboys dragooned for their good; visitors with every shade of interest, from idle curiosity or a policy of thorough to serious study. Not infrequently the student becomes bored and the idle visitor deeply interested. Irrespective of all these varieties and changes, the museum remains a major centre of learning and culture. In similar fashion the pilgrimage was a cross-section of human aspirations and follies; yet at its core lay a serious and profound religious sentiment.

For the modern traveller a host of helpful agents provide brochures, guides and tickets. In similar fashion brokers organized pilgrimages and helpful or hopeful authors wrote guides. The surviving guide takes the pilgrim by various routes through France to Compostela, lists the shrines, the provinces and rivers, and notes which have wholesome water and which are fatal to man and beast. The author urges the pilgrim to venerate the Madeleine at Vézelay – for her love, faults are forgiven, the blind see, the dumb speak, the lame walk (see pp. 91-4). St Léonard at Noblat released captives – iron chains in thousands hung in his basilica, manacles, fetters, padlocks and other instruments more barbarous than he could describe. In the far south by the mouth of the Rhône lay Saint-Gilles, speediest of all the saints to help the unfortunate and afflicted. The author himself had seen a prayer answered on the very same day. The most vivid sculpture in Provence still displays the generous gratitude with which the pilgrims of the 12th century rewarded St Giles for his aid. 10

Pilgrims on their journey passed through some wild, some desolate and some impressive scenery. To cross Les Landes tired pilgrims needed three days. It was sandy, swampy and unhealthy. In Gascony people all ate sitting round the fire, without a table, and drank from one cup. They slept all together on a thin straw mattress, the servants with the master and mistress. But the fish and pork of Castile and Galicia disagreed with strangers who were not used to them and only the very fit and the acclimatized escaped sickness. In summer there was added torment from enormous flies. At some points on the journey rivers were encountered which had to be crossed by boat. The guide called down curses on the boatmen on the rivers by Sorde, who cancelled the good effects of the Gascon red wine by extortionate charges, and worse. Their boat was small, made from a single tree trunk. 'Take care not to fall into the water. It is best to hold your horse by the bridle outside the boat and to embark with few other passengers. If overladen it sinks immediately.' The boatmen rejoiced if pilgrims drowned as they robbed the dead. In the Basque country a high mountain was crossed by the Somport pass – a mountain so high it seemed to touch the sky. 'From the summit one can see the sea and the frontiers of three countries, Castile, Aragon and France.' Charlemagne planted a cross here and pilgrims did likewise. At Lorca they found two Navarrese sharpening knives such as were used for skinning horses. They enquired whether the water was good to drink and were told that it was. 'Two of our horses immediately died and they set to work on them.' He commends or grumbles at the hospitality which may be found by the way – in some places the bread is good and the wine excellent; some are hospitable to the poor. In Galicia each pilgrim who passed through was given a stone to carry to a town further on where they were building a basilica.

The author's greatest eloquence is reserved for the ten churches of Compostela, including the Church of the Trinity, where the many pilgrims who died at their goal are buried, and above all for the Cathedral of St James. He dwells on the large fountain, where excellent, clear refreshing water flows from the mouths of four lions for the use of pilgrims and inhabitants. An inscription announces that 'I Bernard, treasurer of St James, brought the water here and raised this monument for the salvation of my soul and the souls of my family. 11 April 1122'. The provision of public amenities, roads, bridges, water supplies was throughout the Middle Ages and in widely separated parts of Europe regarded as an act of piety. Roads and bridges could be believed literally to carry the soul of the donor across the gulf to heaven. Next to the fountain were stalls where pilgrims could buy the little scallop shells that were the symbols of St James and other things they were likely to want: wine, shoes, medicines. There was money to be made out of badges, charms and souvenirs; and pedlars as well as innkeepers thrived. A pilgrim needed several different currencies on the journey and moneychangers set up stalls at many places along the routes: Vézelay, for example, and Compostela itself.

The pilgrimage to Compostela presents an intriguing puzzle. St James' connection with Spain was not suspected until the 7th century, when a scribal error in an apocryphal list of the apostle's mission fields was responsible for 'Hierusalem' (Jerusalem) becoming 'Hispania' (Spain). In the early 9th century Theodomir, Bishop of Padrón, discovered his body – or what he supposed to be his body – in a neglected tomb in a deserted cemetery out in the wilds. The Reconquest of Spain from the Moors had just begun and St James, so it was thought, had revealed himself to help the Christians in their battles. King Alfonso II informed Pope Leo III and Charlemagne of the good news. The town of Santiago de Compostela grew up on the site of the tomb. But why did this St James, of dubious origins and local belligerence, in a remote and inaccessible corner of the Iberian Peninsula, so capture the popular imagination that a pilgrimage to Compostela ranked second only to one to Rome, which had the bones of two apostles, St Peter and St Paul? His cult survived the Moslem counterattack of Al Mansur in the late 10th century, and attracted pilgrims from all over Europe in the 11th and 12th. The fame of the town, its prosperity, its very existence were owing to St James. In the early 12th century Diego Gelmirez, bishop from 1100 to 1140, rose to become archbishop and papal legate. During his episcopate the new cathedral, begun in the 11th century, was virtually completed. But relations between town and bishop were not happy in spite of their common allegiance to and mutual dependence upon St James. The bishop was powerful, ambitious and acquisitive. In 1116-17 the townsfolk, driven beyond endurance by his pride and his exactions, revolted, and the cathedral had to be turned, temporarily, into a fortress.

Why did so many people make the long, arduous, often dangerous journey to Compostela? Some, of course, went because this was part of the penance imposed on them for wrongdoing, but very many went voluntarily, and their motivation must always to some extent elude us. By the 13th century more emphasis was being placed on their state of mind. Physical endurance tests and mortifications alone were not enough. A 13th-century German Franciscan friar, Berthold of Regensburg, warned his congregation not to put their trust in almsgiving or pilgrimages, for they are all vain without true contrition. What was the point, he asked, of going all the way to Compostela to honour some bones, for the real St James was not in Galicia but in heaven, and did they not realize that by going to mass in their parish church in their own home town, they could enter into the presence of God himself, who was greater than all the saints and angels?

Conques and Sainte-Foy

In the heart of the Rouergue, in the Massif Central of France, lies the little town of Conques, set about the magnificent Abbey Church of Sainte-Foy, St Faith. Here is an enchanting monument to the pilgrims of the 11th and 12th centuries. Faith herself is supposed to have been a virgin and martyr of the late 3rd century, whose relics were preserved where she had died, at Agen on the Garonne below Toulouse and Moissac, far to the west of Conques. In the 5th century a basilica was built there for her and St Carpasius, from which she departed – or, as we should say, was stolen – in the 9th century, and settled in Conques. Here was an ancient monastery, or rather one would suppose from the site a monastic hermitage, recently revived after it had fallen into decay and ruin. In the 10th and 11th centuries first a trickle then a flood of pilgrims came; and in the 11th and 12th her great reputation, and the charm of her resting place on one of the best routes from northern and eastern France to Compostela, made Sainte-Foy an extremely prosperous pilgrim centre.

Walk about Conques and tell the towers thereof, and one cannot help being impressed by the beauty and size and splendour of the church she built. If we were to compare it with the remains of the abbey churches at Wearmouth and Jarrow in which the Venerable Bede had worshipped in the 7th and 8th centuries, we would be struck immediately by the dramatic difference in scale. We have no reason to suppose that the Church of Sainte-Foy was built for a larger community than Bede's; and apart from building this splendid church and adorning it the monks of Conques made little contribution to the culture of their age – nothing at least comparable to the intellectual, devotional and literary achievements of Bede and his circle. Nor had the men who planted the community at Conques intended so great a building. This we can infer from the narrow site on which they built. When the church was complete, the shelf in this narrow, charming, hidden valley had been filled by one enormous, very conspicuous building. To provide themselves with space for the cloister and the domestic buildings which were expected to surround it in any Benedictine community of the 11th and 12th centuries, they had to build up the soil and make a large terrace on which the remains of the cloister now sit. The fashion and the function of the abbey had quite altered.

Beyond the cloister there lay a little town: one can still trace its streets and some of its lineaments, for it has not greatly altered in shape since the 12th century. This shows us one of the many links we shall notice between the flow of pilgrims, merchants, visitors to a shrine and an abbey, and the formation of a town. The fondness for building enormous churches, long, broad and high, can be found in many parts of Europe in this age; to abbreviate a long and complex tale, it is first in evidence in Germany in the 10th century, in the cathedrals and the imperial abbeys of the Ottos; nor is there any church of the 11th century now surviving more massive or weighty, or simply impressive, than Speyer Cathedral, the spiritual home and resting place of the 11th-century German king-emperors, the successors of the Ottos. But by the time that Emperor Henry IV (1056-1106), defiant in spite of the thunders and abuse of Pope Gregory VII, was showing his devotion to God, the Blessed Virgin, and the Salian dynasty by completing its magnificent profile the fashion for enormous churches had stretched in all directions, specially to the west and the south-west. Thus a pilgrim from Speyer who came to Conques would think the church modest compared with his own Kaiserdom; but one who came from most other parts of western Christendom would have found it impressive and exciting.

The church of Conques was a large basilica to house a monastic community and a shrine: so far we are contemplating the image of a modern fashion with ancient roots. So too in function. If we could ask a monk of Sainte-Foy the question 'Who lives here?', he might have said, God, St Faith, a community of holy monks; and we provide shelter and a welcome to all who come here to join in our worship of God and our reverence for his saint. Two points in this statement need emphasis, for they are easily misunderstood. Sainte-Foy had been dead many hundreds of years when the church we know was built. But she was in the eyes of her flock fully as much alive as she had been in the 3rd century, and far more powerful. The relations between God, the dead saints and the living sinners were much more like those in the society of gods and heroes and men in Homeric society than anything with which we are familiar. Faith was the personal proprietor of her church and its domains; and wherever her admirers and her relics spread,

The Last Judgment, Conques. On our left, Christ's right, above the bottom register, St Faith kneels over those admitted through the gate: God's hand indicates her intercessions are granted.

small plots of land were set aside as a second, a third and a hundredth home for her. It was probably in the 11th century that a parish church was built in her honour in the city of London, close by the east end of St Paul's Cathedral. When the Normans brought the fashion for building enormous churches to England after 1066, a great Romanesque cathedral towered over the little church; and in the mid- and late 13th century the Apostle advanced still further east and St Faith was reduced to a modest chapel in his crypt. Sainte-Foy, St Faith in Conques, is a complete church of the 11th and early 12th centuries: a monument to belief in relics in this age, when pilgrims thronged to her for her own sake, and because she lay on the road to St James of Compostela.

All this helps to explain why the space allotted to the monks in the great church seems at first sight relatively modest. They had a part of the east end – such part as Faith herself could spare – and the crossing. But most of the nave, and the sweeping curve of the ambulatory, providing a passage for pilgrims round the saint's shrine, were for visitors to the church. The scale on which it is built is in fair measure an index of the numbers who came; the height and splendour of the building of their generous offerings at the shrine. These are more directly represented by the reliquary of St Faith herself, which can still be seen in the abbey museum, but once adorned the shrine in the abbey choir. It is an object of immense interest, for it is a direct link with the world we are trying to explore: a somewhat doll-like figure in wood coated in

28

gold, encrusted with jewels on no particular plan or pattern by innumerable rich and eminent pilgrims.

The pilgrim who came to the west end, seeking entrance to the church, was not simply invited to worship and pay, but also given fairly sharp and precise religious instruction. On the tympanum over the west door one may still contemplate a Last Judgment – a common sight in such places, yet there is something especially frightening about the Judgment at Conques. It is not a notable work of art, but the point is clear. Mankind is judged, and judged sternly; the recruits for hell are very numerous indeed. The devil and his family first catch the eye; but the observer will presently see that all is not hopeless, even for the laity.

The appeal of Conques and natural beauty

We cannot explore Conques without wondering about the beauty of its setting. Did the pilgrims who came here value not only the shrine and the chance of a holiday but the natural beauty which surrounded them? Did the first founders and re-founders also savour the beauty of the Rouergue? It is often supposed that the feeling for nature which sends thousands to the Alps or the English lakes today is a novel sentiment, invented by Wordsworth and his kind. The delight in hill and wood and water is in its essence as old as human record. The early descriptions of the Grande Chartreuse, or of some Cistercian sites – and most notably Rievaulx – make it abundantly clear that natural beauty could be accepted as an element in choosing a hermitage or a religious home.

Here is the 12th-century description in the *Life of St Ailred of Rievaulx* of the monks settling at the site of the abbey. 'They set up their huts . . . by a powerful stream called the Rie in a broad valley stretching on either side. . . . High hills surround the valley, encircling it like a crown. These are clothed by trees of various sorts and maintain in pleasant retreats the privacy of the vale, providing for the monks a kind of second paradise of wooded delight. From the loftiest rocks the waters wind and tumble down to the valley below, and as they make their hasty way through the lesser passages and narrower beds and spread themselves in wider rills, they give out a gentle murmur of soft sound and join together in the sweet notes of a delicious melody. And when the branches of lovely trees rustle and sing together and

3

the leaves flutter gently to the earth, the happy listener is filled increasingly with a glad jubilee of harmonious sound, as so many various things conspire together in such a sweet consent, in music whose every diverse note is equal to the rest. His ears drink in the feast prepared for them, and are satisfied.' And the biographer goes on to imply that this was part of the appeal for the young Ailred, who joined the community soon after, as well as evidently for himself. In that age as in this some were intensely aware of natural beauty, others no doubt quite unmoved by it.

In a similar way, there were a few, from St Benedict and some of the Celtic saints to Francis of Assisi, who had an exceptional gift with animals and feeling for them. There were more already in the 12th century, though far more in the 13th and 14th, who could portray leaves and flowers and animals with vivid, penetrating observation. Human beings vary enormously: to some it seems natural to hear God's voice in a stream or the song of a bird; to others they are indifferent or distracting. In some measure it has always been so.

Thus the study of pilgrims and pilgrimages reminds us of the variety of sentiment and attitude which attracted men and women onto the pilgrim routes. But it also emphasizes the central significance of saints and relics to the understanding of many aspects of the life of the age apart from the religious. If we consider this variety too curiously, however, we may be led to a superficial view of the cults themselves; and this can only be countered by a deeper enquiry into the meaning of some of the more remarkable cults in themselves.

III

The saints

The cult of the Blessed Virgin

At all periods of the Middle Ages the greatest of the saints was the
Blessed Virgin Mary. The cult of Our Lady represents two rival
aspects of Christian theology. If Christ is both judge and
mediator, then modest and anxious human sinners may well look
for an advocate who will mediate with Him. This function the
Blessed Virgin came amply to fulfil in the late Middle Ages. But
from the 11th century on a greater emphasis came equally to be
laid on Jesus as a man; and if a man, then once a child and a baby;
and the human context of his early life came to be a matter of ever
greater interest and speculation. St Ailred of Rievaulx in the
mid-12th century wrote a book on Jesus at the age of twelve, and
St Francis in the early 13th made popular the Christmas crib.

Interest in Mary as Jesus's mother led in 11th-century England
to a concern for her own family, to the cult of her mother, St
Anne, to the feast of her conception – of Eastern, Byzantine
origin, but diffused in the West from England. The monastic
theologians of England in the early 12th century tried to spread
about the doctrine that her conception was Immaculate, a view at
first ill received by many in Europe. An emanation of the foggy
island, thought one, and St Bernard of Clairvaux denounced the
new doctrine as an aberration. Yet it made steady headway.
Meanwhile, in other respects, Bernard himself was a leading
devotee of Mary; for he was the central figure of the Cistercian
Order, all of whose churches were dedicated to her, from Portugal
to Poland, from Scotland to Sicily. To the new religious orders in
general she was regarded as a patron, and an enormous number of
houses of many complexions were dedicated to her. It would not
be far wrong to say that in the 12th century if a founder had no
special personal or local reason to choose another patron, he
would be expected to dedicate a new religious house to her. In the

13th century she was viewed with similar devotion by the friars, and it was the attitude of St Francis to her which indirectly inspired the notion of the servants or slaves of Mary, enshrined in particular in the order founded by a group of pious laymen in Florence in the 1230s which came to be known as 'The Order of the Slaves of the Blessed Virgin Mary', the *Servi* or Servites, which flourishes still.

From the circle of men in early 12th-century England who fostered devotion to her conception came also the first collections of what grew to be a popular literature in many parts of Europe, the stories of the Virgin's miracles. A young Italian monk in the great hill-top Abbey of the Sagra di San Michele, St Michael of Chiusa, near Turin, dropped the consecrated wine on a white towel when he was serving mass, and after a moment of intense misery prayed earnestly to Mary; the stain disappeared. Later in life he came to England and was made Abbot of Bury St Edmunds; and in England he met and encouraged and fostered the local devotion. From this meeting of native tradition and a devout cosmopolitan spirit – as so often in the 12th century – sprang new ideas and energies, and both the cult of Mary Immaculate and the stories of her miracles spread widely and swiftly.

The miracles are often given a local setting, but it is quite incidental. It was universally believed that she had been assumed into heaven and that there were therefore no earthly relics of her. Images of her and pieces of her veil and the like – even drops of her milk – were to be found in many places; and Chartres claimed to possess the nightdress she was wearing the night she gave birth to Jesus. But although these helped to create local centres for her cult, she was universal in her interests and her appeal. In this she resembled her son. He had one great shrine, the Holy Sepulchre at Jerusalem, and the Holy Land was at once the scene of his early life and the goal of the most adventurous of earthly pilgrimages. He was also present in a precise and local sense in the sacred host whenever it was consecrated in the Eucharist: on every altar at the time of mass. Yet he was omnipresent, universal, in every place at once.

Medieval society was a hierarchy, and the orders of the heavenly host resembled the earthly society. God was supreme and unique, the only king, though spoken of in various modes, as the Holy Trinity or Christ or the Paraclete, the Holy Ghost the comforter. But Mary was the queen of heaven, often so described, often, from the early 12th century, so represented in the scene of her coronation by her son. Next came the apostles and evangelists, also universal saints, but with local habitations, Peter and Paul in Rome, Mark in Venice, James in Santiago de Compostela, and so forth. Below them came many orders of saints, down to those whose cult was only local.

The Blessed Virgin and church dedications

This hierarchy comprising many steps, from the great universal saint to the humble man or woman of purely local fame, is of very ancient origin; as is also the supremacy of Mary. If one takes a simple test of how the saints stood in popular esteem, one can compare the relative frequency of the dedication of churches to Mary and the other saints. By the 10th and 11th centuries a rich variety of cults can be observed all over Europe, in which local saints mingled with the Apostles and Roman martyrs, although Mary was still the favourite of all. In the 12th and 13th centuries her long reign came to its climax, not only in the popularity of her cult and of dedications to her, but in the artistic theme of her Coronation, which spread from Reading and Saint-Denis all over   4
Christendom.

The inclusion of local saints reflects the growing importance of relics. In Italy in the 6th and 7th centuries there was a move to insist that a church should have relics of the saint to whom it was dedicated. It seems that all that survived of this into the central and late Middle Ages was the common practice of setting small relics into an altar, or placing a casket under, or near it, preferably containing at least some items attributed to the patron saint. But the practice of dedication in the 10th, 11th and 12th centuries clearly precluded any insistence: for how could one hope to provide appropriate relics for numerous churches of All Saints, or dedicated to Christ, the Holy Trinity, or the Virgin Mary? It was not wholly impossible to provide relics in such cases: the 12th-century relic list of Peterborough Abbey has introduced us to such surprising items as fragments of the cloth in which Jesus was wrapped, pieces of his crib, his cross and his tomb, and of the loaves which fed the five thousand; of St Mary's garment and veil. Peterborough also had some fragments of its own patron, St Peter, and of other Apostles. Yet the abbey could clearly boast far more substantial remains of Anglo-Saxon saints, as well as the torso of Saint-Florentin (see pp. 14-15). The dedication of churches to other than local saints, the popularity of the Trinity and the Blessed Virgin, all presuppose that relics were not essential.

St Nicholas

This is clearest of all, perhaps, in the spread of some relatively new cults. At some date in the mid-11th century a Norseman living in London (or a Londoner with a Viking name) founded a church dedicated to St Nicholas. At about the same date Nicholas begins to appear in English calendars; and his cult and his fame as a patron of children, Santa Claus, began mysteriously to spread about Europe. It was after this spread, not before, that the Normans in south Italy sailed from Bari to Myra in Asia Minor and stole the body of St Nicholas. It was the cult which led to the search for relics, not vice versa. Yet it is evidently significant of the currents of sentiment that the growth of Nicholas's cult should lead to the remarkable act of piracy on which the noble Church of St Nicholas at Bari is founded. It is implied in the contemporary accounts of the translation that Nicholas himself inspired the deed and favoured it, and was happy to be transported to south Italy; as well he might be, for there he was valued as never before.

St Michael

In Nicholas's case the cult came before the relics. Even more striking is the case of St Michael, for the fighting archangel is exceptional among the saints in having no mortal existence. Yet his cult had a strong material element in it, for it was closely linked to certain places and types of landscape. Michael was a hill-top saint, and doubtless replaced many a dragon who had failed to defend an earlier, pre-Christian cult. He is, or ought to be, the favourite of those who look for a pagan origin in every medieval cult. He is also a warning of the danger of this hunt: for it often leads us to overlook obvious but central facts about the cult in its Christian guise. The cult of Michael is ancient, and perhaps always had something to do with the attraction of strange, unusual, lofty places. Yet this does little to explain the revival of the cult, which spread a mantle of churches and chapels over hill-tops from Italy to Le Mont Saint-Michel and Saint Michael's Mount. The 10th and 11th centuries witnessed ancient chapels grow into great monasteries perched on sites as inconvenient for large communities as one could well devise. These are peaceful shrines to a warrior saint. Doubtless one can say that the spread of the cult was part of the prehistory of the Crusades, and Michael undoubtedly played his part in the growth of militant cults, along with St George and St Maurice. Yet this is only part of the story; for what could be more peaceful than the Sagra di San Michele of Chiusa? – and in such sites, with rare exceptions, a church or monastic complex dedicated to the archangel stands where a great fortress or castle, a real military centre, might have been.

The relics of the saints were never more powerful, never more avidly collected than between 1000 and 1300; but many of the most popular saintly cults had little or no connection with relics. The local saints and local pilgrimages flourished exceedingly; but so did the general cults and the cults of immaterial saints. The paradox is vividly presented in the planning of the great churches of the period.

The example of Winchester: St Peter and St Swithun

Almost every stage in this story is reflected in the present structure of Winchester Cathedral. Like many English cathedrals its original dedication, to Peter and Paul, belonged to the general cults and the Roman links of the age of the conversion, the 7th century; and in basic structure and design it is now a characteristic Norman cathedral of the late 11th century, even if relatively little Norman detail survives outside the transepts. But Bishop Haedde's dedication to St Peter and St Paul (7th century) and the Norman rededication to St Peter (St Paul was never formally deposed but came to play a minor role over the centuries) only represent two moments and two aspects of the church's history. Its first major rebuilding was in the 10th century, and this was prompted by the rediscovery and translation of the body of St Swithun in 971. Swithun had been Bishop of Winchester a century before, and died in or about 862. But it was not until the reign of Edgar that serious interest came to be taken in his miracles and relics. The story begins about 968.

'Three years before' St Swithun was translated into Winchester Cathedral '. . . came the venerable Swithun to a certain faithful smith', wrote a contemporary, 'appearing' in a dream 'worshipfully apparelled, and said to him . . . "Do you know the priest

Plan of Winchester Cathedral. A, late 12th-century retro-choir; B, probable site of St Swithun's shrine from 1093 to the Reformation; C, monks' choir, 12th–14th centuries; D, nave, remodelled in the 14th century.

called Eadsige, who was thrown out of the cathedral with the other priests by Bishop Aethelwold for their misconduct?" (that is, when Aethelwold replaced clerks by monks in Winchester Cathedral). "Long ago I knew him, Sir, but he departed hence and I know not for certain where he lives now." Then Swithun replied, "Of a surety he dwells at Winchcombe. And I entreat you now by the Saviour's name that you quickly announce my errand to him and say to him for a truth that Swithun the bishop commands that he should go to Bishop Aethelwold and say that he himself open my burial place and bring my bones within the church."' The smith was very reluctant to tell his vision, because he thought none would believe him. But repeated appearances of the saint, and a small miracle, stirred him to action, and by chance he met a servant of Eadsige's in the market place, and so delivered the message. Eadsige was naturally reluctant to visit Aethelwold after he had been ejected from the minster, even though he was a relation of Swithun's. But in due course he changed his mind and became a monk at Winchester. And by this and similar means Swithun achieved his purpose:

King Edgar then after these tokens, willed that the holy man should be translated, and spoke to Aethelwold the venerable bishop, that he should translate him with honourable solemnity. Then the bishop Aethelwold with abbots and monks raised the saint with chanting. And they bore him into the church, St Peter's house, where he stands in honoured memory, and worketh wonders. There were healed, by the holy man, four sick men within three days. And during five months few days were there, that there were not healed at least three sick persons – sometimes five or six – or seven or eight – ten or twelve – sixteen or eighteen. Within ten days two hundred men were healed, and so many within twelve months, that no man could count them. The burial ground lay filled with crippled folk, so that one could not easily visit the minster.

The crowded cemetery is an authentic picture of 10th- or 11th-century life, whatever we may think of the miracles and dreams with which it was surrounded; and in fairness we must remember that the author of this account was none too sure about dreams himself. 'Some dreams are in truth from God, even as we read in books; and some are from the devil for some deceit, seeking how he may pervert the soul . . .'. But of the miracles he had no doubt. 'All these were so miraculously healed within a few days that one could not find there five unsound men out of that great crowd.'

Thus the prosperity of the cathedral owed much from 971 on to the fame and the miracles of St Swithun; but it was also a prestigious cathedral in a royal city, and under a saintly bishop whose human life was a great deal better recorded and more impressive than Swithun's, St Aethelwold (963-84), a substantial community of monks came to form the chapter. In recent years the Old Minster, the pre-conquest cathedral, has been excavated with great skill by Professor and Mrs Biddle and their colleagues; and they have shown how the translation of 971 was followed by the building of a great west work, almost a church on its own, centrally planned about the site of Swithun's grave, which remained the centre of his cult. At the same time the main monastic church to the east was enlarged; and from then until the coming of the Normans the Old Minster was in effect two churches set end to end: the church of the dead Swithun and the church of St Peter, St Paul and the living monks.

All this the Normans changed. The Saxon minster was destroyed, and a great Romanesque basilica replaced it. Substantial as the Old Minster had been, it was dwarfed beside the new Norman church, as those who saw the foundations of the Norman west front exposed beside the Saxon church in the 1960s will recall. In 1093 Swithun's shrine was moved to the new cathedral and set in the east end. This second translation showed the Norman devotion to some saints of pure English lineage and their contempt for most other English traditions, for the loving care to preserve the site of Swithun's shrine was abandoned.

Winchester Cathedral and the hierarchy of earth and heaven

In Winchester Cathedral the universal saint and the local cult were both represented. Peter and Swithun lived together in uneasy harmony: Walkelin built a great church for Peter, but in local feeling and custom it became increasingly Swithun's church, so that in later generations, while Canterbury Cathedral has always been Christ Church, Winchester became St Swithun's. Yet the original structure paid considerable attention to the basic principle of the cult of the saints, that of hierarchy. The tomb and the relics of Swithun had been long since the centre of many miracles; and miracles inspired respect, devotion and money, all necessary to the well-being of a great religious institution. Unquestionably Swithun was not a major saint, and it must have cost Walkelin and many of his successors an effort to pronounce his name. At the east end was set the shrine; before it the high altar dedicated to Peter and to the divine presence in the mass. Immediately to the west lay the monks' choir, stretching under the central tower and a little to the west. God, St Peter, St Swithun and the other saintly bishops and less saintly kings whose bones were gathered in reliquaries and tombs about the east end represented the higher regions of the hierarchy of earth and heaven; the living bishop and the living monks came next; and beyond the screen the throng of the laity. In this way the sense of hierarchy, modified and mitigated by the power of a local saint and of his relics, was preserved and turned to stone. God, the dead saints and the living monks – or to put it another way, the hierarchy of heaven and those who enjoyed or endured a brief mortal life on earth – lived together in a structure built to reflect and symbolize a view of society in which all these orders had their place.

Saints and shrines

The structure of Winchester Cathedral can be seen as a set of variations on several themes, of social history, of liturgy and

devotion, of fashion; but for our present purpose, most essentially, on the parts which were played in its history by Peter and
Swithun and Mary. Peter reminds us that the great universal saints
were venerated throughout Western Christendom; in every
church their festivals punctuated the weeks and months of the
Church's calendar. Monks and clergy who could understand the
Latin office of the day – and all who came on major feast days and
tried to learn something of the saints in whose honour they came –
would have the opportunity year by year to remind themselves of
the earthly and heavenly merits of the major saints. Swithun is an
excellent example of the power of relics and miracles. Such power
could be shown in every century from the 4th on. But there was a
remarkable concentration of interest in relics, translations and
rebuilding of shrines and churches about them between the late
10th and the 13th centuries. We have met St Faith, flying in the
arms of her monks to Conques, and the delectable home where
her bones, and her reliquary, have lived ever since. We shall soon
meet St Mary Magdalene, translated, transported or otherwise in
evidence at Vézelay from the mid-11th century; inspiring pilgrim
throngs and offerings on the grandest scale, from which her
church was built and adorned in the first half of the 12th century.
In 10th-century Dijon (so it seems) an obscure saint of uncertain
authenticity was unearthed and identified as St Benignus, a
Roman martyr. For his bones a venerable circular crypt was
devised in rough imitation of that of San Vitale at Ravenna. The
crypt and shrine were so venerable that they alone survive of the
early church; and both were imitated for an authentic confessor in
the person of St Augustine of Canterbury, for whose church and
shrine a rotunda like Saint-Bénigne's was begun just before the
Norman Conquest. Saint-Bénigne became the home of a great
monastic community, a centre of monastic reform; but the living
saints who flourished in the church above never supplanted the
relics in the crypt. Greatest of all the relic churches were the
basilicas of Peter and Paul in Rome; and they needed no rebuilding
in this period, for they had been built on the grandest scale long
before, a reminder of the long history of the martyrium and the
shrine. Their only rival in the West, St James at Santiago de
Compostela, was not only the occasion of a major new pilgrimage
church in the 11th and 12th centuries, but also the inspiration of a
whole chain on the routes which led to him.

Shrines could be placed in many different situations. St Swithun
originally lay in the westwork, where he had first been buried.

Saint-Bénigne lay first and last in a crypt, similar in conception to the common Italian martyrium, whether ancient like St Peter's or Sant'Ambrogio in Milan, or of this epoch, like San Zeno at Verona (see p. 89). Some shrines of major saints lay in transepts or on one side of the choir. In these centuries one of the most popular positions came to be east of the high altar, which made the focus of the whole vista a shrine within the apse. A splendid example of this was the new Saint-Denis built under the patronage of Abbot Suger, and described by him in a famous series of books.

Canterbury and St Thomas Becket

Equally famous is the shrine of Thomas Becket at Canterbury of the late 12th and early 13th centuries. This is part of a remarkable story. Lanfranc's cathedral had been a church without shrines, dedicated to Christ and the Holy Trinity. St Anselm (1093-1109) and his successor presided over a notable extension eastward which allowed more space for the monks, and for the reappearance of substantial shrines to St Dunstan and St Aelfheah, who had been slighted by Lanfranc. But after Becket's murder in 1170 and a timely fire in 1174 the whole east end was replanned and remodelled to allow for the new saint and the new relics. The scale of the rebuilding and the need for it were both the product of the *succès fou* of the dead archbishop. As the echoes of the murderers' shouts and threats died away and before they had time to return and desecrate the body, his disciples gathered the corpse from the cathedral pavement and laid it in the crypt, in a marble sarcophagus 'before the altar of St John the Baptist and St Augustine, apostle of the English. . . . And there', wrote John of Salisbury a few days or at most a few short weeks after the murder, 'many mighty wonders are performed, to God's glory: great throngs of people gather to feel in themselves and witness in others the power and mercy of Him who always shows His wonder and His glory in His saints. In the place where Thomas suffered, and where he lay the night through, before the high altar, awaiting burial, and where he was buried at last, the palsied are cured, the blind see, the deaf hear, the dumb speak, the lame walk, folk suffering from fevers are cured, the lepers are cleansed, those possessed of a devil are freed. . . . I should not have dreamt to write such words on any account had not my eyes been witness to the certainty of this . . . .'.

Westminster Abbey and St Edward the Confessor

On 7 July 1220 the young King Henry III was present when the papal legate and the Archbishops of Canterbury and Rheims led a great concourse of bishops and clergy for the solemn translation of Becket's relics from the crypt to the shrine raised high in the Trinity Chapel to the east of the high altar. The young king may well have reflected that even if Thomas the chancellor had been his grandfather's friend, Thomas the martyr had been his enemy, and that many who came to do him honour delighted in a cult which was against the secular establishment and symbolized resistance to the king. It was partly from such thoughts, maybe, that Henry himself conceived the idea of making of his own Westminster Abbey the centre of a rival cult, to Edward the Confessor and the English monarchy.

In the course of the 1230s he set seriously to work, and through the middle years of his reign he steadily diverted resources into the rebuilding of the Abbey choir, crossing and part of the nave. The cost was prodigious, and it was only one of many building schemes in which this noble patron of architects and masons beautified the land he knew so little how to govern. In the Gothic style of the choir his admiration for all things French, and all that the French kings were building, was mingled with many English features, and with the Italian cosmati of tomb and shrine: this conjunction faithfully reflected the cosmopolitan taste of a king who felt himself a member of the international caste of kings and dynasts, a stranger to his own baronage. Yet all was designed to do honour to a saint with the impeccably English name of Edward by a king who brought English names back into the royal family for the first time since the Norman Conquest, and called his sons Edward and Edmund. It is impossible for us to disentangle all the threads in his complex personality, but two things stand out clear. First of all, the shrine which was and is the centre of the architectural pattern of Henry's Westminster Abbey was intended to form a focus of kingly quality and inspiration, and to be Saint-Denis and Rheims rolled into one; it was already the coronation church, and became the chief burial church of English kings and notables, with a royal galaxy gathering round the shrine. Secondly, as a cult it failed to become popular: Canterbury had been paid for by the pilgrims, Westminster was financed, almost entirely, by the king. Perhaps there was something inherently more attractive in a cult linked to resistance, to denial of the establishment; what is certain is that Thomas Becket's reputation for miracle-working far surpassed the modest efforts of Edward the Confessor.

The saints and their miracles

If someone gave property to the Old Minster at Winchester in the 12th century, the gift was made to God and St Peter and St Swithun and the monks of the Cathedral. If he or she had given a gift to the see of Tours in the 5th or 6th centuries, or to the see of London between the 7th and the 11th, as likely as not they would have thought and spoken of giving it 'to St Martin' or 'St Paul'. The saint was regarded as a personal proprietor of his church and all its land and treasures. In the conditions of the early Middle Ages a saint had been expected to protect his followers and his properties by the use of fairly rough methods – blinding or laming his enemies, for example, or even drowning them, if all else failed. With the rise of papal monarchy and the structure of the Church's law in the 11th and 12th centuries the personal lordship of the saint declined, however much his authority in the spiritual world and in popular esteem might survive and grow. But it is significant that Canterbury Cathedral remained God's church, Christ Church; and that however intimately Becket was associated with the defence of Christ's properties and privileges in his life – unlike St Swithun at Winchester – he never supplanted him as proprietor after his death. His ascendancy in the Cathedral was a more personal one, as the great thaumaturge and model for his

5   successors. Becket's miracles were very numerous indeed. Not all of them were serious. One of the king's favourite falcons was injured, and cured by prayer to Thomas; as the saint had been devoted to hawking and had often accompanied the king in earlier days in this favourite pursuit, it was a singularly appropriate act. Similarly, observed William of Canterbury, one of the chief narrators of the miracles, when a knight lost a horse in a forest in Ponthieu, prayed to the saint and soon after found his horse, this is not to be attributed to chance. Everything has a cause, even if it is not immediately apparent; even a leaf does not fall from a tree

without a reason. The author of all causes is God, and he alone is First Cause, and causeless.

Thus William and his like looked for a miraculous explanation in every strange event, where we would look for coincidence or a natural, scientific cause. This and the love of a good story help to explain the credulity that runs through all medieval collections of miracles. But it would be exceedingly naive to imagine that we can explain all or many of the events which William described. Contemporary, eye-witness accounts of miracles are very numerous; and the vast majority are miracles of healing. In most cases we cannot tell precisely what happened; but the power of faith evidently mingled with quite other circumstances in a fashion largely hidden from us to produce some very striking cures.

Even more interesting is the atmosphere these tales carry with them. The cult of Thomas spread rapidly across France, especially in parts where he had lived or was known. A knight of the Limousin was noted for his ferocity, but also for his devotion to Thomas, for he had been much impressed by the martyr's death in the same year in which he received the belt of knighthood. When fatally wounded (as he supposed) his last despairing thought went to Thomas; and lo! – the 'angel of the English' (an expression even his friends never thought of applying to the living archbishop) stood by him, all in white, dressed in alb and stole. Three times he said to him 'The Lord has risen' and marked him with the sign of the Cross; and after he had for the third time used the words of the angel of the Resurrection, the knight sprang to grasp his hands; but Thomas disappeared leaving him alive and cured. His household fell to rejoicing: they rang bells and sang hymns, and at the thanksgiving mass the priest urged that a chapel be built to St Thomas by the folk assembled. A site was marked out and stones were collected; on the site a paralysed woman was cured that night, and the next night, in spite of the wind, a procession was formed with candles which the wind failed to extinguish.

People tended to be credulous; but there were doubters and scoffers too. One of the miracles publicized by John of Salisbury in another of his letters dealt with one of these. It occurred at Chartres while John was bishop there at the end of his life (1176–80), and is of particular interest because it concerns an ordinary man, Peter, an artisan, and affords us a vivid glimpse of everyday life. One day, he and other stonecutters, working in the Abbey of St Peter's (Saint-Père), Chartres, were having their lunch. They fell to discussing Becket's miracles. Peter burst out laughing and made light of them, boldly asserting they were inventions, and false. He took a mouthful of food and said that if St Thomas had any power he was to choke or poison him. His companions dissociated themselves from such temerity, assiduously protecting themselves with the sign of the Cross. Peter went off home but presently fell speechless and helpless. He was brought to the Cathedral and his mother and friends begged Bishop John for help. The poor mason lifted his hands to the shrine where the Virgin's nightdress was kept, but to no avail. So John washed a phial containing St Thomas's blood and gave Peter the water to drink: he was cured, and went on pilgrimage to Canterbury to give thanks.

The living saint

Both Sainte-Foy of Conques and Saint-Bénigne of Dijon were essentially dead saints – living members of the heavenly host of whose mortal activities little was known; their human lives were of little interest. This was not the whole truth about all the most popular saints of the early Middle Ages. Of St Mary Magdalene and St Peter a little was known and more invented; and there are few figures of the ancient world of whom we have so much evidence as for St Paul. Yet broadly speaking the pious of the early Middle Ages expected their saints to be dead. From the time of Eadmer and St Anselm a new wind blew; a deep interest in the human saint is reflected in many saints' lives of the central Middle Ages. Yet there remains a striking contrast between Thomas Becket and Francis of Assisi. The murderers' swords converted a dramatic archbishop whom some admired and some hated, but few regarded as a model of sanctity, into the most popular dead saint of the century; more popular in his death than St Bernard of Clairvaux, whom many had venerated far more in his life. St Francis, like Becket, performed miracles. But the basis of his reputation was the charisma and charm of his personality; his brilliance as a teacher, his power over people and animals; the spiritual example of his life. He was already a professional holy man many years before his death, and supremely evokes the veneration and love that the pious (and some of the impious) of the central Middle Ages felt for a living saint.

Francis's life, teaching and example helped the Blessed Virgin to a stature even she had never reached before, as queen of heaven

and as the image of all the virtues most admired, from chastity to mercy. She was not a contemporary saint about whom vivid stories could be told by those who had known her in the way that Francis was; yet a great part of her power lay in her capacity to inspire the human emotions which were particularly admired and looked for in the saints. Who could be more the image of pity than Jesus's mother when she witnessed his crucifixion, and held his dead body as it was taken from the Cross? She symbolized many things, most powerfully those elements which had been least conspicuous in the sentiment of the 8th, 9th and 10th centuries: divine mercy and charity; chastity as a virtue and a quality among men as well as women. There are even striking analogies between the language used about her, and that of the romantic poets of the 12th and 13th centuries about earthly, carnal women. These analogies must be delicately handled, for the pursuit of real similarities is like the hunting of the snark – at the moment of capture they swiftly and silently vanish away. But the true significance of the Virgin lies in another world, that of the Holy Family, and of the humanity of Jesus. As crowned queen of the saints she reminds us now, above all, of the rich variety of 12th-century cults, which compassed the human and humane, the militant archangel, the unidentified corpse, the site of a burial, a striking natural feature – what you will.

IV
What is popular religion?

If we go back along the pilgrim road which led to Conques from
the Rhineland and Burgundy, we may find another church similar
in character and function to Sainte-Foy, the Madeleine of Vézelay.
The presence here of St Mary Magdalene in the 11th and 12th
centuries transformed a modest and venerable abbey of no
distinction into one of the great centres of art, architecture and
culture of the West (see p. 92).

In the spring of 1166 the exiled Archbishop of Canterbury,
Thomas Becket, was given cautious and modest encouragement
in his struggle with Henry II of England by Pope Alexander III.
Becket made up his mind that the time had come to excommunicate the king and make a public proclamation of the justice of his
own cause. Today we might seek television time, or buy a page of
a national newspaper. There was no equivalent means open to
Becket; but he could make a public demonstration in the presence
of a large international throng. To this end he made a pilgrimage
to Vézelay, and he arranged to speak from the cathedral pulpit on
Whit Sunday, when the great church was packed with a
congregation drawn from many parts of Western Christendom.
The plan did not go quite as intended, for shortly before the day
he heard that Henry was seriously ill; Becket hastily revised his
scheme, and excommunicated the king's counsellors and his
decrees, the Constitutions of Clarendon, which he had to quote
from memory since he had left his copy behind. But the element
of improvisation did not altogether spoil the effect: Henry and his
counsellors could not pretend that they had no knowledge of the
matter.

All sorts and conditions of men and women gathered in the
Magdalene's church at Vézelay to hear the archbishop: pilgrims,
holiday makers, locals enjoying a day out, devout worshippers at
the shrine of a great saint, the pious and not-so-pious of Vézelay
itself, the community of monks. Clearly their assumptions and

their inspiration were diverse and complex. We can proceed no further in our quest of them without some discussion of what popular religion means and meant.

Twenty years earlier, in the presence of the king and queen of the French, a still greater throng had collected at Vézelay, on Easter Day 1146, so large that the Madeleine could not hold them all, and they met in the open air on a hill slope outside the town. There in a lofty pulpit specially made, St Bernard of Clairvaux himself preached the Second Crusade: the ascetic monk and father of innumerable monks urged the layfolk of Christendom to war. At the heart of the Christian liturgy which Bernard recited every day and knew by heart lay prayers for peace, invocations of the peace of the Lord. Yet here was one of the most inspired Christian preachers of the Middle Ages urging men with all the eloquence at his command to a war which must seem to us today cruel to a degree. To understand this we must go back a little, examine the background to the Crusading movement, and provide a brief frame of events to our story.

Europe 1000–1300: social structure

A king, said the English Alfred, must have three kinds of men – those who pray, those who fight and those who work. Traditional political history was the history of kings; and its central theme from the 11th to the 13th centuries was the apogee and fall of the medieval empire, the rise of papal monarchy, the contest of empire and papacy and the victory of the papacy. What does this mean? In principle there were two kinds of authority in the medieval world: the spiritual authority of which the pope was head, and the temporal authority of emperors and kings and lesser potentates. To this division corresponded a similar division throughout society. Pope, archbishops, abbots, archdeacons and canons; then a great way below, the parish clergy and the clerical proletariat: all these had spiritual functions and most were fathers to flocks of some kind. But they were also the counterparts of secular folk: emperors, kings, princes, great lords, knights, and a great way below, peasants. Alfred's division made the clergy those who pray, the lords and knights those who fight, the peasants those who work. Needless to say it was always a heroic simplification. Bishops worked with him to rule his kingdom and were lords in their own domain; the best of them thought and wrote as well as prayed. The lords dominated their villages and farms and tenants; they and their bailiffs presided over law-courts; they were rulers in a 'feudal' society, landlords as well as warriors. Many of the humbler folk did not work – were idle through necessity or choice; western Europe was underdeveloped territory: the employed tended to be underemployed. Even the peasant sometimes fought and often prayed, however inaccessible his thoughts and prayers are to us today. And the analysis took no account of the merchant or the artisan, of the townsman. This was understandable in Alfred, for when he was a child towns were few. But he himself was a notable pioneer in founding and refounding towns, and in the 10th, 11th and 12th centuries towns sprang up again all over western Europe. They were communities whose centre and *raison d'être* lay in the market in their midst and in peaceful occupations, yet also the home of fierce independence, internal riots and external wars, so that the walls and gates which surrounded them were as characteristic as the markets, as were the innumerable churches which adorned them, of which we shall speak anon.

The religious orders

The 9th and 10th centuries witnessed the beginning of a great revival of the religious life. The monastic cloister was the centre of a deeply influential, deeply admired way of life – a ritual life with elaborate liturgy at its centre – a life for relatively few dedicated monks, not in itself an expression of popular religion. Yet the monastic, ascetic life lay at the root of much which is fundamental in this book: the dominant asceticism which inspired the papal reform of the 11th century; the love of great churches and the ritual they enshrined; many of the devotions which flourished in monastic churches and so became more widely known and more widely diffused – cults of saints and relics, devotion to the Blessed Virgin and the services in her honour; and so forth. The 10th and 11th centuries were the heyday of a traditional monasticism, with the 6th-century Rule of St Benedict at its heart, but rejoicing in a much enhanced liturgy performed in churches where the monks worshipped in the choir, and the laity could gather in groups large and small in the nave. There was a constant flow of influence from the cloister into various channels of popular religious devotion, and the monks in their turn were dependent on the increasingly

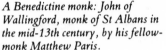

A Benedictine monk: John of Wallingford, monk of St Albans in the mid-13th century, by his fellow-monk Matthew Paris.

wide interest and generosity which gave them the endowment and patronage they needed.

In the late 11th and 12th centuries the pattern of religious life grew more varied. Reformed monastic communities and orders sought a more retired and ascetic life; the Cistercians and their like tried to live in more remote situations and exclude the laity from their churches. Other communities came closer to everyday life and served hospitals, centres of social welfare of all kinds; from one of these sprang the Hospitallers, who became in the end an Order of Crusading Knights – and one of the strangest features of the religious life of the 12th century was the orders of knights, Templars, Hospitallers and others, who combined the monastic and military life. Two strong tendencies governed the new impulses of the 12th and 13th centuries: the tendency towards the more retired, contemplative life; and the opposite tendency towards a life of practical, pastoral work in villages and towns. They sound to us distinct alternatives. In practice they were often combined, as in the life and inspiration of St Francis, and from the pastoral, itinerant, missionary work which he and St Dominic developed were to grow the orders of friars in the early and mid-13th century.

As the religious orders grew in variety and numbers of recruits, a marked change came over their relation to society. Many of the recruits to the traditional monasteries of the 10th and 11th centuries had come as children, 'oblates', offered by their parents. As the variety of choices open to men (and in much less degree, to women) widened and spread in the 12th century, and as new ideals were developed which demanded personal choice and commitment at the outset, the proportion of religious who came of their own volition increased. The religious life became a vocation; the child oblate gradually disappeared. The world of the child-monk is a strange, lost world to us; but a window is opened into it by the moving autobiography of the Anglo-Norman monk Orderic Vitalis, written at the close of his *Ecclesiastical History* in Normandy in the early 1140s, looking back to the moment over fifty years earlier when his father had given him, a weeping ten-year-old, to the Norman monk who escorted him from his old home in Shropshire to his new home at Saint-Évroult in Normandy. 'Weeping, he gave a weeping child to Rainald the monk, nor ever after saw him.' But the life which followed, regular, ordered, contented and devout, evidently reconciled him to the sad memory of its beginning.

Political structure: Church and kings

Northern Europe was dominated by three monarchies in these centuries: the German, whose king was also usually Holy Roman Emperor, crowned not only in Aachen, in Charlemagne's city, but in Rome by the pope; the French, at first more modest in power and pretension, but from about 1200 perhaps the greatest in Europe, seat of the Capetians, descendants of Hugh Capet, a dynasty of remarkable persistence passing from father to son for more than three centuries; and the English, at first alternately ruled by English and Danes, but after 1066 Norman or Angevin, from William the Conqueror to Edward I – the conqueror of Wales – lords of a large part of France, more powerful than the French king until the rising power of Philip II Augustus put them in their place at the turn of the 12th and 13th centuries. In 1000 it was traditional to see in the kings of the West God's earthly representatives; divine right all medieval kings could claim, for without God's permission and blessing no legitimate monarch

might reign. But we mean more than that; for it was widely accepted that kings were God's instruments to regulate the Church as well as the kingdom. They chose the bishops and presided over councils; they reformed and regulated the affairs of abbeys; on all important issues and decisions they expected to be consulted. The *Regularis Concordia*, the solemn agreement by which the English monastic reformers provided for the customs and observance of their monasteries in the early 970s, opens with an address to King Edgar, which makes out that this pious, forceful but not at all monkish young man was the director and inspiration of the whole movement, a sentiment familiar from the adulatory literature of modern totalitarian states, but in the *Concordia*, honest in intent.

When the Danes came to this country with a great army, Aethelred the Unready (978-1016) issued the following edict: so that 'we may obtain God's mercy and his compassion and that we may be able through his help to withstand our enemies. Now it is our will that all the nation shall fast as a general penance for three days on bread and herbs and water . . . and every man is to come barefoot to church, without gold or ornaments, and to go to confession. And all are to go out with the relics [in procession] and to call on Christ eagerly from their inmost hearts. And one penny . . . is to be paid from each hide [and . . .] distributed . . . and the food also, which each would have consumed if the fast had not been ordained . . . is to be willingly distributed for God's sake after the fast to needy men and bedridden persons. . . . And slaves during those three days are to be freed from work, in order to go to church, and in order that they may the more willingly observe the fast.' And in every minster masses are to be said, and the psalter sung, until things become better; 'and all in common, ecclesiastics and laymen, are to turn eagerly to God and to deserve his mercy.' Such an edict seems to us ecclesiastical rather than royal, and it was composed for the king by the Archbishop of York, the famous preacher Wulfstan. But there was no division of spiritual and temporal into watertight compartments in law or in life. The king expected his subjects to be good, Christian citizens. Aethelred commanded them to cast off every heathen practice, to form the habit of frequent confession, to go frequently to communion, to keep oath and pledge, to shun false weights and measures and fraud. In the same breath he denounced perjury, murder, stealing, avarice and greed, over-eating and drinking, injuries to the clergy and breaches of the marriage law.

51

The papal reform of the 11th century: papal monarchy

In the mid-11th century, the papacy itself, which had passed through some dark tunnels and witnessed some heroic efforts at improvement, was captured by a small international group of zealots, led by the German Pope Leo IX (1048/9-1054). He was the nominee of the pious Emperor Henry III, and worked with him to reform the Church and the world. But he was also the mouthpiece of a popular religious movement whose origins we have met in the pages of Raoul Glaber, first visibly stirring in the years about 1000, though owing many debts to earlier times; it came to its height in the mid- and late 11th century. In the late Middle Ages popular religious movements commonly took little notice of the pope or else attacked him; the papal reform movement of the mid-11th century was a remarkable example of a popular movement in which the pope took the lead.

Direction was given by the simple, revolutionary, yet also deeply traditional programme of the movement. The reformers attacked simony, that is, the sale of church offices. The name derived from Simon Magus, whose story is told in the Acts of the Apostles. Simon saw the apostles Peter and John bestowing the gift of the Holy Spirit upon recently baptized Christians through the laying on of hands. He offered the apostles money for a share in their spiritual power and was sternly rebuked by Peter. Medieval legend embellished the tale. Simon Magus, with the help of the devil, was able to fly through the air, but the prayers of Sts Peter and Paul deprived him of this magic power and he fell headlong – a dramatic subject for painters and sculptors.

After simony, the reformers attacked the marriage or concubinage common among the clergy; and Pope Leo the Great in the 5th century, to look no further back, pronounced the law on which they acted, that no bishop, priest, deacon or sub-deacon might marry. They declared the authority of the pope supreme on earth in all spiritual matters, and found a variety of ways in which his power should be wielded over secular rulers when occasion demanded. In their eyes this was only to put into effect what Jesus had given to Peter; and no one now doubts that similar claims had been made in principle for many centuries. Yet there was something new in the way the popes of the late 11th century exercised their authority. Leo IX had worked in harmony with Henry III: Gregory VII quarrelled with Henry IV. Whatever the rights and wrongs of that dispute, it marked a parting of the ways.

The pope was no longer a remote, prestigious, charismatic figure presiding over the immense treasury of Roman relics, Peter's successor sitting on Peter's tomb, but a king to be reckoned with by all who owed allegiance to him in western Europe. In all sorts of ways his kingship differed from the secular monarchies: its sanctions lay mainly in heaven and its justification wholly in the Catholic faith and its preservation and spread. The secular monarchies all enjoyed a curious mixture of hereditary and elective succession; but however much a formal ritual governed the process of kingmaking they became increasingly hereditary – save only the German, and even that remained in practice confined to two or three families. But the popes were elected, from 1179, by a clear-cut two-thirds' majority, and the popes were usually intelligent, elderly, and short-lived.

The special character of the reformed papacy is most clearly revealed in its alliance with the *Patarini*, the movement for religious reform and social revolution in Milan. This was a term of contempt aimed at them by their enemies, and which stuck – like Whig and Tory in 17th- and 18th-century England. They were largely humble folk, the underprivileged citizens of the city, but included a few of the nobility and a number of lower clergy: the combination of elements across the social hierarchy from which revolutions often spring. Milan had been dominated by an alliance between the landed nobility of its neighbourhood and the established, worldly, married upper clergy, led by the old Archbishop Guido. The religious programme of the *Patarini* was perfectly orthodox, by the standards of the 1060s and 1070s: the enforcement of celibacy on upper as well as lower clergy; moral reform in general; and the boycotting of the sacraments of sinful priests. They went further, and declared these sacraments invalid, a very extreme view, but one shared by some (though far from all) of the papal reformers.

It has rarely been the case that the hierarchy of the Church has supported social revolution – much the reverse on the whole; but the situation was new and exciting. Milan was the ancient seat of St Ambrose and traditionally very independent in its attitude to Rome; in the 11th century very close to the emperors on the whole. The temptation to the reformed papacy to ally itself with men who preached its doctrines, attacked the old guard and undermined the traditional regime, and turned to Rome for help, was overwhelming. Yet for a long while the Curia was (so it seems) divided in its attitude, and tended to look for peaceful solutions to Milan's problems. In 1059 Anselm of Lucca (later Pope Alexander II) and the great ascetic Peter Damian, as papal legates, quelled a riot against the *Patarini*; but the pope, Nicholas II, reinstated Archbishop Guido in the same year. In 1066 the Patarene leader Ariald was murdered, and in the next year two papal legates came to make the peace again. The late 1060s saw the rise of the most brilliant leader of the *Patarini*, Erlembald, himself a layman of high class, but also a demagogue; he won steadfast support from Hildebrand, especially when he became Pope Gregory VII in 1073. Meanwhile, in 1071, the old archbishop had died, and Milan suddenly became the theatre of war between pope and emperor, each supporting a rival candidate, each seeing in Milan a symbol – in Henry IV's case, of imperial authority, in Gregory's of reform and papal authority in north Italy. This was the beginning of the great war between Henry and Gregory; after some vicissitudes, Erlembald was killed in a riot in 1075, Henry invested his candidate for the archbishopric, and the stage was set; the *Patarini* disappeared in the *démarches* which followed – and by 1077 Milan had become a small part of the issues which were debated in the castle of Canossa. Yet the *Patarini*, though they came and went in so relatively short a time, were of great significance, for they show us the papal reformers in direct touch with a notable popular movement.

In northern Europe the papal monarchy competed with the old established Frankish monarchies in France and Germany, and with the English. The situation in the Mediterranean lands was more complex. In Italy itself the Emperor, or King of Germany, ruled as heir and successor of the Lombard kings and, more remotely, of previous Roman emperors; and beneath him there remained till the turn of the 11th and 12th centuries some vestiges of the old high aristocracy. But more and more initiative was passing in north and central Italy to the cities great and small; they were reviving and flourishing as they had not flourished since the decline of the ancient world in the West in the 5th century. In the south of Italy a remarkable new power had arisen dominated, like the English kingdom, by Norman invaders, who presided over a group of duchies and counties – a kingdom by the mid-12th century – nominally Christian and Catholic, yet containing and for a while tolerating the presence of numerous Greek Orthodox Christians, and Moslems.

Poised between the Normans in the south and the city states of the north, the pope presents a complex image both as a political and a religious potentate. The medieval popes claimed substantial temporal authority in the papal states and, in a measure, elsewhere. As Vicar of Christ – a title which came to be especially the pope's in the 12th century – St Peter's *alter ego* and successor, with St Peter's keys, the pope claimed the loftiest, most sublime authority. But he was also the head of an international spiritual government, presiding over a bureaucracy in regular contact with every corner of Western Christendom, and even beyond, for the popes attempted to enter diplomatic relations even with distant oriental potentates who did not always exist: a spiritual monarch, but still a ruler in a very ordinary sense of the term. In the 11th century bureaucracy is a somewhat misleading term: Gregory VII may have issued as many as three letters a week from his chancery; but as its effective influence grew, and especially when a host of litigants brought their affairs to the Curia in the mid- and late 12th century, it came to be one of the most elaborate governments in medieval Europe.

Meanwhile, in almost all the cities of central and northern Italy there had grown up a spirit of independence and enterprise, bellicose, capitalist, anti-clerical and devout, all at once. The old order naturally fell under attack as the citizens became more involved in politics and more violently factious, and the old order was commonly represented by the local bishop. In city after city his temporal authority was dethroned; sometimes the process was violent, sometimes peaceful – for the new men commonly included the bishops' own lay friends and relations. The new order also had a strong element of piety, for the citizens expressed their new-found wealth most evidently in building and beautifying their churches. Rome itself was one of the great city states, and in Rome we see the pope had yet a third hat, as a petty tyrant, the supreme representative of the old order. 'The medieval Romans loved and hated their father the Pope – hated him because every good citizen of every medieval city (like every medieval student) was in a state of rebellion, against authority, against tyranny, against freedom or against rebellion itself. They loved him because he was their father, the earthly presence of their own Apostle, and because his court was the centre of the tourist trade on which the economy of Rome has been securely based since the early middle ages. Call them pilgrims, call them suitors, call them ambassadors: without the visitors to the Roman curia the hoteliers of Rome would starve; and so while the Romans drove out the Pope again and again when the call to freedom stirred them, hunger and penitence turned them almost at once to fetch him back.'

Thus Italy was a land of cities with a partly Moslem kingdom in the south. And Spain was in the first act of the *reconquista*: the great Moslem caliphate of Cordova had broken up in the 11th century, and the cultivated and relatively peaceful emirates gradually fell victim to the bellicose little Christian kingdoms of the north, until by the end of the 11th century the greater part of northern and central Spain had fallen, for a time at least, to the king–emperor of León-Castile. His reconquest was essentially a political affair. Medieval Christianity was usually intolerant – that is to say in its official aspect, for there were evidently many medieval Christians who found it natural to be on friendly terms with pagans, Moslems and even with heretical Christians. But in Spain Christendom had so long lived under the umbrella of Islam as to take a measure of tolerance for granted. It is one of the strangest and saddest paradoxes that medieval Spain, once the most liberal in its treatment of other faiths, a land where Jew and Moslem lived at peace, became by the end of the Middle Ages a scene of extreme religious and political intolerance. But it was not so in the 11th century, and although the end of the 11th and 12th centuries witnessed the first serious confrontations between major Christian and Moslem powers, the fanatical spirit of the Crusades was not born in the Iberian Peninsula.

The Crusading movement

Christianity had once been a religion of peace, and throughout the Middle Ages there were many vestiges of this early and deep tradition. Theologians frequently, indeed normally, accepted the notion of a just war, but that usually meant a war in self-defence. Nor were the Church's leaders passive in their attitude to the violent military aristocracies with whom they dealt. St Odo, Abbot of Cluny in the early 10th century (926-44), propounded an ideal of Christian knighthood in his *Life of St Gerald of Aurillac* which savours more of the monastic life than of the full-blooded militarism of the Crusades. He makes Gerald learned and ascetic, a model of chastity whose rare concessions to lay standards included the eating of meat. He promised peace and reconciliation to his enemies, and if he was forced to fight to protect the poor from depredation, he instructed his men to fight with the backs of their swords and with their spears reversed. He was never wounded nor did he wound anyone. He would have seemed ridiculous to the real soldiers of the 10th or 11th centuries, though he was saved from absurdity in Odo's pages by a piety which made him invincible. But other measures were needed to deal with the horrors of contemporary life.

In the 11th and 12th centuries attempts were made to set a religious seal on knighthood. The traditional ceremony by which a great lord placed armour on one of his knights had been purely secular, though a religious aura surrounded the oath of obedience and fealty which the knight gave to his lord. But in the 12th century an elaborate religious ritual was developed; it came to be the practice for a devout knight to spend hours, sometimes the whole night, in church before the ceremony, and to receive the clergy's blessing on his arms. We may doubt if this made warfare much less brutal; but it represented a real attempt to reconcile the ideals of clerical and lay society, to provide the Church's sanction for some sort of code of behaviour.

In the early 11th century strenuous efforts were made to set a limit to local violence and private war: councils were held in France and Germany, and in 1043 the Emperor Henry III proclaimed peace from the pulpit of Constance Cathedral. Truces were arranged for periods of time: the peace of God was proclaimed for periods of months and years, truces for particular days of the week; all manner of devices were considered and urged. But in the end if Europe became modestly more peaceful it was a war which made it so; for the chief effect of the Crusading movement on western Europe was apparently to rid it of a large proportion of its most unruly and adventurous folk. The success of the Crusading movement is exceedingly hard for us to understand; but at its root lay a whole complex of popular religious ideas which worked at several different levels, some cruder, some more elevated.

The idea that God could specially favour warfare in 'Christian' causes gained ground in the mid-11th century with extraordinary rapidity. The Normans invaded Moslem Sicily with a papal blessing. Their cousins who invaded England in 1066 claimed a papal banner; but the truth of this claim is far from certain, and papal legates visiting the island a few years later exacted elaborate penances from Normans who had killed Englishmen at the Battle of Hastings. In both cases divine intervention was assumed by many contemporaries: God would wish to recover Sicily for

Christendom, and although it had been Moslem for a considerable period, it could be plausibly presented as a defensive war; similarly, William the Conqueror claimed that he went to remove a perjured usurper who had broken an oath sworn on holy relics, to recover a land which was rightly his. But the Crusade which Pope Urban II preached in 1095 and St Bernard preached again in 1146 was on a grander scale and had a larger theme. Urban may have been stirred by requests from the Byzantine Emperor, Alexius I Comnenus, for troops to help defend Byzantium, 'East Rome', against the Seljuk Turks; but he also opened the path to Jerusalem and inspired his audience with a vision of the holy city, the aim of the greatest of earthly pilgrimages, of all places in the world the most naturally Christian in the eyes of a medieval Catholic, and urged its deliverance. If the invasion of Sicily was defensive, by that token the more was the liberation of Jerusalem and the defence of East Rome; and however little we may approve any of these criteria, there is something inspiring in Urban's vision of a righteous and just channel for the warlike proclivities of the semi-barbarous peoples of western Europe. It was also a great stroke of statesmanship, for at a blow he restored the union of papacy and popular religious movements, and turned the tables on the silent, excommunicate Emperor Henry IV, who allowed the Crusade to flow past him. Urban's call to arms rebuilt papal prestige from the ruins in which Gregory VII's last years had left it. But this does not explain his success.

It only makes sense if we appreciate the alliance Urban inaugurated with a crusading doctrine far cruder than his own. It is true that the Crusade appealed to all manner of adventurous instincts: for the ambitious it offered gain of territory, gain of wealth; for others an escape from a humdrum life at home; some, like the Duke of Normandy, William the Conqueror's son, ran happily away from inheritances that were beyond control; others, like the Count of Blois, the Conqueror's son-in-law, were urged to the front by their wives. Count Stephen returned early, and ingloriously, from the First Crusade, and his imperious and bellicose wife – not the Conqueror's daughter for nothing – sent him back again. But the vast hordes who followed the call of Peter the Hermit were inspired by a fanatical enthusiasm whose inner meaning is hinted to us in the contemporary version of the Song of Roland, and made quite explicit in the later German version of the Song, the *Rolandslied*, written by a younger contemporary of St Bernard. The heathen are cattle for the slaughter: war in a holy cause is good, and to destroy the infidel is to do God's work, for which he will reward you; death in such warfare is martyrdom. Jerusalem is the earthly image of the heavenly city; those who die on the way there go straight to heaven. War has always been a savage thing, but atrocity was an inherent element in the Crusading movement, as inspired by the popular doctrine, to a quite horrifying degree. The followers of Peter the Hermit could not wait to reach the Bosphorus before encountering infidels; they found them on their way in the peaceful, prosperous Jewish communities in the Rhineland. The most spectacular relic of Western Jewry in this age is the ritual bath-house under the 6 synagogue at Speyer, which has always been a fearful reminder of what the German Jews suffered in the First Crusade, and has in recent years been made a place of pilgrimage by the deliberate act of the German authorities atoning for a more recent atrocity.

In fairness to Pope Urban it can be said that a great gulf separated his conception of the Crusade from this popular doctrine; and this helps us to understand and define the nature of popular religion. It can be utterly divorced from the official teaching of the Church or the lofty speculations of the theologians. Yet the Crusading movement also makes clear that this divorce was often far from complete. Before long, the popes rewarded faithful Crusaders with a promise of plenary indulgence: that is to say, if they died in a state of grace, their sins shriven and pardoned, they could be sure of heaven and be spared any cleansing of sins in purgatory before they went there. Historians have long puzzled about how much of this was already included in the promises of Urban II, and we shall never fully know the answer, for there are inescapable ambiguities in our understanding of his doctrine of heaven and hell. He was a Cluniac monk by origin, and doubtless brought up to the kind of doctrine popular in monastic circles in the 11th century, that the population of heaven was small, and consisted largely of monks. In the 12th century the population of heaven increased substantially – in many folk's opinion – partly because of a greater optimism, partly because God became in human eyes more humane, less severe and harsh than he had been, partly because the doctrine of purgatory was elaborated and popularized. The earlier view had been that most folk went straight to hell at their death – where else could such sinners go? – but some might, under God's providence, later escape elsewhere (see pp. 147-50). Once purgatory was defined, the sinners could be purged there; those in hell had no hope or chance of escape, but the large majority of mankind, who were a mixture of good and evil, might be sorted out and prepared for heaven after their death. This, however, was far from clear in the days of Pope Urban, and his own doctrine seems most intelligible if we accept the statement of the contemporary Guibert de Nogent, who tells us that he promised that death in the Crusade would be tantamount to martyrdom. 'Now you may enter the fight without danger', said St Bernard of Clairvaux, 'where to conquer is glory and to die is gain. . . . Take the sign of the cross and you will obtain indulgence for every sin which you confess with a contrite heart.' And again: 'how glorious are the victors who return from battle! How blessed are they who die as martyrs in the fight'; both ways success is sure.

This echoes the teaching of Turpin, the warrior archbishop of the late 11th-century version of the *Song of Roland*, urging Charlemagne's troops to battle:

> 'Barons, my lords, Charles picked us for this purpose;
> We must be ready to die in our King's service.
> Christendom needs you, so help us to preserve it.
> Battle you'll have, of that you may be certain,
> Here come the Paynims – your own eyes have
>   observed them.
> Now beat your breasts and ask God for His mercy:
> I will absolve you and set your souls in surety.
> If you should die, blest martyrdom's your guerdon;
> You'll sit on high in Paradise eternal.'
> The French alight and all kneel down in worship;
> God's shrift and blessing the Archbishop conferreth,
> And for their penance he bids them all strike firmly.

Here the papal doctrine and the popular doctrine seem for a while to meet. Death on Crusade opened the gate to heaven. If we reflect on the conditions of Crusading warfare we can hardly avoid the suspicion that this is a parody of the doctrine of martyrdom among the early Christians. Yet at this point we meet a paradox very near the heart of our subject. A Crusading historian like William Archbishop of Tyre can recount without any squeamishness how the natives of Antioch knew the Crusaders had arrived when a shower of two hundred heads, severed from slaughtered Turks, came over the wall. This was the kind of activity Urban and Bernard were launching. Yet both were in their hearts men of peace; and Bernard – when not actually engaged in preaching a

Crusade – was a great deal more interested in the heavenly than the earthly Jerusalem. Your canon Philip, he said in a letter to the Bishop of Lincoln, setting out for Jerusalem has found it sooner than he expected – not the earthly Jerusalem which is somewhere near Mount Sinai, but the heavenly Jerusalem in my abbey.

Popular religion

If we were to put all the books which were written in the 12th century into a single library, we should find that a great preponderance represented the studies and the interests and the outlook of the learned: that they have far more to tell us about the devout meditations of monks and the scholarship of the schools and incipient universities than about the thoughts of ordinary folk. More popular works of devotion and sermon literature sometimes bridge the gap; but when written down much of this has an inexorable tendency to become more ethereal, more removed from the lay mind. It is where bridges could be built that we are best informed: in the literature on pilgrimages and relics, in the design of churches and their adornment, in the less sophisticated vernacular literature; most of all perhaps in story-telling. For this was a golden age of literary history and chronicle, and the First Crusade was described in vivid and gory detail by a knight who fought in it, the anonymous author of the *Gesta Francorum*, and by Anna Comnena, the Byzantine princess, who witnessed the coming and going of the barbarous Western hordes from the great walls of Constantinople, by others who went and many more who did not – so that we know in sumptuous detail how the Crusaders behaved and can judge something of what inspired them.

Yet a great deal is missing. We have enough evidence to be sure that various magical practices, witchcraft, necromancy, and other activities which we should call superstitious were widely used; and some by drawing together the threads have tried to weave a history of medieval witchcraft or have found traces under every stone of some rival religion to the official Church. These efforts fail because they attempt to make a single jigsaw out of the fragments of several dozen. Even in a single place at a single time religious life was complex. 'In Venice in the early middle ages, the merchant lived a spiritual life different from the sailor of the same town', wrote Professor Manselli, 'yet both their religions were popular and different from the religion of the learned.' This is no invitation to despair or scepticism, however; it urges us to concentrate our attention on the known and the knowable; and if it obliges us to see popular religion most fully where it is nearest to the religion of the learned and of the hierarch, we shall find copious hints by the way of what else lies hidden from us.

Let us begin with the creed of a simple man, highly intelligent but not a theologian of the schools. In 1179 Waldo, a merchant of Lyon who had cast away his wealth and sought God in poverty, gathering round himself a community of poor evangelists, came before the pope in the Third Lateran Council in Rome. A strenuous and sincere attempt was made to keep him within the Catholic fold, and the next year an ample profession of faith was prepared for him which reveals in a concrete and clear way the bridge between one man's popular religion and the official doctrines of the Catholic Church. As a bridge it failed, for within a few years Waldo had left the Church and founded what is now the most venerable of Protestant communions, the Waldensian; but as a bridge between the religion of the pope and the lay evangelist it may yet prove more successful.

'In the name of the Father and of the Son and of the Holy Spirit and of the most blessed and ever Virgin Mary.' It opens with a very formal statement of faith in the Trinity and adherence to the Creeds. It goes on to talk of God the creator, the Old and New Testaments, the incarnation of the Son, 'born of the Virgin Mary with a true human birth; and he ate and drank and slept; fatigued with the journey he took rest; and he suffered truly his passion in the flesh and died a true death of his body, and rose by the true resurrection of his flesh and truly came again to life. . . . This we believe with our hearts and confess with our lips.' Waldo was made to state his faith in the Catholic Church and the sacraments – baptism, confirmation, eucharist, penance, extreme unction, marriage, and the Church's orders and so quite specifically to reject current heresies (see pp. 99–102). 'We believe the devil became evil not by God's creation but by his own will. We do not at all condemn the eating of meat; we believe in' the resurrection of the body and the Last Judgment, but also that alms and good works may help the dead. 'We have renounced the world' and live in poverty, but accept that those who live in the world and enjoy their possessions may also be saved. Thus Waldo held, by what seems to us no narrow thread, to contemporary Catholic doctrine; but presently the tensions grew, the thread snapped, and like John Wesley he became the unwilling founder of a new communion.

V

Popular and unpopular religion

Churches as evidence – their sites

The central theme of this book is the meeting of Church and people, and we try to view it especially through the visible evidence by which the building, adornment and furnishing of churches reveal and reflect the attitudes, aspirations and fashions of medieval society. The survival of enormous numbers of medieval churches in almost every part of Europe tempts us to think that everyone was united in the faith and practice which they represent; they are dramatic evidence for the notion of the age, or ages, of faith. There is much truth in this, and in all sorts of ways their site and setting, their design and style and ornament, have much to tell us of the interests and devotion of their builders. They also disguise the hidden world of the heretic, the blasphemer, the dropout, and the pagan.

The vivid sculpture of the west front of Saint-Gilles unites the culture and the artistic creativity of the Roman and Romanesque worlds with a church which was a centre of pilgrimage. It looks out on a small town which was a major centre of travel and trade: here the routes from northern Europe down the Rhône impinged on the world of the Mediterranean. In Toulouse and Saint-Gilles in the 1130s a powerful preacher called Peter of Bruis urged on the faithful the doctrine that God had no use for churches and 'inflamed [them] with an immense hatred of the cross, and one and all were armed with swords and with fire to revenge upon the cross the torments of the crucified'. He invited his followers to gather any crosses they could find and make a bonfire of them. Many of the citizens of Saint-Gilles were enraged: the physical presence of their church, its relics and its images, was the centre of their faith and their devotion; the pilgrim traffic was equally the source of their earthly prosperity. They saw to it that Peter of Bruis was burnt on his own bonfire of crosses, and this fire melts

10

together the themes which make this chapter: the Church as a positive witness of medieval popular religion; its enemies, the devout heretics who saw the visible Church as a distraction and a barrier to true devotion; and the scoffers to whom it was offensive or irrelevant.

High on a rocky cliff above the valley of Poschiavo, where a finger of Switzerland points down into Italy, stands a lonely church. It is the Church of San Romerio, and his shrine is set actually in the cliff edge, at the summit of a precipice. In the shrine traces of prehistoric use have been found, which may suggest that it replaces an ancient, pagan, holy site. Of the saint we know only his name, which may be a corruption of San Remigio, but it is most probable that in the course of the Middle Ages it became the home not of the great Apostle of the Franks, Saint-Remi of Rheims, but of an obscure hermit who affected a cell high on a cliff. The site is similar to the less dramatic cell of St Francis on a cliff ledge at the Carceri above Assisi, now enclosed in a charming convent set about it in the 15th century by San Bernardino. Francis's cell sat on a cliff no more than 30 metres high; but the principle was the same. Sites such as this are as important as the surviving saints' lives as evidence for the life of the hermits who flourished in 11th-century Italy and elsewhere. The hermits were among the creators of the religious aspirations of this book; and especially in the 12th century we find them appearing in every part of Europe, their function often not confined to prayer and contemplation. In a brilliant article Dr Henry Mayr-Harting has evoked the little world of Wulfric of Haselbury, the English village hermit who was sage, counsellor, banker even, to his community, and shows many of the traits already associated with the resident holy man of the late Roman world.

The valley of Poschiavo is ill-documented between the 9th and the 13th centuries; but three churches tell us something of its history. San Romerio tells of a hermit and his cult; far below, in the valley, the large Romanesque tower of the main church of Poschiavo is clear testimony that this was the mother church of the region already in the 12th century. On the western slopes lies the Alp of Selva, a modest settlement with a tiny chapel, Romanesque at heart but much altered in more recent centuries. Then as now, Selva can only have been accessible and habitable in the summer: the chapel is witness that the life of the Alpine peasant, and his use of the high Alpine pastures in the summer, was not so different then from what it is now.

1 The reliquary of Sainte-Foy, a doll-like figure of wood coated in gold, mostly of the 9th and 10th centuries, though incorporating a head from a late antique bust; the crown was added in the 10th century, and some of the jewels later (pp. 28-9).

2 The Abbey Church of Sainte-Foy, Conques (Aveyron) (pp. 26-9).

3 Rievaulx Abbey from the air. 'High hills surround the valley, encircling it like a crown. These are clothed by trees of various sorts and maintain in pleasant retreats the privacy of the vale, providing for the monks a kind of second paradise of wooded delight' (pp. 29-30).

4 The Coronation of the Virgin: the earliest known representation, on a capital from Reading Abbey, *c*. 1130 (p. 33).

5 A miracle of St Thomas Becket, from a 12th-century window in Canterbury Cathedral, illustrating the cult of Becket's blood. Here it cures a young woman, Etheldreda of Canterbury (second from left). The shrine has a candle on it like an altar (pp. 40-44).

6 Speyer: the ante-chamber to the subterranean bath-house for the purification of Jewish women, early 12th century (p. 59).

7 The fall of Simon Magus, watched by Sts Peter and Paul; on the right the Devil waits for his victim. A capital by Gislebertus at Autun (p. 52).

8 The Church of San Romerio, Graubünden (Grisons), Switzerland, set on a cliff edge: looking south towards Italy and the Valtelline (p. 64).

9 Wells Cathedral, nave, late 12th century, completed in the early 13th century (pp. 84, 86).

10 Saint-Gilles, the west front of the Abbey Church: a great Romanesque set-piece, with entablature and frieze evidently based on classical models, and animal heads vividly portrayed above the frieze (p. 63).

11 Amiens Cathedral nave (p. 85).

12 The font in Saint-Barthélemy, Liège, cast in bronze by Rainer of Huy, *c.* 1107-18, showing John the Baptist baptizing penitents in the Jordan (pp. 84, 107).

13 Toothache and footache in the 12th century – from the south transept of Wells Cathedral (p. 86).

14 San Zeno, Verona: from the north aisle of the nave we see the crypt below and the choir and lofty vault above it (p. 89).

15 San Zeno, Verona, bronze bas relief on the west door, c. 1138: the consequences of the Fall – man and woman must work, spinning and ploughing, with the murder of Abel by Cain.

16 Vézelay Abbey: the great Romanesque nave, *c*. 1120–40, with the choir of *c*. 1200 beyond (pp. 91–4).

17 *Right,* Malmesbury Abbey: the south porch, *c.* 1160-70, richly decorated – the entry for visitors and layfolk coming from the town, since the cloister lay to the north, and doubtless the scene of many marriages (p. 113). In the medallions scenes of the Old and New Testament alternate, and virtues combat vices.

18 Amiens Cathedral: the woad merchants of the surrounding district showing the source of their wealth – on the exterior of their chapel, late 13th century (p. 121).

19 A northern font: the baptism of Christ at Castle Frome, Herefordshire, 12th century (pp. 105, 107).

20 Amiens Cathedral: the rose window in the south transept with the rim of a wheel of fortune round its upper half (p. 121).

21 Pisa Cathedral, pulpit by Giovanni Pisano, 1302–11 (p. 121).

22, 23 *Above,* Duccio, *Maestà,* for Siena Cathedral, now in the Museo dell'Opera del Duomo, 1308–11 (p. 122). *Below,* Detail from Ambrogio Lorenzetti's allegorical fresco of good government, Siena, Palazzo Pubblico, completed 1339. Wisdom hovers above the enthroned figure of Justice, holding balances, on each of which is a winged figure. The one on her right, distributive justice, beheads and crowns; on her left, commutative justice hands out a weapon and money. A double cord runs from the scales to the left hand of Concord, seated below Justice, and from her into the hands of the citizens (pp. 122–3).

24 The Last Supper, from a tympanum at Saint-Bénigne, Dijon, 12th century (p. 134).

25 The death of Saul, from the Lambeth Bible, mid-12th century (see pp. 133-4).

26, 27 *Above left,* Saint-Savin-sur-Gartempe, Noah's ark in the act of being launched, with men clambering aboard; from the nave ceiling, end of 11th century (pp. 135–6). *Above right,* Lincoln Cathedral, bas relief of Noah's ark from the frieze on the west front, mid-12th century. Here the animals are boarding at the last minute (p. 136).

28 Autun: the flight into Egypt, by Gislebertus, *c.* 1125–30 (pp. 137–8).

29 Zillis, the life of Christ: the nave ceiling of the church of St Martin, 12th century (pp. 137-8).

30 Zillis: fishy monster with elephant's trunk (p. 137–8).

31 Zillis: Joseph equipped for the flight to Egypt 'with contemporary luggage and a stout whip' (p. 137).

32 Zillis: the Gadarene swine (p. 138).

33 Christ appears to Mary Magdalene, 'Noli me tangere': nave capital by Gislebertus, *c.* 1130–35 (pp. 141–2).

34 A detail of the Resurrection of the Dead, from the tympanum over the west door, Autun Cathedral, by Gislebertus, *c.* 1130–35. An angel lifts a saved soul heavenwards while another clings for protection (p. 152).

35 From the Last Judgment, by Gislebertus at Autun: condemned sinners, including a miser and an adulteress, leaving their tombs to face serpents and the devil's grip (p. 152).

In these three cases site and structure combine as historical evidence. Sometimes the sites of churches talk in quite a different way. For many centuries the Archbishop of Mainz, from a headquarters safe within ancient walls beside the Rhine, presided over a province which stretched far and wide to the east: the pattern of a missionary province devised by St Boniface in the 8th century remained until the next step forward in the advance of Christendom, with the formation of Magdeburg, soon to have a similar province stretching far beyond the Elbe, in the 10th century. The pattern of provinces and sees in central Europe, especially in Poland and Hungary, and in the far north, in Scandinavia, reflected missionary enterprises linked to the kingdoms of these regions, and still in active progress in the year 1000. In England the see of Dorchester, a modest town in Oxfordshire, stretched over seven shires to the north-east, covering much Viking territory in process of reconversion. By the 1070s the missionary age was past, and the Normans moved the see north to Lincoln. Likewise, in the 10th and 11th centuries, the holder of the ancient see of York often had his base in securely Christian territory at Worcester; and the diocese of York itself stretched over a great area of Danish and Norse settlement in the north of England, from the vale of York in the east to the coast of north Lancashire in the west, and as far north as Whitehaven, near which lay at that time the frontier with Scotland. In England the successive invasion of Angles and Saxons and Vikings had erased all but an antiquarian memory of Roman provinces; but over much of the continent the structure of Roman provincial and municipal organization survived in the provinces and dioceses of the medieval Church. This led to smaller and more coherent units in France, and far smaller sees in Italy, where almost every town of any pretension had a bishop. The Cathedral of Lincoln, splendidly set on a hill, is a monument to Norman planning of the 1070s; the Cathedral of Milan, a much younger building, none the less covers the remains of a great double-cathedral of early Christian times, and the baptistery in which St Augustine was baptized; and in the Basilica of St Ambrose, Sant'Ambrogio, a kilometre away, on the edge of the ancient city, the bones of Ambrose and the Roman martyrs for whom he originally built the church in the 4th century still lie. Most of what we see at Lincoln or in Sant'Ambrogio is of our period, but the sites represent historical situations of very different epochs, and Sant'Ambrogio a continuity of cult and aspiration covering many centuries.

In its own context, a village church can tell its story as plainly as those of a great city. The titular churches of Rome tell us where leading Roman Christians lived in the 2nd and 3rd centuries AD. The little church of St-Just-in-Roseland, by a hidden creek in Cornwall, commemorates a saint as obscure as San Romerio and serves a community on the heights above it; presumably its site, and many like it, reflect the landing point of early missionaries and a world in which communication from the world and the Church elsewhere came by water. Similarly the Church of St Eata at Atcham, 'by the mighty river Severn' where the historian Orderic was baptized in the 1070s, owed its origin to Northumbrian missionaries of perhaps the 7th or 8th century; and the Church of Kirkby Ireleth, near the Duddon estuary in the north-west of England, sits where the converted Norse built it, near the water; in the Middle Ages it served a community stretching 18 miles inland to the head of the Duddon Valley; here as in many such cases the dead had to be brought long distances for burial, and one is left guessing how often the living saw their pastors.

This parish was very likely formed about the year 1000, and remained for many centuries of extraordinary size because the process of forming new parishes in town and country became fossilized in the 12th century. This was because of a strengthening of episcopal authority, which made the informal establishment of parishes impossible, and of the Church's courts and canon law, which provided a legal framework much more difficult to break. The pattern of country parishes became fixed in many parts of Europe at this time; and the uneven progress of development is still reflected in the huge country parishes of Italy, the *pievi*, the relatively small country parishes of France and southern England, and the very large parishes of north-western England, culminating in Kirkby Ireleth, one of the largest of all. In the towns, more changes came later. In Italy it was still often reckoned that each city had a single parish; and the great baptisteries, often rebuilt in this period, remain a monument to the doctrine that the children were taken to the city baptistery to be christened. English towns were commonly much more modest than Italian in the 12th century; but oddly enough they had far more parish churches. In most English towns, indeed, the number of churches declined in the late Middle Ages – some churches became larger, some towns became smaller; we cannot attribute the decline to any measurable decline in fervour. But in London the shape of innumerable tiny parishes still reflected down to 1907 (long after many of the churches had disappeared) the pattern of settlement of 11th- and 12th-century London.

Style and furnishing

We look to churches as historical evidence not only for their sites but in themselves, in their image and style and furnishing. Doubtless there are many difficulties. A fashion came in with the 14th century in many parts of Europe for much more elaborate furniture of wood than had hitherto been used; and the appearance of church interiors before that is often wholly obscure. Even the late Gothic wooden furniture survives very patchily, for the ideals of the Counter-Reformation and the age of the Baroque swept Gothic clutter from the interiors of innumerable churches, and opened vistas which might have been acceptable to some Romanesque builders, but were evidently anathema to most of their Gothic successors. Only in Lutheran Germany and Anglican England, paradoxically, does there survive any great number of the screens which wholly enclosed the chancels and choirs of late medieval churches in most of western Europe, setting them off as separate chambers for parsons or canons or monks, and for the altar and the holy sacrifice. Romanesque and Gothic churches survive, beyond counting; but they are usually shells, refitted and refurbished time and again, and eventually restored with the ruthless affection of a Viollet-le-Duc or a Gilbert Scott.

Romanesque and Gothic: the labels are arbitrary and may easily mislead. They may invite us to a summary of the history of architecture which would lead us far astray. They imply a contrast which is real, and was felt by contemporaries, but dissolves the more closely one inspects it. Romanesque is the architecture of the 11th and early 12th century, of the great churches and the small, the oratories and parish churches which spread all over Europe in that epoch. Gothic was the predominant fashion in many parts of Europe from the mid-12th to the 15th or 16th centuries. In 17th- and 18th-century England Gothic and classical churches were being built side by side, sometimes designed by the same architect. In a somewhat similar way Romanesque survived alongside Gothic in many parts of Europe for several generations. It is conventional to describe the Abbey Church of Abbot Suger of Saint-Denis, just outside Paris, begun in the 1120s, consecrated in 1144, as the first building truly Gothic. In the next century

Romanesque and Gothic buildings were still growing side by side in Germany. Mainz Cathedral was largely rebuilt, and a new design made for Cologne, in the 13th century. One is mainly Romanesque, the other Gothic. The crossing and nave of Wells Cathedral are of the last quarter of the 12th century, and the purest surviving example of the earliest English Gothic. Six miles away is the western chapel of Glastonbury Abbey, identical in date, but essentially Romanesque. Subtlest of all is the contrast in the Basilica of St Francis at Assisi. Over the Italian Romanesque structure of the lower church, of *c.* 1230, its builders went straight on to build a beautiful Gothic church in the French style, without any break in time, so far as we can tell.

It is an exceedingly delicate matter to define these labels: much better to contemplate acceptable examples. Let Compostela speak for Romanesque, and Laon and Amiens for Gothic. The great Cathedral of St James, Santiago de Compostela, lies in north-western Spain far from most other famous Romanesque centres; but it was the terminus of many popular pilgrim routes and it serves to remind us of the cosmopolitan character of some of these fashions. It is immensely long, and the style is heavier and darker now than originally intended, for it was originally painted with brilliant colours and lit by a thousand candles; but it never enjoyed much natural light. Many Romanesque basilicas seem relatively squat today. But Compostela is very lofty, and the appearance of height is enhanced by great vertical ribs going right up to the vault, and over; the church is thus punctuated by a series of immensely lofty arches, and it seems a *tour de force* to keep so much heavy stone aloft in a building of relatively simple structure. The pilgrim who travelled through France in the 12th century would have seen several very similar, at Tours and Conques especially. The present church at Compostela is supposed to have been started about 1078, completed about 1140. In 1140 Suger's Saint-Denis was well under way, and such buildings as Laon Cathedral not far in the future. At Laon stone oxen contemplate a busy town and pleasant pastures beyond it from the twin western towers. In conception they are extremely like their cousins which support the famous font in Saint-Barthélemy at Liège; and they are not widely separated from them in time. The font is of the 1110s; the cathedral was built between *c.* 1150 and 1200. There are mouldings and piers in the cathedral which might have been designed in the 1110s, and many elements to remind us that its architect was born in the heyday of Romanesque. Yet all the

9, 13

12

84

Laon Cathedral, south-west tower, late 12th century. From a drawing by the architect Villard de Honnecourt, c.1235. The mason's hand is poetic licence.

arches are pointed; there is a lightness about many of the columns, a geometry traced by slender clustered shafts that helps to make the church feel much lighter in weight than Compostela; it is also lighter in the other sense, and the windows are tall and large; there is a large, ornate rose in the east; the stone frames the great expanses of glass, instead of the windows piercing gloomy walls. One could pursue the comparison through the style of glass and sculpture, through the whole conception of a church.

If we pass into the mid-13th century, and to Amiens, we see all the tendencies of Laon brought to astonishing fulfilment. Amiens is the loftiest of the Gothic cathedrals, and all the arcades, all the lines, are calculated to emphasize the fact. The clustered columns seem even more slender; the windows have tracery and are much enlarged; the sense of an immensely lofty building frame of glass is carried to perfection.

The contrast is great, but not complete. The ground plan of Gothic churches varied much, but the fundamental cross of the

11

great Romanesque basilica remained the norm. The east end grew larger, to allow for more space for pilgrims and shrines and altars and liturgy and stalls for canons and monks and subordinate clergy and choirboys. But crossing and nave sometimes changed little; and two of the greatest of Gothic naves, at Winchester and Canterbury, are Norman structures refaced. No Romanesque architect attempted to scale the heights of Amiens. But Compostela is a lofty building; so is Conques; so are many others like them.

Romanesque and Gothic are not 12th-century terms; the builders of that age would hardly have understood the distinctions we are making; the kind of profile they designed and executed changed almost imperceptibly. Right through the 12th century the masons' ideas of how a church should be laid out, of the schemes of proportion appropriate to it, of how to use stone, changed very slowly. Yet the 12th century was a period of creative change. If we compare St James's Cathedral at Compostela with St Andrew's at Wells we see at once a striking difference. The shapes of the arches, the mouldings, the whole impact of Wells is different; and if we look closely we find heads and comic scenes, a riot of inventive sculpture. At Wells, however, there is no aspiration to height. Not only does a part of its charm lie in the very modesty of its proportions, but the designers avoided any sense of height. The soaring ribs of Compostela and Amiens are not to be seen at Wells; instead the vertical line is broken, and the eye is carried horizontally along the triforium by the pattern of an unbroken line of arches. It has sometimes been said that the masons of Wells and other English Gothic churches had no head for heights and could not aspire to the glory of their French contemporaries. But Wells and its sisters have their own idiom and their own sentiment. The English masons rejoiced in the inventiveness of their world; but like St Bernard they condemned the excessive loftiness of their French rivals. To Bernard everything excessive was distracting; the French architects on the other hand saw soaring arches, as Abbot Suger saw glittering ornaments, as attracting the mind heavenward. But such speculations have limited validity: all that is certain is that these splendid buildings enshrined ideas aesthetic and religious which their patrons and builders tried to harmonize.

At the root of the transition from Romanesque to Gothic there lies a puzzle. It is far from clear how 'Roman' the architects of Romanesque churches imagined them to be; but it is clear that many patrons and builders of the 11th and early 12th centuries were aware of the appropriateness at least of their style to a world

'A congeries of little chapels and churches' (p. 87): St Augustine's Abbey, Canterbury, before the Norman Conquest, with 7th-century churches of St Mary and Sts Peter and Paul, and later additions, linked by the 11th-century rotunda.

which looked to ancient Rome as a supreme authority in matters of taste and culture. At Autun or Saint-Gilles one can see the direct use of Roman models in architectural design. In some respects this continued, and in sculpture the great works of the early 13th century, especially those of Chartres of the 1220s, show classical influence which has worked deep into the sculptor's mind and inspiration. But the Gothic arch, to put the matter in its simplest and crudest terms, is a deliberate denial of the Roman past. They arrived at it by what seems to have been a strange alliance between technological advance and stylistic imitation. The high vaults of the nave of Durham Cathedral come to a point, doubtless because the architect-engineers had appreciated that they would be easier to build and more secure once built. But the pointed arch was also copied from some Islamic buildings. How conscious Gothic architects were of this one may well doubt; but it must have been widely observed that the architects were turning their backs on Rome.

It is an extraordinary change in fashion and sentiment, however one views it; and this emphasizes to us the advantages they gained – in variety of design and lightness of touch, in paint and glass and the play of light. All these effects were used to provide a setting of surpassing beauty for the worship of God and the many other activities of the Church. In earlier centuries the major churches had been much smaller, divided into little compartments, some-times, indeed, a congeries of little chapels and churches. Each compartment had its separate function, though these are very often quite imperfectly known to us. Some porticos and porches were used as law courts or for storage of documents and books. Others were chapels for particular seasons of the year. The great westworks which one finds in so many different forms all over northern Europe contained upper and lower chambers and chapels in which particular feasts of the Church's year were appropriately celebrated. The great cult of the archangel Michael, patron of lofty places, flourished from the 8th and 9th centuries on, and right through our period, and sometimes his devotees gathered on mountain tops, or built churches in his honour on lesser eminences; sometimes they contented themselves with chapels in a western tower or over a transept. These chapels survived, indeed, into a different world, and there is a striking example in the narthex or westwork of Vézelay of the mid-12th century.

The Romanesque basilica, however, tended to become an enormous single room, like a great castle hall. It was commonly cruciform in shape, and often had nooks and corners set apart from its main functions, for treasuries and other purposes. The westwork at Vézelay is an example of an element from the earlier world which quite commonly survived, attached to a great basilica in other respects of more unitary character. The laity still had their own place in the nave, with a nave altar, sometimes dedicated to the Holy Cross, before the rood screen, for their especial use. But it seems likely that in many churches of the 11th and 12th centuries lay people in the nave could look east across relatively modest screens to the monks or canons in the choir and beyond them to the high altar, so that they could feel themselves participants in the community's mass; and in many cases they could see beyond the high altar the lofty shrine of the major saint, or boxes of relics supported on beams. But the evidence for the furnishing of early Romanesque basilicas is exceedingly spare and perplexing. In Rome in the early 12th century the newly built Basilica of San Clemente had low screens which still survive; the whole church is visually one. But this is a small Roman basilica, a deliberate reproduction of the main elements of its predecessor, destroyed in the Norman sack of Rome in 1084. It was archaic when it was built, and it would be rash to deduce that screens in other parts of Europe were so low. Some screens survive elsewhere in Italy, and they are higher, though not substantially higher, than in San Clemente. A common arrangement in northern Italy placed the shrine in a crypt which could and can be viewed from the nave; and surviving examples suggest that though the choir was often much higher than the nave, it was at least partly visible. At San Miniato outside Florence or San Zeno on the edge of old Verona, we can still visit churches of this age where the worshipper in the nave can look upward into the choir and down into the crypt and the shrine of the saint; and so in a single instant worship Christ on the high altar and the saint in his tomb. The mid-12th-century choir screen of Ely Cathedral survived into the 19th century, long enough for us to be able to inspect reliable drawings of it, and these show an arcade. Through the arches one could have seen monks, high altar, and St Etheldreda; but if the arches had curtains across them, all would have been hidden; if they were surmounted by a rood beam and a rood, or crucifix, even the east window would not have been clearly visible. We do not know if curtains were used at Ely, nor anything about the design and construction of a rood. All that we can say is that the general conception of a great basilica presupposes a new desire in the 11th century for buildings to be regarded as single enormous rooms; that no surviving evidence contradicts the possibility that low screens were the norm. All that we know of screens in the late 12th and 13th centuries suggests that they were growing higher and more opaque. Our very ignorance may suggest a simpler chronology than really occurred. It may well be that there was much difference of taste and practice in 11th–13th century Europe, in all kinds of furnishing. But the general picture, of increasing furniture and growing segregation of nave, choir, sanctuary, shrines, chapels – this seems inescapable. In domestic building, in the 14th and 15th centuries, the great halls and chambers of earlier castles were accompanied and in a measure replaced by a multiplicity of rooms for special purposes. The break-up of the large church into separate spaces and rooms in part reflects this new attitude to domestic organization and comfort; and not comfort only, but ritual too, for the great house was designed like the great church to suit the ritual of royal and princely and aristocratic courts. But in church another effect was clearly sought. Religious sentiment, the search for sanctity and holiness, whatever one calls it, demanded in the 11th century a great space; in many situations, especially in 13th-century France, it demanded too an enormous height. In the 14th and 15th centuries the choir and high altar, the most sacred parts of the church, had once again, in most parts of Europe, to be enclosed, to be hidden, secluded, to have privacy. In great measure, this change in religious sentiment lies beyond our

14,15

period; but not wholly, for it was foreshadowed by the mighty screens built for Italian and French churches already in the 13th century.

Beside the great cathedrals grew up thousands of smaller churches. In the 11th century in many parts of Europe the majority of these were little boxes, emphasizing the contrast between the two styles of worship most affected in that age – the intimacy of priest and congregation in the small church, the remoteness and cosmic scale of worship in a great basilica. But in a variety of ways the contrast grew somewhat less in the 12th and 13th centuries. Many parish churches grew larger by the extension of chancels, the building of aisles and the addition of chapels. This partly reflected growing population and wealth, growing multiplicity of cult and sentiment; and every generation wished to rebuild and alter as the expression of the pious and generous feelings of communities and patrons, so that many churches were subjected to almost constant tinkering. Another common reason for extensive building works was the frequency of fire – either to replace its ravages or build stone vaults and screens less inviting to it than wooden ceilings and open draughty spaces. Fire was an ever-present risk: furniture and ornaments of wood, as well as ceilings, were easily ablaze; altar clothes and other linen stored under altars or near shrines fell easy victims – as happened at Bury St Edmund's – to candles guttering in a draughty church.

The urge to rebuild meant that the noise, dust and discomfort of building works in progress were a familiar, indeed a normal part of the life of churches great and small. The changes affected furniture even more than structure. We cannot be sure that the very extensive wooden furniture of the late Middle Ages was common before 1300 – certainly very little survives of so early a date; but there is no doubt that furniture had as much to do as the size of congregation with church planning in the later Middle Ages. Meanwhile, there had always been many intermediaries between the tiny box and the cathedral. In the 12th century substantial castle chapels and the parish churches intended also to house small religious communities were extremely common; and some parish churches, or mother churches serving a wider district or a *pieve* in Italy, had a scale and a port suited to their standing. Many of the hundred parish churches of London remained tiny; some were already buildings of more ample stature. Almost all of these have disappeared or been replaced. But we can still walk about Lucca and observe that large and sumptuous churches were

Building works in progress: a 13th-century impression of the building of St Alban's Abbey, by the monastic historian and artist Matthew Paris.

built in great numbers in the prosperous towns of 12th-century Tuscany.

The example of Vézelay

The heroic efforts of church builders in these centuries reflect a society deeply imbued with Christian devotion, with the belief that it should be expressed in visible building, with a sense of sin and judgment that could only be expiated by immensely generous gifts to fabric funds, in awe of a divine being who rejoiced in the beauty of human craftsmanship and welcomed the dedication of all that was richest and best to His own worship. But this inspiring statement hides a deeper truth: that in this society, as in all, there was much variety of approach and faith and sentiment; that there were many who protested, or happily ignored the collecting boxes; that there were many who gave lavishly to one church while trying to destroy another.

Where could we find a more eloquent expression of 12th-century devotion than in the great Abbey Church of the Madeleine at Vézelay? It has few competitors for sheer beauty among Romanesque churches; it holds much of the finest Romanesque sculpture which survives. Even shorn of most of its paint and all its ancient glass it is marvellously beautiful and a document to inspire the historian. Beside it we may set a contemporary chronicle, written by Hugh of Poitou, monk of Vézelay, one of the community which enjoyed the basilica in its first beauty. The story he tells is of a proud, self-centred community, harshly jealous of its rights, tyrannical to its tenantry, at odds with its superiors, in conflict also with its secular neighbours and the local nobles. The two documents, the church and the chronicle, seem to tell quite incompatible stories; and yet each in its way must tell the truth.

'Many people ask,' wrote the author of the *Miracula* of the Madeleine, probably in the late 11th century, 'how the body of St Mary Magdalene, whose native land was Judaea, could have been translated to Gaul from a land so far away. To such doubts we may return a brief reply. All things are possible to God . . .'. In the mid-11th century, under extremely – as some would say, suspiciously – obscure circumstances, the monks of Vézelay discovered that they had the body of the Madeleine. Between 1050 and the early 13th century pilgrims came in great throngs to Vézelay, bringing bountiful offerings to supplement the building funds the monks could extract from their own resources and tenants. By the late 13th century the prestige of a rival set of relics of the Madeleine at Saint-Maximin in Provence had diverted the flow of pilgrims away from Vézelay. By a strange mercy the pilgrims ceased to come to Vézelay, and the monks never had the wealth in later centuries to rebuild their church in the fashion of a later age. Many miracles were wrought by the Madeleine at Vézelay; and the greatest of her miracles, as has often been observed, was the church itself.

It was said that the abbot who first discovered her relics planned a translation into a lofty shrine in the choir; but a cloud of impenetrable darkness filled the church while he was discussing the plan, and was taken to demonstrate her wish to stay in the dark crypt where she was supposed to have been found. By 1100 funds were sufficient to pay for a new choir and transepts; and the abbey's place in the Church was strengthened for a time by its subjection to Cluny herself – a subjection which helped her to prosperity at first, but like everything else in her history led to bitter conflict within half a century. In 1120 a serious fire broke out on the eve of St Mary Magdalene's day, consuming the ancient nave and numerous pilgrims. Over the ashes rose, in the next twenty years, the nave and narthex which are the glory of the present church. Here the young Peter of Montboissier, the future Abbot Peter the Venerable of Cluny, was brought up as a young monk. Here Gislebertus, the great sculptor of Autun, spent some years between apprenticeship at Cluny and his maturest work at Autun. The Madeleine and her community made the great hill-top shrine and the town – and all the country about it – rich and famous.

16

The local townsfolk, however, far from savouring this prosperity, rose in revolt against Abbot Arnaud early in the 12th century and murdered him. The history of the town for the next fifty years, when it is best recorded, shows that mixture of strife, faction, bitterness and prosperity which marks the history of so many towns and cities in 12th-century Europe. The Madeleine was their patron, the source of all their wealth, their guide on the path to heaven; her community, however, was the very symbol of tyranny in the age of the communes.

Relations between the community and the counts of Nevers were equally dramatic. As he gets nearer to the time when he was writing, Hugh of Poitou's narrative becomes shriller in its denunciation of the counts and their wives; for one of these Jezebel and Herodias were almost too kindly labels. But it is clear that he portrays a tradition of enmity which was firmly established at least as early as the time of Count William II, who died about the middle of the century. By great good fortune we have from other sources evidence to give us something like a rounded picture of this extraordinary man. There is no doubt that he was notorious for acts of cruel tyranny to churches and other landlords whom he thought to be interfering with his own rights. There is equally no doubt that he was a man of great prestige and ability, held in the highest respect by King Louis VII of France, who tried to make him regent, with Abbot Suger, when he set off on the Second Crusade. The count, however, refused and presently withdrew from the world, became a humble lay brother at La Grande Chartreuse itself, and died in the odour of sanctity. He had lived long enough to be known to the young Hugh of Avalon, later bishop and saint of Lincoln; and Hugh's biographer has preserved the tradition of a remarkable character. While still in secular life, he combined military and lay authority with a reputation for being pious and austere. When Louis VII was relaxing over a game of chess and heard the count was visiting him, he hastily hid the board for he knew the count's disapproval of jests or 'idle amusements'. We are told a delicious story of how the count not long after came in unexpectedly and finding the board still set rebuked the king roundly for wasting his time. There are other stories which reveal both the downright common sense of the intelligent layman, and an extreme case of 12th-century piety – he allowed the lice to eat him, he told his son after his retirement to the Chartreuse, in the hope 'by God's mercy to escape the insatiable appetite of the worms of Hell'.

There are few labels more opaque than 'anti-clerical': the word is used of people who have a deep hatred of everything spiritual and of those whose enmity is solely for the clergy, and may themselves be fervent believers; it is used of people like Count William and his family, who had a feud with one particular clerical or monastic institution and its inmates. Yet the word is not wholly without meaning, for the feeling which William and his kin had towards Vézelay was evidently similar in many respects to that which many laymen have felt in all ages of the Church's history for the clerical élite in the Church militant, claiming 'naked to follow the naked Christ' while clothed in remarkable temporal prosperity. If we use the word in this sense we may say that the Count of Nevers united in his person, as many did, two of the motives most common and powerful in his society: an austere, fervent and lofty piety, and a violent anti-clericalism.

Anti-clericalism, dissent and heresy

A similar combination helps to explain the success of the ex-canon regular and ex-abbot Arnold of Brescia in the mid-12th century. Like many of the monastic leaders of his age, he was a popular preacher. Arnold went further and roused the rabble against inadequate bishops and clergy. 'He said things that were entirely consistent with the law accepted by Christian people, but not at all with the life they led', observed John of Salisbury with characteristic irony and relish. Arnold roused Brescia against its bishop and was chased to France; there he sat at Abelard's feet and railed against St Bernard of Clairvaux. St Bernard 'prevailed on the most

Christian king' Louis VII of France to return him to Italy. He did not preach any precisely heretical doctrines; but his preaching was totally destructive of the ecclesiastical hierarchy, so that it was not unreasonable to regard him as an enemy of Church order. 'Whilst dwelling in Rome under pretext of penance' he allied himself to the forces of unrest (see p. 55), and the pope who had reconciled him found himself denounced as a 'man of blood'. If a few of his sermons had survived we might well have supposed that he was a fiery preacher orthodox in intent; indeed, he may have said little that was not said by the allies of the reformed papacy in Milan in the 11th century, or by the saintly ladies of 14th-century Italy in their denunciation of the Avignon papacy. In his context he was a social revolutionary and he was eventually caught by the Emperor Frederick Barbarossa in a rare moment of accord with the pope in the mid-1150s, and executed.

If not a heretic, Arnold was a dissenter, a man who disputed the order of things as he found it; and the growing variety of expression, attitude and outlook in the 12th century proved fertile ground for dissent. This took many forms, social and political as well as religious. It could be skin deep, or profound. Many of the great religious leaders began as dropouts, nor are the frontiers ever clear. In our own society dissent has often become the arch-orthodoxy, to the discontent of its truly dissenting followers. St Francis rejected the wealth and all the social assumptions of his father, threw at him even the clothes that he wore, and refused to touch or handle money. Could rejection of the values of Assisi go further than that? Yet not long after he was setting off for Rome to lay himself, his followers, his rule, at the pope's feet, in total obedience. Never have dissent and conformity lived more closely together than in Francis.

Scoffers and blasphemers

As in every age, there were many scoffers and blasphemers; and there were some who seriously doubted the truth of the Christian faith, or were totally indifferent to it. Sometimes blasphemy sat on a throne, as in the person of William Rufus, King of the English (1087-1100), whose lively wit so fascinated and appalled his more sober contemporaries that even Eadmer, the devout biographer of St Anselm, portrays a king whose wit and humour make him much more entertaining than Eadmer's saintly hero. A new pope was elected in 1099, Paschal II. What was he like? – asked the king; and his advisers enjoyed a little joke at the king's expense by saying that he was the exact image of Anselm, whom the king could not abide. But most of the humour tells the other way to a modern audience; and we cannot refuse our sympathy to a king who looked coolly at the Church's attitude to the Jews, and evidently thought it plain injustice.

The scoffers also included those who enjoyed the parody of holy things and lofty sentiments, and this we may interpret as we will as a common feature of every age of faith or an expression of hidden dissent. Probably it held elements of both. Thus the cult of courtly or romantic love often produced parodies of Christian doctrine and practice, such as the Cave of Lovers in the *Tristan* of Gottfried von Strassburg, which has many features of a Gothic cathedral, or the passage in the slightly later *Lay of the Reflection* by Jean Renart, written about 1220, in which a courtly lover asks his lady to love him as an act of charity – 'Such charity would be tantamount to making a pilgrimage to the Holy Land' – in which we may perhaps suspect that it is courtly love as much as the pilgrimage which is being laughed at. Among the lightest and most famous of such parodies is the pretended confession of the Archpoet to his patron, Rainald of Dassel, Archbishop of Cologne (1159-67) and arch-chancellor of the Emperor Frederick Barbarossa. He confesses his three 'sins' and enjoys the vision of the angels hiccoughing a prayer for his repose, as he lies dying in a tavern.

Presul discretissime,	Pardon, pray you, good my lord,
veniam te precor:	Master of discretion,
morte bona morior,	But this death I die is sweet,
dulci nece necor,	Most delicious poison.
meum pectus sauciat	Wounded to the quick am I
puellarum decor,	By a young girl's beauty:
et quas tactu nequeo,	She's beyond my touching? Well,
saltem corde mechor.	Can't the mind do duty?
Secundo redarguor	Yet a second charge they bring:
etiam de ludo.	I'm for ever gaming.
Sed cum ludus corpore	Yea, the dice hath many a time
me dimittit nudo,	Stripped me to my shaming.
frigidus exterius	What an if the body's cold,
mentis estu sudo,	If the mind is burning.
tunc versus et carmina	On the anvil hammering,
meliora cudo.	Rhymes and verses turning.

Tertio capitulo	Look again upon your list.
memoro tabernam.	Is the tavern on it?
Illam nullo tempore	Yea, and never have I scorned,
sprevi, neque spernam,	Never shall I scorn it,
donec sanctos angelos	Till the holy angels come,
venientes cernam,	And my eyes discern them,
cantantes pro mortuis	Singing for the dying soul,
'Requiem eternam'.	Requiem eternam.
Meum est propositum	For on this my heart is set:
in taberna mori,	When the hour is nigh me,
ut sint vina proxima	Let me in the tavern die,
morientis ori;	With a tankard by me,
tunc cantabunt letius	While the angels looking down
angelorum chori:	Joyously sing o'er me,
'Sit Deus propitius	*Sit Deus propitius*
huic potatori'.	*Huic potatori.* *

* The toper, where the reader is expecting *peccatori*, the sinner.

Missionaries and toleration

In the far north-eastern frontiers of Europe there was some intercourse between Christian and pagan. On the frontiers of northern Europe, indeed, there was an ancient tradition of missionary activity, in which from the days of Charlemagne conquest and baptism had been combined: sometimes baptism was accompanied by serious preaching, sometimes by force, occasionally by both. St Olaf, King of Norway in the early 11th century, converted many of his subjects by the most ruthless methods. Bishop Otto of Bamberg, in the early 12th century, appealed successfully to the Pomeranians by fervent preaching and by the display of wealth and pomp which revealed the prosperity his God might be reckoned to bring to converts. Bishop Diego of Osma in northern Spain was inspired by a sudden enthusiasm in the first decade of the 13th century to abandon his diocese and to take his young disciple Dominic to preach to unconverted Scandinavians. An exasperated pope returned them both to Spain; but St Dominic never forgot the heathen and they remained a part of the work and inspiration of the Order of Friars Preacher after his death.

Elsewhere, the only non-Christians regularly encountered were Moslems, for those who lived in Sicily or Spain or went on Crusade, and Jews; and the presence of the Jews was a great trouble and anxiety to orthodox churchmen. To most modern Christians it seems strange and inexcusable that even the most enlightened Christians of the early and central Middle Ages were normally intolerant; but so it was. There were exceptions, probably more than the documents reveal to us – for there is a strong prejudice in surviving records in favour of the orthodox, and of polemic against the heretic. The attitude of live-and-let-live which subsisted in Spain and south Italy in the 11th century, and in many parts of western Europe before the Jews fell victim to the Crusading movement, is very ill-documented.

By inference we may be sure that much personal tolerance is hidden by the nature of surviving records; and so in effect we have to wait for the *Willehalm* of Wolfram von Eschenbach in the early 13th century for a positive call to tolerance. Wolfram's *Parzival* in the 1200s portrayed a man who lost his faith – not in the sense of becoming a convinced intellectual unbeliever, but in the sense that trust in God and in himself evaporated, and had to be revived by a long, slow, difficult process of conversion. The theme of *Willehalm*, of the 1210s, at first sight seems much simpler and more primitive. It is in form a Crusading epic, full of blood and thunder, and sensational changes of fortune, with a cast of thousands; a *chanson de geste* from the world of a century before. Wolfram, furthermore, betrays no knowledge of Islam, little if any of Jewry. But one of the central themes of the poem is the relation between Willehalm's queen, a converted pagan, and her own kith and kin. 'Hear a simple woman's counsel, and spare God's handiwork': even the heathen are God's handiwork. Wolfram's mind was sophisticated, and he saw some of the problems of his plea for tolerance. What difference does baptism make if we are all, pagan and Christian alike, God's handiwork? The question is perhaps implicit in the poem, rather than explicit; but such is the power of its conclusion that no imaginative reader can escape it. Implicit in both Wolfram's greatest poems is a distaste for the Church's intolerant authority and for clericalism in most of its forms. There is more than a trace of anti-clericalism. But there also underlies both poems a deep orthodoxy: Wolfram can see the problems which lie on the frontiers of simple faith as he knew it – of doubt, anxiety, and of the problem of the heathen and of a Christian's attitude to unbelief and false belief. But we may be sure he remained, according to his lights, and so far as was compatible with a passionate loyalty to his knightly order and vocation, a pious Catholic.

Heretics: Waldensians and Cathars

The most radical dissenters of 12th- and 13th-century Europe were the folk whom we usually call heretics, following the contemporary usage of that epoch. Western Europe had been strangely little touched by anything recognizable as formal heresy before the year 1000. In the early 11th century several groups of heretics are reported, then silence falls again soon after 1050. From the early 12th century we meet first a trickle then a flood of evidence of them; and as the century advances they fall more and more clearly into two types, ultimately crystallizing as Waldensians and Cathars. The followers of Peter of Bruis (the 'Petrobrusians') and Henry of Lausanne have evident links with later, puritanical, Protestant sects and communions; and their successors the Waldensians, who broke with the Church in the 1180s, still survive and are now the oldest surviving Protestant communion.

The Cathars derived their faith from a near-Eastern sect, the Bogomils, originating in Bulgaria. The increased contacts between western Europe and Byzantium stimulated by the Crusades may have played some part in spreading new ideas; but it was the improvement in long-distance communications established to cater for the rapidly increasing volume of trade that seems to have been primarily responsible for the speed and the direction of the penetration. Trading links brought Bogomils from Bulgaria to Constantinople, which became the centre for expansion and propagation. In the 1140s, when they were being subjected to persecution by the authorities in Constantinople, Bogomil missionaries penetrated both to Bosnia and, via the Danube–Rhine route, to the Rhineland. Thence they spread again along routes trodden by merchants and pilgrims, to Flanders, to England and to Champagne. The Cathars discovered at Cologne and Bonn in 1143 were burnt, the former by the populace, the latter by the local count. In 1163 five Flemish immigrants, again at Cologne, were denounced by their neighbours for not going to Church, convicted and burnt. Two years later, in the winter of 1165-6, a group of about thirty immigrant Cathars were apprehended in England, and adjudged heretics by a panel of bishops at Oxford.

Henry II ordered them to be branded, stripped and whipped out of the town. So far, the Cathars seem to have found the regions they penetrated inhospitable. Only small groups seem to have been involved, usually immigrants and weavers. Weavers became synonymous with heretics in Flanders and the Flemish towns were the centre of the cloth industry. Itinerant weavers carried their beliefs with them, and itinerant missionaries and pastors might use the convenient occupation of weaver as cover for their activities. For the Cathars in northern Europe for the most part did not flaunt their beliefs. They tried to live quietly, even practising occasional conformity to divert attention from themselves, and when questioned could be reticent. Their caution is hardly surprising when one considers how they were treated by suspicious neighbours, fanatically hostile crowds and stern rulers.

'Cathar' is derived from Greek and means 'pure', and the Cathars were those who had broken, as far as possible, all ties with evil, material things. It was, and is, a dualist faith. They believed that only the spiritual world is good, that God is wholly and essentially spirit. The visible world was created by the power of evil, either seen as an autonomous deity or as Satan, the leader of the fallen angels. In this life, the soul, the divine spark in man, is imprisoned in a fundamentally wicked body. They therefore preached, for those who wished to be perfect, an extreme asceticism. They must live in complete poverty and simplicity, like the apostles. They must abstain from everything connected with the flesh: all sexual intercourse and all food associated with animal intercourse – so, not only meat, but milk and eggs as well. Curiously they were not forbidden fish. They must never tell a lie, swear an oath, or renounce their faith. Such rigorous demands were only attainable by an élite, and were only required of such. There were different categories of adherents, different stages of progress. The ordinary believers, the *credentes*, provided the Cathars, the *perfecti*, with food, shelter, any necessary help or protection. They might delay till old age or mortal sickness, when purity need not be sustained too long, the sacrament, the *consolamentum*, which enrolled them too among the perfect. The austere, moral lives of the perfect were admirable and came to be widely admired in Languedoc and northern and central Italy. Their dedication, courage and constancy were an inspiration and example. The services and sacraments were serious, simple and devout. They met in some convenient large room: a Cathar would preach, bless them, distribute bread after reciting the Lord's

Prayer. At the solemn sacrament of the *consolamentum* the candidate for purification was given the book of the Gospels to hold and addressed by one of the perfect in some such words as these: 'You wish to receive this holy baptism of Jesus Christ?' The Gospel book was placed on his head and all the Cathars present laid their right hands upon him. The Lord's Prayer was recited and a few other short prayers were said, the beginning of St John's Gospel was read and the purified *'Christianus'* kissed the book and bowed three times.

Ordinary, unsophisticated people, townsfolk and peasants, were not likely to recognize at once how radically this faith differed from orthodox Christianity. Familiar passages from the New Testament, the Lord's Prayer, dire warnings of the wickedness of the world and the snares of Satan, stress on the spiritual merit of chastity – all were commonplaces of Catholic services and preaching. The lives of the perfect, who travelled around in poverty, preaching and ministering, recalled primitive apostolic practice. People could be won over without understanding the full implications of the doctrine. The dualist belief that spirit is good and matter evil logically necessitated the denial of the humanity of Christ. If He came from God he was a spirit and could not become flesh and blood. The facts of his earthly life then were not real, but an appearance only, an illusion. He was not born of Mary, was never actually hungry or thirsty or tired, and could have felt no pain on the Cross. There could be no resurrection of a non-existent body. The Church, by accepting lands and wealth, had compromised with the world and therefore with the devil, and so had forfeited all claim to apostolic authority. The true Church, the true successors of St Peter, were the Cathars. The teachings, sacraments, institutions of the evil, worldly Church were all wrong, or useless. It was wicked to venerate the Cross. Prayers for the dead or gifts to the Church for their repose were pointless as there was no purgatory or hell after death. Hell was now, in this life. So (as the more fervent held) marriage was wrong as it led to children, to more souls being imprisoned in evil flesh. Church buildings were unnecessary; monks, clergy, priests to be repudiated. In short the 'Roman Church is the devil's church and her doctrines are those of demons. She is the Babylon whom St John called the mother of fornication and abomination, drunk with the blood of saints and martyrs'. The Cathars would have none of it. They acknowledged a pope of their own and developed a completely independent, rival organization. They had their bishops, with their own ritual of consecration.

The Cathars flourished especially in southern France and north and central Italy. So rapid was their spread, so deep their roots, that they inspired panic in the Catholic hierarchy. At the turn of the 12th and 13th centuries brutal instruments of persecution were devised by men often of the loftiest moral convictions. The lands in which they flourished most and where they had been tolerated, around Toulouse and throughout the Languedoc, were subjected to the Albigensian Crusade, launched by Pope Innocent III in 1208-9, a movement in which political brutality, clerical alarm and many qualities less repellent were mingled. Amid fruitless efforts to win the Cathars back by persuasion, a system of enquiry and inquisition was gradually developed, to be perfected under Pope Gregory IX (1227-41). The obdurate heretic was handed over to the secular arm; and the Church had an understanding with the secular authorities in those countries in which the Inquisition was allowed free play that obdurate heretics would be burnt. In north and central Italy, where the independent spirit of the city republics made persecution very ineffective – even in cities like Perugia and Assisi officially under papal control – groups of heretics were relatively undisturbed. They were countered, however, by orthodox preachers like St Francis, whose inspired demonstrations that birds and flowers and sun and moon were God's creatures, and not the devil's, did much to undermine the Cathar hold on the popular imagination. The question will be asked till the end of time: were the Cathars more effectively countered by peaceful persuasion or by persecution? Did St Francis or the inquisitors have more to do with the decline of the Cathars? Such a question can never be answered; but it is abundantly clear that both took their toll. The Cathar churches went underground. When we meet Cathars at close quarters in the Inquisitors' records in the Pyrenees in the early 14th century – made famous in *Montaillou* (see pp. 125-6) – we meet them far from the main centres of population, strangely intermingled with the Catholic population – as indeed they had been in their heyday. The Cathars gradually faded away in the 14th century, and virtually disappeared in the 15th.

Meanwhile the other sects survived, persecuted likewise but not destroyed, to provide a slender link with the new movements of the late Middle Ages, and eventually with the Reformation. They had often shown elements of common ground in early days with the Cathars, as in their doubts about marriage or their rejection of infant baptism; but each movement showed also its own special features, not least the Petrobrusians with whom we began. They say that 'it is not necessary for Christians to have sacred places for prayer, since God, when invoked, hears as well in the tavern as in the church, in the market place as in the temple, before the altar or before the stall, and He will listen to those who are deserving'. Thus Peter the Venerable's summary; and he goes on to describe the extreme point of their rejection of the material Church: their insistence that 'holy crosses be broken into pieces and burnt since they are the symbol or instrument with which Christ was so horribly tortured and so cruelly killed'. From this sprang Peter of Bruis's own tragedy; for on such a bonfire the folk of Saint-Gilles laid the heresiarch himself, and thus the 'impious man was made to pass from fire to fire, from a transient to an eternal'.

VI

The laity and the Church

Baptism and Confirmation

Few questions are more difficult, or more essential to our enquiry, than the problem of the ways in which the Church impinged on the lives of ordinary folk. Then as now, it was perhaps most immediate to them at the central events of life, birth, marriage and death, but in a rather different way. It was generally assumed by the central Middle Ages that unbaptized babies had little or no chance of heaven; and thus very early baptism was favoured. So many died in infancy that this could sometimes mean informal ceremonies by midwives or parents; the books of instruction and the synodal statutes of the 13th century contain careful prescriptions for lay baptism. But the clergy much preferred that the babies be brought to church and be received in as public a fashion as possible.

The fonts which survive in great profusion from the Middle Ages are a vital witness to medieval baptismal customs. In early days baptism had been generally conferred on adults or grown children; and this was performed in public ceremonies in large buildings specially designed for the purpose. In Italy the baptisteries survived; old ones were restored and new ones built. In Florence, Pisa and many other cities we can still visit them; and they continued long after our period to play something of their original role. In the baptistery in Florence – dedicated, as was common, to St John the Baptist – a series of circular holes in the marble seem to have functioned as fonts. Dante apparently broke one of these in order to free someone trapped in it, and the incident inspired his description of the holes in the sides and bottom of the third circle of Malebolge in the *Inferno* (XIX, 13-20), into which the simonists were thrust head first. 'They seemed to me neither less spacious, nor larger, than those in my beautiful St John, made as places for baptism, one of which, not so many years ago, I broke as someone was drowning in it.' By the 11th century catechumens no longer came when they were grown up; they were brought by their parents and godparents as tiny babies. But they entered the Church and the civic community in a baptism service in the large baptistery adjacent to the cathedral. In northern Europe by this date innumerable tiny churches had their 19 own fonts. Here the baptism was normally an intimate affair in which the family brought the baby to be welcomed by the community in which they lived, sprinkled with water and anointed with holy oil by the priest. Of this the baby would remember nothing, but for his older brothers and sisters, and for the children of the neighbourhood, it would serve as a reminder of how they came to join the community, and of their first contact with their parish priest.

More occasional and more remote was their contact with the bishop. It was noted of several saintly bishops that they were assiduous in their duty of visiting their flock, preaching and confirming the children; we are left in the dark how effectively this was fulfilled by the majority of bishops; and even the more conscientious never seem to have engaged in the regular yearly round of confirmations to which we are accustomed today. William of Malmesbury, the biographer of St Wulfstan, Bishop of Worcester from 1062 to 1095, describes how the saint put everything aside when on tour and busied himself from morning till night – even in the long days of summer; not only in youth but in maturity and even when he was white-haired and decrepit he toiled all day long, wearing out eight clerks carrying the chrism for him in the process. But the biographer also says that 'in a single day he confirmed often as many as two thousand, often three thousand or more, as is established by witnesses of weight'; and allowing for the habitual exaggeration of medieval chroniclers, the figures suggest that confirmation was not a frequent event in any local region, even in Wulfstan's diocese. Usually he refused to eat until the job was done, but on one occasion his distinguished friend Abbot Serlo of Gloucester, a Norman from Mont Saint-Michel, insisted that he have lunch with the monks in their refectory while the children were marshalled in the cemetery outside, and there the parents sat and chatted and waited for the bishop. But one foolish young man staged a parody of a confirmation, laying mud on the forehead of any child who came to him and uttering blasphemous words. The people laughed, but the young man was cut short in his folly (so the biographer asserts), suffered a fit, and tried to drown himself; the bishop blessed him and the fit subsided, but the young man died not many days later. The story gives us a vivid glimpse of Gloucester in the late 11th century, under the shadow of the mighty choir built by Abbot Serlo, the main structure of which still survives. We are shown a strange mixture of feelings: the people queueing to have their children confirmed by a holy bishop, yet swayed and amused by the kind of parody of holy things which was evidently a common element in medieval humour – then terrorstruck by what they took to be divine wrath and vengeance.

Wulfstan himself was a friendly and peaceable man, and his sermons commonly had happier results; yet he could be fierce in the face of what he thought evil. When he went to Longney on Severn to consecrate the church built by an old Saxon thegn there, he found that a nut tree in the churchyard was the scene of feasting and gambling; of this he could hardly approve, but it was the tree and not the gamblers who suffered, though doubtless they were duly impressed when it withered. Nothing was more bitter than Wulfstan's curse, said his chaplain and assistant, and William's informant, the monk Coleman; nothing sweeter than his blessing. His curse fell heavily on many wrongdoers, including the slave-traders of Bristol. Wulfstan condemned them for selling English slaves to Ireland, an established practice, he says, so that people even sold their relations. He denounced it sometimes for two, sometimes for three months at a time, coming every Sunday to preach against it. Eventually he had such success that the practice was abandoned, and one obdurate slave-trader was blinded by the mob and thrown out of the city. 'I applaud their devotion, but condemn the deed', commented William of Malmesbury.

The diocesan statutes of the 13th century make clear that by then confirmation was a regular practice, but that you had to be prepared to travel in search of the bishop. 'Let the priests frequently admonish the people to have their children confirmed', says one statute of the 1220s. 'For after baptism one should receive the sacrament of confirmation. But if any is confirmed as an adult, let him be admonished by the priest of the place that he make confession before and after he is confirmed. And let the priest say often to the lay people not to put off confirmation till the bishop comes that way, but to take their children to him as quickly as possible when they hear he is in the neighbourhood, and carry with them suitable bandages, sufficiently broad and long'; and in

1240 Wulfstan's successor as Bishop of Worcester spelt out in his diocesan statutes what all this meant. The bandages of new cloth would be bound over the holy oil on the forehead, and oil and cloth were to be washed off in the font three days later; the bandages were then to be burnt.

The fonts with which we are most familiar in English parish churches are comparatively small stone basins on a pedestal, often carved, sometimes with inscriptions, figures or scenes appropriate to their functions. Some are of metal, as is the magnificent bronze font at Liège, surrounded with bas-reliefs of John the Baptist and his baptism of Jesus, supported on splendid oxen, symbols of the Apostles, to whom the sacrament of baptism was first delegated. There were clearly many larger fonts which have not survived, fonts large enough for total immersion, large enough to drown in. For the font in the 10th, 11th and 12th centuries had a further role as one of the possible means of determining innocence or guilt, in the ordeal by water. The Laws of the English King Athelstan (924-39) explain the procedure in detail.

19

12

If anyone pledges (to undergo) the ordeal, he is then to come three days before to the mass-priest whose duty it is to consecrate it, and live off bread and water and salt and vegetables until he shall go to it, and be present at mass on each of those three days, and make his offering and go to communion on the day on which he shall go to the ordeal, and swear then the oath that he is guiltless of that charge according to the common law, before he goes to the ordeal. And if it is (the ordeal of) water, he is to sink one and a half ells on the rope; if it is the ordeal of iron, it is to be three days before the hand is unbound.

At Canterbury we know that ordeals took place in the baptistery, a separate building to the east of the church, where also the bodies of the archbishops were buried. The accused was tied and thrown in: if he floated he was guilty; if he sank he was innocent, though he might of course drown in the process of proving it. By the 13th century more rational procedures had found favour and this type of ordeal was discontinued. A decree of the Fourth Lateran Council of 1215 forbade the clergy to administer the ordeals, and thereafter the practice withered away.

Burial

The statutes of the Bishop of Worcester of 1240 lay down that proper care is to be taken to keep churchyards clean. 'Cemeteries which contain the bodies of those who shall be saved, many of them now purged of their sins and waiting for the new garment of their glorification, we reckon are scandalously defiled by the droppings of animals'. However much it might be accepted theologically that the new body and the old were not physically connected, it entered very deep into the consciousness and sentiment of medieval pious folk that the dead waited in their tombs for the Last Judgment and the resurrection. In portrayals of the Last Judgment the dead are commonly shown coming naked to learn their fate. Mistress Quickly assured the dying Falstaff that he 'should not think of God, I hoped there was no need to trouble himself with any such thoughts yet'. This may be the *reductio ad absurdum*, but the idea was normal in the Middle Ages that what a man did and said at the moment of death was crucial to his destiny; that a thoughtless man might escape the fire by a deathbed repentance.

In the 5th Canto of his *Purgatorio*, Dante makes Buonconto da Montefeltro tell how he fled mortally wounded from the Battle of Campaldino in 1289 – a battle in which Dante fought on the opposing side – and with his dying breath he called on Mary. 'La parola del nome di Maria finii'. The angel of God took charge of his soul and the devil complained bitterly at finding his prey snatched from him because of one little tear.

> *L'angel di Dio me prese, e quel d'inferno*
> *gridava: 'O tu del ciel, perche mi privi?*
> *Tu te ne porti di costui l'eterno*
> *per una lagrimetta che il me toglie'*
> (V, 100-7)

'God's angel seized me, and the infernal one cried out: "O messenger from heaven, why have you robbed me? You carry off his soul eternal, because of one little tear that deprives me of him."' Thus a sinful man might escape the fire by a deathbed repentance; and death and all that goes with it have been the nearest meeting-point of most pious people and their God. If the laity met the Church in baptism and confirmation, they assuredly met it most forcibly when they came to the funeral obsequies of their friends and relations.

Many non-Christian cultures have had the practice of burying with their dead, when they could afford it, all the wealth and trappings that might be needed in an after-life. In the Sutton Hoo Ship Burial of the early 7th century there is a strange mingling of grave goods and Christian symbols: it probably commemorates a king who tried to keep on terms with his pagan gods and with Christendom. Later Christian burials were relatively plain, though they will sometimes yield fine clothing and ornaments. Many a bishop was buried in full pontificals with his pastoral staff; and in 1214 the English queen of Alfonso VIII of Castile, Eleanor daughter of Henry II and Eleanor of Aquitaine, was buried in their foundation at Las Huelgas at Burgos in fine linen garments lined with fur, with a pillow for her head exquisitely embroidered. The shrine of a saint could be as sumptuous as the burial of a pharaoh. The pharaoh was equipped for his life after death; the saint was surrounded by works of art and jewels reflecting the honour due to one whom God had glorified. The function of Eleanor's pillow is not quite clear: perhaps it was thought fitting that her head should rest in death as in life, so that she appeared to await the Judgment in reasonable comfort.

But then as now there were many customs hard for us to penetrate. We may be touched by, without fully comprehending, the sentiment which led the Lady Dervorguilla, foundress of Balliol College, Oxford, to carry her dead husband's heart about with her for years, and eventually to build Sweetheart Abbey, a Cistercian house in southern Scotland, round its final resting place. But the whole process of requiem mass, committal and the tending of the grave, even for the relatively humble, was something which impinged very much on the consciousness of the laity; and in a world in which infant and child mortality was by modern standards incredibly high, and when death came unawares, even more than to us, at all ages, they were more frequently at church for such a purpose than we.

In early days only the great were buried in church. Cemeteries large and small, sometimes close to the church, sometimes away from it, provided space for the growing numbers of the dead; visible monuments were rare. As time passed space for larger cemeteries in towns had often to be sought in suburbs. But more of the dead were laid in churches too; memorials became commoner, and in due course larger and more expensive; prayers and offices and masses for the dead flourished and multiplied. The change was due to grounds of convenience and to fashion and sentiment. As parish churches in towns grew in number, and the towns grew about them, space for cemeteries could be very limited, and burial in church – where a suburban cemetery was not acceptable – almost a necessity. In the 11th and 12th centuries changing attitudes to human destiny and Judgment made the felt need for prayers for the dead and for masses to relieve them of punishment in purgatory, more imperative. The beginning of this was the spread into general use of the office of the dead, which began as an occasional, special devotion in the monastic houses of the 9th and 10th centuries. The end was the establishment of regular masses for particular souls, the chantries, which by the early 13th century were beginning to be a recognized institution, and before 1300 had already developed so far that many masses were said in chapels specially built and by groups of clergy specially appointed and paid for this specific purpose. By the late 14th century, when they were past their peak, there were well over seventy chantries in St Paul's Cathedral in London; and the growth of chantry chapels, the bustle of chantry priests and the singing of chantry masses helped to make large churches resemble vast mausolea. The dead played a very active part in the religious sentiment of the late Middle Ages.

Marriage

Between birth and death lay marriage, which was celebrated as one of the Church's sacraments, but which separated the clergy, who were celibate, from the laity, who were not.

In the 12th century the law of marriage became exclusively a matter for the Church courts. This may seem strange, and it had not always been so. The early Church lay under the jurisdiction of the Roman Empire, and the law and sentiment of marriage were Roman, even though the Church laid down some striking ideals for married couples which went far beyond the letter of the law. The most fundamental was Jesus's saying: 'Those whom God has joined together let no man put asunder' – whose splendid simplicity did not solve all the problems of ordinary life. By what test did one know which marriages God had blessed? What made a binding marriage? What of marriages between Christian and heathen? What of the marriages of slaves? What of the widely accepted second-rate marriage of man and concubine? All these questions were asked, and none was given an entirely lucid answer before the 12th century. Then it came to be accepted that marriage was a sacrament of the Church, that Church courts had a special jurisdiction in marriage cases, and it became a little clearer what kind of marriage was binding. Yet the change took place in paradoxical circumstances. It was due partly to a marked improvement in the honour given to Christian marriage, in part to a resounding statement from many quarters that marriage was second best; celibacy was a loftier state. Some of this becomes clear if we consider a well documented example.

The *Life of Christina of Markyate*, recluse and prioress of the mid-12th century, gives an exceptionally vivid account of the struggles of a young girl, bent on celibacy, to evade the matrimonial snares set by her parents and their friends. It was written by one of her chaplains, and much of it was evidently based on Christina's own reminiscences. A critical reading of the book leaves little doubt that she was given to romancing in her later years, and we need not believe implicitly every detail of the story. But its essence and assumptions are entirely convincing. She was the daughter of a well-to-do burgess of the small town of Huntingdon. While she was still in her teens a young nobleman of the region called Burthred – egged on, so the story tells us, by the notorious Bishop of Durham, Ranulf Flambard, whom Christina claimed had tried to seduce her himself – asked her hand in marriage. The parents evidently thought that this was entirely their affair, and agreed; but Christina refused.

They brought her gifts and made great promises: she brushed them aside. They cajoled her; they threatened her; but she would not yield. At last they persuaded one of her close friends and inseparable companions, named Helisen, to soothe her ears by a continuous stream of flattery, so that it would arouse in her, by its very persistence, a desire to become the mistress of a house. We saw this same Helisen afterwards when she took the veil for the purpose, I believe, of expiating this criminal behaviour. She left no stone unturned in her efforts to undermine her friend's resistance, deriving hope of ultimate triumph from the proverb: 'Constant dripping wears away a stone'. But she was quite unable to extort one word signifying her consent even though she had spent a whole year trying out these stratagems. Some time later, however, when they were all gathered together in the church, they made a concerted and sudden attack on her. To be brief, how it happened I cannot tell. All I know is that by God's will, with so many exerting pressure on her from all sides, she yielded (at least in word), and on that very day Burthred was betrothed to her.

It is not clear whether the betrothal took place within the church or 'at church door' as was coming to be the custom; and perhaps had already been for some time past. The liturgical books which survive from England and north-western Europe in this period containing marriage services show that the various elements in marriage were coming under the Church's shadow more fully and effectively than hitherto. They unite in a single whole, betrothal – the exchange of promises and gifts – at church door, nuptial mass within the church, and the blessing of the bridal chamber which preceded consummation of the marriage. The story of Christina shows that the elements were still commonly kept separate. First of all, it was simply taken for granted by her parents that marriage was to be their daughter's lot and the choice of partner essentially theirs. But Christina had a will of her own, and she was already set on a life of celibacy. She insisted that consent was her affair; and the story illustrates very clearly that in such cases, and especially when one of the partners sought what many churchmen reckoned a higher vocation than marriage, consent was essential to a valid marriage. Yet in the end Christina was worn down and gave her consent. Consummation did not immediately follow; doubtless her parents reckoned that they must proceed in stages, and the separation of betrothal – which in this case as often evidently involved a firm promise to marriage, not just an engagement to marriage some time in the future – and consummation was quite normal. She made it clear to her parents that she was determined to avoid consummation; and they tried various methods of wearing down her resistance. They cut her off from her spiritual advisers; they took her to 'public banquets' and especially to 'one of the merchants' greatest and best known festivals', the Guild merchant – for 'guild' could be an assembly for pleasure as well as for profit. There 'they commanded her to get up and lay aside the mantle which she was wearing, so that, with her garments fastened to her sides with bands and her sleeves rolled up her arms, she should courteously offer drinks to the nobility'. They hoped that ribald compliments and sips of wine 'would break her resolution and prepare her body for the deed of corruption'. When this failed, 'they let her husband secretly into her bedroom in order that, if he found the maiden asleep, he might suddenly take her by surprise and overcome her'. But she was awake and dressed and sat up most of the night regaling him with stories of chaste and saintly virgins, so that the young man naturally came to think she was not the partner for him. Stirred on by his comrades, he tried twice more; but in the long run (after various rather improbable adventures) she was allowed to escape his embraces, and he became her ally in the long struggle to break the marriage, which ended in her becoming a recluse, a nun and head of the small community at Markyate.

The conclusion of the story illustrates how necessary consummation was to 12th-century ideas of marriage: because the marriage had not been consummated and Christina was determined on a life of celibacy, the local bishop in the end, very reluctantly, agreed to dissolve the bond. His reluctance was understandable, since a generation later it was laid down by Pope Alexander III (1159-81) that consent to a marriage here and now *(de praesenti)*, made an indissoluble bond by itself – and that marriage could only be dissolved by a declaration that it had never been valid or by *both* partners entering religious orders. From the 12th century to the 16th entry to marriage was based fundamentally on exchange of oaths, on the formal consent of the partners. Naturally enough this hid a great variety of custom; and it was precisely. the variety of custom which made the popes seek so elementary a basis: to have demanded marriage in church, or at church door, would in effect have defied the customs of many lands and implicitly declared invalid many successful marriages. We know little in detail of the customs of these centuries, but it is evident enough that even this simple insistence on a contract in the presence of witnesses was not compatible with every local practice. Over the centuries the authorities steadily encouraged marriage in church to the point that the Roman Catholic Church reckoned in the 16th century that it could be enforced; and the growing number, size and splendour of church porches from the 12th century on bears witness to the practice. They had other uses: for burials, and for meetings of different kinds; they often had rooms above for priest's lodgings, for schools, for strong rooms, and for guilds. They gave shelter too for bridal parties and indicate the slow but steady success of the Church, till Chaucer's Wife of Bath could claim that 'husbands at churche doore she hadde five'.

17

None the less, consummation was a vital feature of all normal marriages and a marriage could be annulled if it never took place – though the theologians denied that it was essential to the sacrament, since they denied that it had occurred in the most perfect of all marriages, that of Mary and Joseph. But in ordinary life the carnal side of marriage and the rearing of children were vital; the story of Christina, which assumed parental authority and the central importance of the marriage bed, would have been perfectly intelligible to innumerable parents of the Middle Ages. The celibate theologians and canon lawyers, however, emphasized other elements; and in their idealism especially emphasized the need for both partners to give their consent. We may believe that this insistence had a very variable success; but in the long run it won many echoes from the marriage partners themselves, and this is most clearly revealed in some of the vernacular poetry of the 12th and 13th centuries.

Thus in the *Parzival* of Wolfram von Eschenbach we are far from the world of ascetic theologians: the author is a layman who took for granted the pleasure of the marriage bed – 'the old and ever new custom of love'; he has no place for the ascetic insistence of many theologians that these pleasures were sinful if they were too much enjoyed. But Wolfram was also extremely devout and an ardent disciple of some of the theological fashions of his age, the opening decades of the 13th century. Many and diverse are the relationships he shows us between men and women, in and out of marriage, in his poem – he illustrates and criticizes in diverse ways the current romantic or courtly fashions of his age. But the marriage which he shows us as most perfect is that of Parzival himself. The hero comes to a besieged city and a people on the verge of starvation ruled by the queen and heiress Condwiramurs. An enemy is at the gate claiming the queen's hand. Condwiramurs pleads with Parzival to be her champion; and in a great combat he worsts the enemy champion and lifts the siege. We have had a little preparation for what follows, but not much. The author has dwelt from the outset on the radiant beauty of the queen; and how Parzival spent all the time of mass on the morning of his combat gazing at her. We are also told that she reckons, as queen and hostess, to lead the conversation and do the wooing herself. When Parzival has triumphed, she 'embraced him, hugged him close and said "I will wed no man on earth save him, whom I have just embraced" . . . .'. After a suitable celebration – for which food and wine by happy chance arrived in time – 'the question was asked: Should the bridal bed be got ready? He and the queen said, Yes.' Yet they did not immediately consummate their marriage: the poet dwells complaisantly on the courtesy with which he allowed a respite before full union took place.

So he whom they called the Red Knight left the queen a maid. She, however, thought she was now his wife, and in token of his love bound her hair matronwise next day, with a fillet. The virgin bride then openly bestowed both land and castles on him, who was the beloved of her heart.

So they remained, glad in their love for each other, two days and a third night. Often he thought of embracing, and recalled his mother's advice, and how Gurnemanz, too, had said that man and woman were one. And now I may tell you, he soon discovered the old and ever new custom of love, and found it pleasant.

In a strange and moving way the Church's view of marriage, of assent and mutual giving, is here mingled with a layman's. He allows something for the natural setting of marriage – for a marriage settlement and a great celebration; and it is completed by consummation and the conception of children. But the heart and essence of the union is mutual giving, mutual surrender; there is a total rejection of ascetic doctrine – courtesy governs Parzival's acts, not any sense of guilt; yet the idea of marriage as a sacrament is implied. In these centuries, as always, marriage customs, marriage laws, the ideals of theologians and of lovers were often in conflict; there were many strains and tensions; but the marriage of Parzival and Condwiramurs shows that a deep alliance was also possible between the most secular and the most theological impulses of the age.

The eucharist

On the carved stone fonts of the late Middle Ages it was not uncommon to place baptism in its setting and represent the seven sacraments. The number was not entirely stable in our period, but well on the way to being established – the seven special marks of divine grace, in which outward ceremonies and objects represented inward graces, seven specially chosen modes for God's operations among men. Of these we have already met four – baptism, confirmation, extreme unction (which immediately preceded death, where possible), and marriage; and a fifth, holy orders, separated the clergy from the laity so does not immediately concern us. Two remain, eucharist and penance.

The eucharist had always been the chief sacrament of the Catholic Church; but communion had long ceased to be its centre. In the early Church the eating and drinking together of the bread and wine had been a communal activity, presided over by the clergy. By the 11th and 12th centuries the mass was far more a priestly ceremony at which the laity were present, only in a minimal sense participating. So rare had communion become that at the Fourth Lateran Council in 1215 it was thought necessary to insist that layfolk communicate at least once a year; whereas attendance at mass was expected every Sunday and on all important festivals. The English king in the 12th century seems

115

normally to have attended mass in the royal chapel every day, and Henry III (1216-72), a man noted for a rather eccentric piety, heard three masses daily when he could. Ordinary folk could not command such leisure, and weekly mass was probably normal, for those who did their duty. The Latin of the mass was unintelligible to most people, and it had become increasingly a dialogue between the priest and his maker. The custom that priests should celebrate daily was well established as a norm, though not a rule; and in large churches where there were many clergy this produced a multiplicity of private masses. In all churches, however, save those of enclosed religious orders, there were masses specially arranged in which layfolk were expected to be present, commonly solemn celebrations with singing and ceremonial in the larger churches, and in principle at least the laity were instructed how to follow these masses. But following did not mean understanding: they were told how to recognize the salient features of the service and make appropriate gestures and say suitable prayers. When they communicated, it was still sometimes in both kinds, partaking of the wine as well as the bread; but this practice was dying out. When efforts were made to increase the frequency of communion, it was in one kind only.

One could go further, and say that there is much evidence of extreme ignorance, not only among the laity, but among the humbler parish clergy, as to what the mass meant and what happened in it. Contemporary satirists delighted to tell such tales, and they have been repeated very frequently since; doubtless if we were transported to a 12th-century village church we should be astonished by the ignorance and illiteracy of most of its worshippers. Yet it could well be that we were impressed and moved by what we found; for there is another side to the story.

The solemn mass of the great church was a public ceremony of great magnificence; the ordinary weekly mass of the small parish church was much more modest, but also more intimate. The characteristic parish church of the 10th and 11th centuries, and still in many places and parts of Europe in the 12th, was a small box with a tiny chancel, the whole being no larger than a moderately large living room in a modern house. Here priest and people were far closer than in most modern churches; and even if the priest commonly turned his back on the people, the practice of elevating host and chalice was coming in so that they could at least see the consecrated elements. One of the earliest surviving books of instruction and devotion for the laity attending mass was the *Lay*

Folks' Mass Book, composed by Jeremiah, one of the archdeacons in the diocese of York, in the mid–12th century. It was written in French for the landed gentry and aristocracy among his flock, but it survives only in a much more popular English translation of the late 13th century. When the elevation takes place lay worshippers should be on their knees, and lift their eyes so that they can view the elements. Since the elevation was introduced precisely so that everyone could see host and chalice, the instruction seems obvious and natural. But it was not perfectly satisfactory to the hierarchy or the religious sentiment of the later Middle Ages; in the early 13th century Pope Honorius III (1216-27) laid down that when the elevation took place the faithful should show their devotion by bowing their heads in reverence. In practice both were expected – they looked, then bowed; and that was the general practice of later centuries, down to the Reformation.

There is a famous story of an over-zealous magistrate during the Catholic reaction of the reign of Queen Mary I in England, who 'hid in a rood loft so as to spy on the congregation, and punished those who failed to gaze upon the consecrated host'. In later copies of the *Lay Folks' Mass Book* the double act is specifically enjoined, and this reflects the change in sentiment: in the late Middle Ages the host and even more the chalice ceased to be near at hand, close to the worshipper; it became, like the holy grail, something remote and mysterious. In the late Middle Ages great houses, which had consisted of a very small number of huge rooms, came to be increasingly subdivided. By the same token, large churches, which had retained some measure of unity, became increasingly divided; and the devotional attitude to the eucharist made it seem more and more appropriate that it should be performed behind deep and dark screens in whose lofts magistrates could hide. In the ordinary parish church the screen became almost opaque: a heavy screen was surmounted by an ample loft in which choirs could sing and some parts of the liturgical drama be performed; and above the loft stood the great rood or crucifixion, commonly backed by a complete wooden frame. These screens emphasized the tension between the two attitudes to the host: it had to be worshipped with bowed head; but it still had to be just visible at the moment of elevation.

Confession

In the early church the good had gathered to the eucharist as a common meal, and the bad had tried to clear themselves by public confession in the presence of the whole community. More personal consultations took place on individual problems of conscience; but confession and absolution were essentially communal activities. When Christianity became the accepted religion of the Roman Empire much larger communities of variable quality were formed. After the barbarian invasions the clergy were faced by numerous recently converted, half-converted layfolk. Both changes made the old discipline somehow inappropriate, if not impossible; and the practice came increasingly to be to confront the barbarian peoples with formal rules and penalties, with lists of penances for particular offences, some of them of draconian severity. The more sophisticated and more personal religious sentiment of the 11th and 12th centuries rebelled against these penances, and against the external nature of earlier codes and practices.

Gradually the custom of private, personal confession came to take the place of earlier rites. At first confession was informal, and so far as we can tell laymen confessed as often to fellow-laymen as to priests. But presently a new ritual of absolution and penance came to be attached to confession, and it tended to become a priestly activity; and confession to a priest came increasingly to be expected from the 12th century on. Indeed, the same Lateran Council of 1215 which prescribed annual communion also demanded annual confession to a priest. By then penance was well on its way into a formal place among the seven sacraments. The pattern is highly characteristic of the whole history of religious sentiment in the Middle Ages. In the 11th and 12th centuries we witness an increasingly personal, individual approach to the problems of the Christian life, of the soul's destiny, and of human devotion; but the structures then devised received more formal, legalistic shape as time went on, and external forms returned in a different guise. The calculation of penances in the late Middle Ages – so many days' penance, so many prayers, so many masses – became increasingly mathematical, and with all differences allowed, almost as mechanical and external as the harsher penances of the early Middle Ages. Yet the possibility of a more personal, individual approach to the sacrament of penance survived.

Thus the world of lay sentiment of the 12th century had strong elements both of individual and of communal piety; but for the majority of layfolk it must be supposed that it was the communal activities of the Church which chiefly impinged on their lives. Of these the great festivals were the most conspicuous. At the Feast of Pentecost in 1166, Thomas Becket preached at Vézelay, and we have observed how great a throng came to a famous abbey church on a major festival (see p. 46). We may be sure that all great festivals brought some increase to a major church, and especially the feasts of saints whose relics it contained. But Pentecost was a special case. To the cathedral on the feast of Pentecost, in many parts of Europe, there came by custom a large part of the population of the diocese; it was the central event of the diocesan year. The custom was not universal: we know that it first came to England with the Normans. But wherever it existed it reflected the sense that a cathedral was the personal home of the people of the diocese at large. A community could have the same feeling for any large church, especially for a great abbey church replete with relics; and so Vézelay, the great pilgrim church, could be in competition with the Cathedral of Autun. Yet not necessarily in competition: for these were churches for occasional use, to which throngs might come on special occasions and particular festivals. The smaller, parish, churches were for every day, or at least for every Sunday.

To the community of an Italian city the cathedral and the baptistery were ever-present facts. Their relation to their bishop and the clergy of the cathedral might have a Don Camillo flavour: in the 11th and 12th centuries the bishop often represented ancient domination and tyranny, and the struggle for self-expression and independence in the community was closely bound up with the effort to be free of his control. But the cathedral remained the centre of many people's pieties, and into its building and adornment they poured much of their surplus resources. Something of the same mixture of love and hate may often have obtained in other European cities too, like Compostela, where the cathedral clergy and the community were huddled together in a small town, too close for comfort; and such conflicts are one of the theme tunes of more than one monastic chronicle of a great abbey with a town about it. This is especially true of the Vézelay chronicle, with its long tale of disputes and riots. Yet the costly splendour of the abbey church still shows that the citizens loved their church too, for it was not wholly built by the offerings of pilgrims from afar.

Amiens

Not all towns embarked on such bitter feuds as characterized Vézelay. A number of documents registering concord, *concordia*, officially drawn up and deposited in the archives, punctuated the history of Amiens in the 12th and 13th centuries; and although concord presumably followed dispute and discord, they do reveal genuine areas of common interest and common action. In 1145 Nicholas, son of Mainer, a burgess of the town, granted properties, including wharves, to the cathedral chapter. This important benefaction secured for the chapter a stake in the new Great Quay, itself the culmination of an extremely ambitious and impressive civic enterprise, the achievement of a remarkably industrious and resourceful people. Amiens' economy was based upon industry and commerce. From locally grown plants they produced and processed woad, a blue dye, for which they had a market in the cloth industries of England and Flanders. They also traded in wine. To facilitate the transport of goods they not only, in the 12th century, dredged the numerous canals by which the city could be traversed, but, diverting the course of the River Somme, constructed a watery bypass, the Chemin de l'Eau, so that laden barges could move round the circumference of the city, unimpeded by the congestion within and rejoin the river where all its various waterways converged, west of the city at the new port. The charter guaranteeing Nicholas's gift was laid upon the altar of the Virgin, in the presence of all the cathedral dignitaries, clergy and people of the diocese assembled on Christmas Day 1145. Nicholas and his wife also instituted an annual feast, every 8 September, for the clergy of the city.

In 1218 positive advantage was taken of a destructive fire to create a masterpiece. In the course of the 13th century the cathedral was entirely rebuilt, two successive bishops, both intelligent and active builders, and a distinguished dean combining to realize a conception architecturally inspired by but surpassing Chartres. The generosity of bishops and chapter was supplemented by the generosity of the commune, the guilds, and individual merchants. A mayor gave one of the rose windows, and the wealthiest of the woad merchants paid for no less than half the stained glass lancets in the nave. All but one window of this glass was destroyed at the time of the French Revolution, and much was never recorded, but in one vanished scene merchants offered sacks of blue dye to purchasers with glinting coins in their hands. Among the chantry chapels, that dedicated to St Nicholas was founded by the woad sellers of the surrounding district. The 18 woadmen's guild also supported its own parish church, St Martin aux Waides, in which a priest regularly invoked God's blessing on their working day with a merchants' mass at 4 am. This church was situated next door to their mercantile headquarters, the Hôtel du Noir Chevalier, where the dye was assayed, weighed and packed for shipment, and the tax on sales collected. A proportion of this was assigned to the pious and benevolent activities of the confraternity.

Gifts of the citizens to the cathedral and the parish churches were part and parcel of an involvement in their city which touched every aspect of life. They worked on and contributed towards a wide range of projects, some designed to make life for themselves more profitable – as the dredging of the canals, the building of the new port – some to improve the amenities, some to defend their liberties, such as a watch-tower symbolically built on the site of the count's castle, razed in 1117. The cathedral was at once an expression of this common purpose, a mixture of civic and religious commitment and aspirations, a symbol of praise and thanksgiving to God and a status symbol too, eloquent of pride in human endeavour and success. At Pisa a sea victory over a Moslem fleet in the 1060s opened up rich opportunities for her sailors in Mediterranean trade. As a thank offering to God the citizens set aside a whole corner of the city, just inside the walls, purchased with a share of the booty, for the purpose of erecting ecclesiastical monuments. The cathedral and baptistery, begun in the mid-11th century, were triumphantly completed in the 13th, enriched without with costly green, red and white marble and within with the magnificent pulpits of her own sculptors, Nicola 21 and Giovanni Pisano. This 'tithe' has adorned Pisa ever since. At Amiens the cathedral is dedicated to the Virgin and three rose windows remind us that the Virgin is compared to a rose. Round the upper half of the great rose window in the south transept is the rim of a wheel of fortune, the figures rising well dressed on the left 20 and falling dishevelled, barefoot and in rags to the right, perhaps a comment on the risks of commerce, appropriate here.

Siena too felt herself beholden to the Virgin, patroness of the cathedral and of the city, honoured her and associated her in her affairs. The official seal of the commune bore the image of the Virgin Enthroned with the inscription *Salvet Virgo Senam veterem quam signat amenam*, May the Virgin preserve ancient Siena whose beauty she seals – or represents – and the citizens believed that in very truth her intervention gave them the victory over a stronger Florentine force because they prayed to her before the Battle of Montaperti in 1260. The painted representation of her that relayed their prayers, the *Madonna degli Occhi Grossi*, had the place of honour on the high altar of the cathedral.

But in 1308 Duccio was commissioned to paint a replacement for this. He responded to the challenge and the opportunity by
22 creating his *Maestà*, the richest and most complex of Italian altarpieces. The main front panel depicted the Virgin Enthroned surrounded by angels and saints; on the back the story of the Passion unfolded in twenty-six scenes. Below on the predella and above on the pinnacles were further 'histories', scenes of the early life of Christ, of the Ascension, of the last days of the Virgin. When it was completed, in 1311, its installation was made the occasion for a public holiday and public celebration. A Sienese chronicle described the event which was also an act of civic dedication. The shops were shut and by order of the bishop a large company of priests and members of confraternities, accompanied by the Signori of the Nine and all the officials of the commune, escorted the noble panel in solemn procession from Duccio's studio outside the Stalloreggi Gate. The most important representatives of church and city had places nearest to the panel and carried lighted candles in their hands. Behind them came the populace, women and children first. On their way to the cathedral they processed round the great piazza, the Campo, while all the bells rang out in jubilation. The day was devoted to prayer, almsgiving to the poor, and the evening, no doubt, to feasting.

Only four years later, in 1315, Simone Martini was employed by the commune to decorate a wall of the great Council Chamber of their new and splendid town hall, begun in the 1290s, with a frescoed *Maestà*. Here the Virgin sits on a throne under a canopy, surrounded by saints. In this context, she sits both as queen of heaven and as head of state, presiding over the deliberations of her devoted citizens. Logically from this follow Ambrogio Lorenzet-
23 ti's dramatic representations of good and bad government in the adjoining room completed in 1339. The personification of good

government, which is also the personification of Siena, sits enthroned, flanked by the cardinal virtues, justice, temperance, prudence and fortitude, and the civic virtues of peace and magnanimity. The theological virtues, faith, hope and charity, hover in blessing and inspiration about his head. The citizens are ranged along the ground floor level, filing up to take their part. On the adjacent wall the results of good government are depicted in town and countryside. Siena is recognizably portrayed with the elegant Torre of the Palazzo Pubblico on the extreme left. A circle of young girls country dancing in the street evokes civic harmony and peace, which enable leisure and sport to be enjoyed as well as business and trade profitably conducted. Opposite, the violence, extortion, uncertainty, ruin attendant on bad government pointed the moral. These walls convey a political programme in pictorial terms. Peace is given prominence, concord holds a smoothing-plane, justice crowns a king with one hand while executing a criminal with the other. Labels are provided as well in case the pictorial message is not clear. Peace and justice are social virtues; as urban life developed these came to be increasingly emphasized, changing circumstances bringing them into fashion, just as fortitude was lauded where martyrs were needed and chastity where population pressed hard on the means of subsistence.

23

Moral teaching and the preacher

Doubtless an exile from the Siena of the Lorenzetti would have given a cynical commentary on this fervent presentation of civic virtue, just as the exiled Florentine Dante portrays again and again the vices of Florence in his *Commedia*. By the same token, we may ask how effective was all this contact between clergy and laity, between the Church's teaching and ordinary Christian folk? What moral impact did the Church have on the Christian laity? If we reflect for a moment on our own experience – on the answer to such questions we might give in late 20th-century Europe – we shall expect no simple answers. It would be as naive to suppose Christian teaching everywhere effective in the 12th and 13th centuries as to suppose its impact negligible. We cannot even tell to what extent many of the laity were exposed to the Church's teaching. Preaching was one of the clergy's most fundamental duties, and every age produced manuals for preachers, often of the most practical, down-to-earth character. But every age brought warnings of the dangers of false teaching. As time passed the education of the clergy improved: this might lessen their tendency to get their teaching wrong, but it might also widen the gap between them and their congregation. Laymen and ignorant priests were forbidden to preach, and this may greatly have reduced the opportunities for ordinary folk to learn. In 1222, when Oxford and Cambridge were already fostering growing universities, the Dean of Salisbury investigated the clergy of the parish of Sonning which lay in his jurisdiction. In the many chapels of this parish he found clergy ministering who showed quite amazing ignorance; of the best of them the record says 'Sufficienter illiteratus est' – 'he is thoroughly illiterate'. Such stories can be paralleled time and again. Their ignorance seems mainly to have been of the Latin tongue and the Latin services, but it is evident that these men could have given little instruction to their flock. Yet only a few years before, the Bishop of Salisbury, Richard Poore, had issued injunctions to the clergy of the whole diocese of a most elaborate kind on how they should teach the people of their parishes, which presupposed a much higher level of instruction, anyway among the parish priests themselves.

The spread of heresy in the 12th century brought great anxiety to the Church's hierarchy: it might be bad for the ordinary folk of Western Christendom to be taught nothing, but how much worse that they should be taught what was false. This anxiety led to restrictions and precautions which have inspired some modern scholars with the thought that the hierarchy's real wish was to stop preaching altogether. What happened was the exact opposite: the 12th and 13th centuries were among the great periods in the history of preaching, and we have copious evidence of the fervour and energy and sheer hard work put into the preparation of sermons in this age; and in the 13th century the friars devised a kind of church whose function was to provide a setting for the preacher's art as truly as the great Nonconformist chapels of the 18th and 19th centuries. We may doubt indeed if there was any very radical break in the tradition that preaching was a fundamental pastoral duty. English vernacular sermon literature has survived from every generation from the mid-10th century on and illustrates very clearly this continuity. But there is a notable change within the medium in the preacher's theme and emphasis. Judgment and penance and the fear of hell were dominant in the 10th and 11th centuries; in the 12th and 13th a new spirit takes over, the preaching of the good Christian life and of practical morality to lay men and women whose destiny is by no means so gloomy as before. We can see the issue of this tradition in the plain, sensible, pastoral instructions passed by 13th-century English bishops to their parish clergy in synodal statutes and like documents; and we can see it in a more sophisticated, educational, imaginative form in the surviving sermons of the early friars.

Lambert le Bègue

Occasionally the curtain is lifted to reveal a model priest, deeply influencing his community. Lambert le Bègue, the stammerer, was ordained priest in the diocese of Liège in the early 1160s. He was full of enthusiasm. He was parish priest of a half-ruined church; he repaired it with his own hands, put in windows, painted it, provided candles and other equipment. He inspired his congregation, especially the women, with a fervent devotion to the Sacrament, and he produced a rhythmical translation of the Acts of the Apostles into the vernacular for their information and use. Under his direction many, after church, spent the rest of Sunday in prayer and hymn singing. He disapproved of Sunday sports, especially dancing and singing in the churchyard, telling drunken revellers they would do better to work on Sunday than so misuse their leisure. Though poor, he preached against priests who charged fees for baptizing children, administering the sacrament to the sick and dying, and burying the dead. He disapproved of pilgrimages because he thought it more important to concentrate on good works urgently needing to be done at home – the redemption of prisoners, the relief of the poor, the consolation of the bereaved. In short, Lambert was a shining example of an earnest, dedicated enthusiast, to whose virtues his parishioners testified; an exemplary parish priest. His bishop, however, imprisoned him on trumped up charges of heresy in or about 1175. He was soon released, but died in 1177. It was not easy to pursue the path of reform, and tackle the pastoral implications of urban poverty, and retain the repute of orthodoxy.

Montaillou

At the other extreme and just beyond 1300 lies a vivid example of a permissive society led astray (in terms of conventional Catholic teaching) by an unworthy priest, in the village of Montaillou, made famous in the 1970s by the brilliant evocation of Emmanuel le Roy Ladurie, a village utterly remote and little known in its own day. The patient care of a group of devoted inquisitors elicited a mass of detailed evidence about 1320; this reveals a priest who was at least half a Cathar, and practised both Catholic and Cathar rites; he was also a free-living, easy-going man with many lovers. A note of caution must be sounded: M. Ladurie's reconstruction of life in *Montaillou* is based on too simple a faith in the truth of all the gossip so lovingly recorded by the inquisitors. We cannot trust the details. We may believe the account given by one of his lovers, a widow with legitimate offspring, of the charms she used to avoid unwanted conception; but the extraordinary effectiveness of her charms may be a warning to us not to believe the literal truth of all the sexual charges brought against the priest; there is hardly any theme on which human beings lie so readily. Yet when all is said and done *Montaillou* provides a picture of a permissive society far removed from any impact from a devout, effective orthodox preacher; one in which fornication and contraception – whether effective or ineffective – were freely practised; in which we can penetrate a complex world of human relations of fascinating variety; a world at once utterly remote from ours, yet strangely familiar, and familiar above all in the range of qualities which it enshrined. Much other evidence would suggest that the deadly sins and cardinal virtues were as active in the central Middle Ages as in more recent centuries; *Montaillou* distils in the compass of a single village the measure of the Church's failure to penetrate many areas of medieval society.

St Francis

Montaillou can be made the text for a sermon on the vices of the medieval peasant, or of the shortcomings of the medieval Church; it can also be seen as a commentary on the mingling of Catholic and Cathar elements in the Pyrenean world. We can see in some of its magic practices and superstitions pagan survivals; just as the mingling of Christian and pagan stories and teaching may be seen in numerous surviving monuments of the Middle Ages. Early examples are the burial and memorial crosses on the Isle of Man. In a very different context at the end of our period, Dante imagined on the inner wall of the first terrace of Purgatory (canto

X), marble sculptures in which the Annunciation was set in a scene adjacent to one of the Emperor Trajan granting justice to a poor widow. These elements in the record of the central Middle Ages have led, or misled, many historians into reading lectures on the moral or intellectual failings of the medieval clergy. But history is full of strange revenges; and few can read the stories about St Francis told by his companions and disciples without learning some profound lessons.

Francis's vocation was to the poor and ignorant, and from his approach to them we can see in a mirror something of their world. And not only theirs, for he was the son of a rich merchant and was on terms of personal friendship with bishops, cardinals and popes. His life is a satire on the whole of his world, usually benign, sometimes savage. In early youth he reacted against his father's values – he repudiated the counting house first of all for chivalry; then, after a spell in a Perugian prison, he turned to beggars and lepers for inspiration. His breach with his father was harsh and total, and left him with a profound suspicion of money and all it bred. The Church surrounded the rich with rules and regulations, some bizarre – the total rejection of usury was extended in principle to all levying of interest – some self-interested, such as the conventional assurance that a rich man's soul could find its way through the needle's eye if his body had given enough in charity, especially to the Church. There were many qualifications: the prohibition of interest came to be hedged round with innumerable qualifications inspired by shrewd observation of the facts of commerce; many students of the Bible, and many preachers, saw quite deeply the irony of the needle's eye and were not afraid to expound it. Total rejection of money was rare. When Francis had undergone his conversion, and begun to gather disciples (1206-9), he insisted that they reject the use of money quite literally: they might not even handle a coin.

From one aspect, Francis's special achievement was to reconcile the Church's hierarchy to ordinary, humble folk. He made a simple rule, based on Gospel precepts, and (in his own words), 'the Lord Pope confirmed it for me'. But his call was to the urban poor of Umbria, and beyond that to the whole of Italy – to the whole of mankind, Christian and pagan, Catholic and Cathar, rich and poor; the special genius of his teaching was to put his message to the ordinary people among whom he lived, by example, by vivid lessons, and by informal preaching. In course of time his order acquired many conventional features; it became more clerical, more learned, more organized than Francis had at first intended. In the early days and with intent he attracted far more laymen than clerks; and although they acquired a certain clerical character by taking the vows of friars, they remained 'lay' in name and in many characteristics; they never became book-learned or formal preachers. The call to the Christian life was no new thing, but the way in which he presented it was fresh and original. He was a highly gifted and imaginative teacher; and he demonstrated, by living it with all his energy, and by gathering disciples who lived it too, that the Christian life was no fairy tale but a challenge. He attached paramount importance to example. He did not just tell people what they ought to do but did it all himself, exaggerating even, and dramatizing, to drive his lessons home. He taught the poor to see a blessing even in their poverty, by embracing it himself, by being poorer than they were. There was indeed a romantic quality in his erection of poverty to a holy virtue, in the concept of 'Lady Poverty'; but it was no false romance he wove round her, for he and his followers knew only too well the harsh and hideous face of actual want.

His effect on the men and women among whom he worked none can doubt. There is a charming story of a simple peasant called John who joined him early in his new life, and imitated Francis's every act: 'If Francis bent his knees or clasped his hands to heaven or spat or coughed he did the same.' Francis was much amused, and remonstrated with him. 'Brother,' said John, 'I have promised to do all that you do. So I want to do all that you do.' Many were less simple; and his converts included leading doctors from Paris and Padua; even his greatest patron, Cardinal Hugolino (later Pope Gregory IX), consulted him about becoming a friar. Francis sent Hugolino back to the Curia; and often showed a shrewd judgment of would-be converts. But his inspiration and his charity flowed so deep that the order grew in an untidy, shapeless way; and some of those most under his influence none the less tried to infuse some method into its organization. There is a celebrated tale of how some of his followers tried to win Hugolino's support to enforce one of the existing religious rules upon him. 'My brothers! My brothers!' Francis retorted, 'God has called me by the way of simplicity and shown me the way of simplicity. I do not want you to name any Rule to me, not St Augustine's, nor St Bernard's, nor St Benedict's. The Lord said to me that he wished that I should be a new-born simpleton in the world' – and he went on to a passionate denunciation of '*your* learning and *your* wisdom'. Doubtless Francis was utterly exceptional in his methods and in his successes. He shows us not only the possible reconciliation of the discordant elements in his world; but also, very vividly, the crags and precipices that might be encountered by one who tried to embrace the whole of humanity in a single religious experience.

The Beguines

Somewhere below the peak of the Franciscan movement, but equally near the heart of the religious sentiment of the 13th century, was the lay movement which produced the groups and communities called by their enemies the 'Beguines'. They started in Liège, in the world of Lambert le Bègue in the generation after his death. They began as groups of women without any fixed rule or community centre, who wished to lead an ordered life, sometimes within, sometimes apart from, marriage and family. They enjoyed the help and patronage of some enlightened bishops and clergy, they spread about the Low Countries and north Germany, and they flourished exceedingly especially in and around Cologne. Like the members of all such movements, they encountered persecution, and after a time were confined to religious communities under a rule, or driven into the wilderness. Meanwhile they had established that it was possible for women in the world to have a vocation as surely as men – a fact which St Clare had tried to enforce on St Francis in Assisi with somewhat modest success, for after a while she was confined, like the later Beguines, in an enclosed convent. The influence of the Beguines ran so deep that the Low Countries and Germany became in the 13th century the first substantial area in Europe in which we can suppose that there were as many female religious as male; normally in the Middle Ages (in marked contrast to the modern world), men greatly outnumbered women in the religious life. In due course the Beguines came much under the influence of the friars; but that is not how they began. They are above all a testimony that the ideals of the Christian life could spread widely and deeply quite apart from the teaching of a great religious leader, like Francis, or of an influential religious order. The fervent Bishop Jacques de Vitry met and admired some of the earliest friars; but his greatest admiration was reserved for Marie of Oignies, the Beguine, whose life he wrote.

VII

The Bible

The Bible and the laity

The Bible was at the centre of medieval religious thought; it is the supreme textbook of the medieval world, essential for understanding its attitudes, its beliefs, its enthusiasms, its culture and its art. Yet how can this be? Have we not been told, times out of number, that medieval Catholics neglected the Bible, that it was brought into the home of ordinary Christian people by the reformers of the 16th century, by Luther in Germany, by the Protestants and Puritans in England and New England? – that it was forbidden to the laity in the Middle Ages? We have indeed a problem here. How can we penetrate to what ordinary laymen and women knew or understood? The best we can hope for, most of the way, is that the efforts the learned made to put across the message and content of the Bible will show us as in a mirror what the uneducated could receive. At times there was a large gulf between them; at times they were surprisingly close. Always there was some contact. In the Middle Ages a teacher of theology was a Master of the Sacred Page, whose first and main business was to expound the Bible. In the schools in these centuries teaching depended essentially on the learning, interpretation and exposition of the authoritative statements of the great writings of the past; and of all these the Bible, God's word, was supreme. It was the only book which was in every library. Its story and its message were the preacher's basic fare (see p. 141). Extracts from it were being constantly sung and recited in churches all over Christendom, especially in monastic churches; echoes of biblical texts can be heard in every corner of the Latin literature of the age and very frequently in vernacular as well; stories from the Bible meet us wherever we find painted books and walls and religious sculpture. The Bible was everywhere.

Yet the strange fact remains: for most orthodox Catholics acceptable translations into the vernacular were not readily available in the central Middle Ages. Among the first books to be written in vernacular German were the Gothic versions of the Gospels of the 4th century; after the conversion of England translations and paraphrases of many parts of the Bible were made in Old English. But in the 11th and 12th centuries the vernacular versions languished; and in the 12th and 13th centuries they came to be suspect. No doubt a suspicion had lingered from earlier days as to the accuracy and orthodoxy of these translations, for the Gothic Bible had been the work of an Arian heretic. But it was essentially in the lay religious groups of the 12th century that the passion for the vernacular Bible most strongly revived, in the circles of men like Peter of Bruis and Waldo of Lyon; and vernacular bibles became associated with the heretical movements of which these men were the leaders.

This is not the whole story, and in the past historians much exaggerated the Church's opposition to vernacular versions of the Scriptures. Many versions similar to Lambert le Bègue's Acts of the Apostles (p. 124) may well have been lost; and it was in the nature of the case that the laity relied on word of mouth for most of their knowledge of the Bible. It was uttered, and the wind has blown it away. Yet in the charged atmosphere in which heresy grew and flourished in late 12th-century Europe, the hierarchy naturally looked at popular renderings with doubtful eyes. Their answer was to condemn suspect translations, and to encourage priests and other clergy to pass the scriptures on to the people in oral and visual form. In this age many churches told the biblical story in stone and paint and glass, as never before.

As early as about 600 Pope Gregory the Great had spoken of painted churches as books of the unlearned. To us (whatever our religious beliefs) there is something repugnant about this extreme dependence on visual aids and on the clergy for knowledge of the main sources of Christian revelation. But in the central Middle Ages it was normally assumed that literature of all kinds passed from the literate – or the professional raconteur or minstrel – to the illiterate by word of mouth. Kings and great nobles were often able to read, but had little need to, for they had clerks to read and expound everything from the Gospel to the latest romance when they wished. In an age when books were laboriously copied by hand and were by our standards incredibly scarce, even the most learned depended in large measure for their knowledge of books on hearing them read and recited. To leave the Bible to the clergy was in many ways quite reasonable, although many clergy were almost as ignorant as their flock. But this leaves us often guessing how much lay people commonly knew. This is the more obscure since we know that many of the parish clergy were relatively ignorant, unlettered folk; sometimes very garbled versions of biblical stories must have filtered down. It used to be said that the Bible was read in every English home a century ago; the truth is much more complex and obscure. In so far as lay men and women of the 12th and 13th centuries studied the Bible for themselves, they did it mainly by listening to sermons and looking at pictures, and we can look at some of the same pictures.

Much of what they saw has disappeared; nor can we hope to study what survives quite with their eyes. It is as much a mistake to suppose that every visitor to a medieval church had taken a course in iconography in the 12th or 13th century as it would be today. Furthermore, how much could they actually see? Medieval churches are commonly far lighter today than they were originally intended to be. In the early Middle Ages windows were few and small; heavy painting on extensive walls, lit only by small lamps and candles, must often have been difficult to grasp. Some of the finest sculpture at Vézelay or Autun, for example, is (or was) high in the church, out of range for normal eyesight. In the 12th and 13th centuries the architects devised ways of making the windows of churches larger: the fully developed Gothic cathedrals of the Île de France are miracles of engineering in stone providing frames for ever larger expanses of glass. But who can make out all the pictures in the glass at Chartres on a dull day, especially in the numerous roundels telling complex tales? None of it is visible at night. Anyone who has seen modern lighting play on the frescoes at Assisi will know how much more easily we can study them than could their medieval viewers. Some of the planning of medieval wall painting and sculpture is so cunning and sophisticated it can hardly have been intended for popular instruction. Yet when all is allowed, it would be preposterous to suppose that so many immense and splendid pictures were commissioned and painted to no purpose. Probably a bevy of guides greeted the medieval traveller to Chartres or Bourges, eager to explain what the wealth of glass and sculpture was about. Medieval visitors came with minds much less attuned to rival media. They were accustomed in a measure to miracle plays, mystery plays, processions which celebrated or symbolized events of the

Church's year and so of the biblical narrative, and (increasingly as time went on) to the sermons of popular preachers. But none of this filled their attention or their leisure so that they could not give time to marvel at and study the bibles of the unlettered.

The Bible in art

The Bible is full of marvellous stories and its medieval students were well aware of them. St Benedict was probably not the only spiritual director to prohibit the reading of the Books of Kings in the evening for fear of stirring his disciples to excessive excitement. The study of the Bible as story, and in its literal meaning, flourished at all periods. But from the early centuries of the Church's history much more had been read into it than lay on the surface of its meaning. It was widely reckoned to have both a literal and a spiritual sense. Learned interpreters from the great fathers of the 3rd and 4th centuries on discussed and disputed how many different types and layers of spiritual meaning the Bible might hold, and arrived at a number of different conclusions. Some parts of the Bible were scarcely allowed to have a literal meaning at all, and it seems strange to us that a joyous love song like the Song of Solomon should be regarded as suitable reading in a monastic cloister. Yet it forms the theme of some of the most inspired sermons of St Bernard of Clairvaux himself. This was possible because it seemed entirely natural to him to read it allegorically: as a fervent description of the relationship of Christ and his Church; and so not only as allegory but as a type, foreshadowing the New Testament as so many passages in the Old were reckoned to do. In art the apposition of the Old and New Testaments was most vigorously revived in the work of Abbot Suger at Saint-Denis in the second quarter of the 12th century. Allegory and type were only two out of many ways of finding spiritual meaning in the Old Testament; but they were two which even layfolk might grasp, and the two which we must grasp if we wish to understand medieval art.

Narrative art entered a new phase in the late 11th century in the dramatic presentation of the Norman Conquest of England in the Bayeux Tapestry. Many surviving examples from the 12th century represent biblical stories, and the art and fashion of narrative combined with a great renewal of interest in the literal meaning of the Bible. Large and ambitious designs in plenty were

25

24–5

A biblical scene vividly presented in the Winchester Bible, second half of the 12th century: the burial of Judas Maccabaeus by the 'Master of the Apocrypha Legends'.

devised to tell the Bible story, or some part of it. Two of the grandest which survive will serve as illustrations: the majestic Pentateuch of Saint-Savin and the provincial painted ceiling of the church at Zillis in the Graubünden in Switzerland, the most perfect surviving example of the poor man's bible.

Saint-Savin and the Old Testament

We can wonder at the monks of Saint-Savin who filled the whole nave vault with only a modest part of the Bible story, or the monks of Peterborough, whose complex and beautiful nave ceiling can be read only with difficulty with the naked eye; we may marvel at the way in which elaborate biblical scenes were sometimes lavished on objects, like the imperial throne of Maximian, which few would ever be allowed to see, and fewer still to contemplate and study. But we can hardly doubt that Saint-Savin, like other monastic churches, welcomed many visitors to its nave; and that the visitors to Saint-Savin were given ample opportunity to study the drama of the Pentateuch; and we may follow in their steps.

Saint-Savin-sur-Gartempe in Poitou is a fine example of a lofty Romanesque monastic church of the 11th century with an immense nave. It was on the barrel vault of this nave that a group of painters added, probably in the early 12th century, the Pentateuch, the story of the first five books of the Old Testament. It was only one of several themes painted in the church – a vivid apocalypse adorns the porch, and the sufferings and death of Saint-Savin and another Roman martyr make the crypt where they were buried a place of torment still. Yet the Pentateuch dominates the whole building. The scale of the great church had caused a quarrel between the abbot, its chief sponsor, and his prior; and the prior had left a few years, perhaps, before the painting of the frescoes began. Prior Bernard was later to be the founder of Tiron and was one of the men whose life combined most succinctly the religious urges of the age: the ascetic life, the flight from riches and the urge to peripatetic popular preaching. Evidently the idea of a monastic community as a source for public instruction lived on after Bernard's departure, and it is vividly represented in the nave ceiling. His connection with Saint-Savin is a reminder of the diverse forms instruction could take, ranging from the popular preacher's tirade against sin, sometimes very informally conducted by the roadside or in the woods, sometimes in the pulpit of a parish or monastic church, to the guided tour of a great cycle of mural paintings or glass or sculpture.

The ceiling of Saint-Savin is the most remarkable surviving example of Romanesque narrative art apart from the Bayeux Tapestry, to which it has been compared – the painting is more monumental, more subtle as a work of art, the tapestry more exciting as narrative. Yet the designer of Saint-Savin has allowed himself plenty of scope for stately drama. There are a few isolated episodes; but for the most part he has selected major themes in the story (as it was then understood) and shown several stages in each. Under a majestic presentation of God in the act of creation, the story of Adam and Eve is told, from her formation to the tragic denouement in the Fall and condemnation to work; next the life and death of Cain, the Tower of Babel and the stories of Abraham and Noah. Noah's ark fascinated Romanesque artists and they 26

26–7   portrayed it in a number of ways, as on the west front of Lincoln Cathedral. Here the story is divided into various episodes, with the representation of the ark itself, in the act of being launched, with men clambering aboard, at their centre. But it was the stories of Joseph and Moses which especially captured the designer's or the patrons' imagination at Saint-Savin, and each has half the space above six bays of the nave, one on the north, the other on the south. The designer evidently enjoyed telling a story, and the narrative element in 12th-century art is very common even in the more limited space of a capital or group of roundels of stained glass. This makes the more remarkable the absence from Saint-Savin and most churches of the age of any representations of the dramatic stories of David and Solomon and the kings of Israel and Judah. David plays his harp here and there in stone, and very frequently in the pages of psalters; and occasionally he is portrayed in his shepherd days or slaying Goliath. But the story of Bathsheba, which so greatly fascinated Rembrandt, or the king-making of Solomon, which dominated contemporary coronation rituals, are hardly to be found in contemporary art.

The last omission is particularly striking. The coronation of Queen Elizabeth II in 1953 was a public event, witnessed by millions of viewers the world over. How public the anointing and coronation of a medieval king was expected to be it is hard to say; but the attendant acclamations and processions must have been intended to parade the royal unction and its sublime significance. The English rituals of 973 and 1066 and 1953 opened with the anthem 'Zadok the priest and Nathan the prophet anointed Solomon king', an anthem which draws attention to the model on which the king-making processes of the early Middle Ages were chiefly based, and to the part played in them by the Church. Those who thought that the divine unction of kings placed them too high, and wished rather to exalt the authority of popes and bishops, might wish not to have David and Solomon too much in the public view. But learned papalists like John of Salisbury filled their writings with examples drawn from the Books of Kings; the puzzle remains. Noah's ark or Samson's pulling down the pillars of the house of Dagon, from Genesis and Judges, combined allegory and drama and doubtless appealed to Gislebertus and his patrons at Autun for that reason. Elsewhere prophetic figures and visions can be shown or assumed to prefigure the Gospel and the coming of Jesus. But the poor man who relied on pictures for his knowledge of the Bible story would have found some large gaps.

Christ visits Martha and Mary, the Biblical exemplars of the active and contemplative lives, from a late 13th-century Bible moralisée.

Zillis and the life of Jesus

Narrative art was a new adventure in the 11th and 12th centuries; and for a number of scenes, especially in the New Testament, the inspiration of narrative combined with the growing fashion for liturgical drama. At Autun Gislebertus has made out of the nativity story – especially the adoration of the Magi and the flight into Egypt – the most touching and vivid of his narratives; and distilled in the single capital showing the journey to Emmaus one of the most powerful stories portrayed in contemporary drama. The circumstances of Jesus's birth, death and resurrection were naturally most fully portrayed in medieval art, though many scenes from every part of the Gospel story can be found, from the temptations and baptism to the marriage at Cana and the raising of Lazarus – all favourite themes. The passage of the Church's year doubtless made easier the explanation to the ignorant of the Gospel story and ensured their grasp of it.

Nowhere is this more fully told than at Zillis. The whole ceiling 29 consists of 153 panels – the number of the miraculous haul of fish in St Peter's boat at the end of the Fourth Gospel (John 21:11). In case we should miss the point, the outer row the whole way round is filled with watery scenes and fishy creatures as far removed from ordinary experience as Zillis from the sea; one of these delightful and probably diabolical creatures sports a fish's tail and 30 an elephant's trunk. But the Gospel stories in the seven panels in each row within are homely and natural, with the costumes and some of the furniture of the day; Jesus the baby is lying in a rough wooden cradle, Joseph embarks on the flight to Egypt with 31 contemporary luggage and a stout whip for the donkey, though the animal, like his more sophisticated cousin at Autun, seems to 28 be standing on a frame of wheels, and may owe more to the wooden theatrical donkey of Zurich than to the live animals of the Graubünden.

The narrative is relatively simple, relatively clear, but the balance is strange to modern taste. More than half of the panels are devoted to the birth and childhood of Christ and to John the Baptist, the baptism and the temptation of Jesus. There is, however, a full portrayal of some of the miracles: the marriage at Cana, with resplendent wine-jars, several healing miracles, including a dramatic vision of the Gadarene swine, and the raising of Lazarus. There are scenes of Jesus teaching, the Samaritan woman at the well, preaching in Nazareth, sending out the disciples; then an impressive Transfiguration. As we should expect, the drama quickens and the scenes grow more ample again as the Passion approaches: the entry into Jerusalem has five panels, and is followed by the cleansing of the Temple, and the story of Holy Week, with a table well furnished for the Last Supper. But after the agony, arrest and the crowning of Jesus with thorns, the tale comes to an abrupt end. There is no crucifixion, no resurrection. It was not that they ran out of space. The last row of panels portrays the church's patron, St Martin. These panels are inferior in design and execution and it has been conjectured that the chief artist had died before they were added. However that may be, we are shown the life of Jesus, but not his death or resurrection. Perhaps they were once portrayed elsewhere in the chancel; very likely there was a rood or crucifixion on or over the altar. In any case the effect is the same: this portrayal of the life of the Son of Man, bounded, as the artists thought the world was bounded, by the great sea, separates the earthly life of Jesus from his return to heaven. Jesus is presented to us in human guise. It may be that the strange fishes are not innocent creatures; that they represent the monsters of the deep and the devils who hedge our life around. There is more symbolism in the plan than we have quite allowed, for Bethlehem's star rises in the east and sets in the west of the church and there are subtle hints of thought and interpretation in many of the pictures. But the general effect remains simple and plain: here is God made man as baby, child, and as a healing, teaching, suffering, human leader.

Whatever the reason for the abrupt conclusion of the life of Jesus at Zillis, it has deprived us of the designer's solution to the deepest problem of Christian iconography: how to portray human death and divine triumph in a single set of pictures of the crucifixion and the resurrection. This was no novel problem: if we could be sure that the original portion of St Mark's Gospel ends where its author intended, on the verge of the resurrection, we would say that the problem went back to the first generations of Christians.

The Passion, and the Dream of the Rood

It is presented in a brilliant literary fantasy in the Old English poem, *The Dream of the Rood,* of the 7th or 8th century. 'Wondrous was the cross of victory', the dreamer tells us, 'and I, stained with sins, stricken with foulness; I saw the glorious tree joyfully gleaming, adorned with garments, decked with gold; jewels had fitly covered the tree of the Lord. Yet through that gold I could perceive the former strife of wretched men, that it had once bled on the right side. I was all troubled with sorrows; I was full of fear at the fair sight. I saw the changeful sign alter in garments and colours; at times it was bedewed with moisture, stained with the flowing of blood, at times adorned with treasure'. Then the cross speaks to the dreamer and tells its story: how it grew in the forest, was cut down, taken to be a gibbet – 'I saw then the Lord of mankind hasten with great zeal that he might be raised upon me. . . . Then the young hero – he was God almighty – firm and unflinching, stripped Himself; he mounted on the high cross' – and we are told the anguish and the glory of carrying Jesus. 'All creation wept, lamented the King's death; Christ was on the cross . . .'. It is an intensely moving, powerfully imagined evocation of the two-fold vision: the suffering and the victory of the Cross.

In the early Middle Ages it was commoner at first for the crucified Jesus to be portrayed as a king and in triumph; the power of this image was still felt in the days of St Francis and the crucifix which spoke to him in San Damiano. By the late Middle Ages Jesus is commonly enduring human agony. But in English books of the 10th and even more of the 11th century the suffering Saviour is movingly portrayed; and in *The Making of the Middle Ages* Sir Richard Southern spoke of the Weingarten Crucifixion, by an English artist of the period *c.* 1050–1065, as

the high point of this compassionate tenderness for the suffering Christ in pre-Conquest England. The picture dates from the time when Anselm was becoming a monk at Bec, and before he had written any of the Prayers or Meditations which are so full of this compassion. The artist – working in a monastery far removed from any strong theological impetus and remote (it would seem) from the centres of devotional innovation – had reached the same position as St Anselm was led to by his monastic experiences and theological speculations. Elsewhere the new impulses came more slowly and arrived with the flood of French influence in the 12th century. In Denmark, for instance, where the heroic traditions were strong, the mid-11th century figures of Christ on the Cross gave a powerful local interpretation to the theme of the triumphant Prince.

Southern describes the gradual modification which produced even in Denmark in the course of the 12th century a crowned figure visibly suffering on the Cross.

Drama and the Friars

In the same concluding chapter of *The Making of the Middle Ages* Southern looked forward to two movements which deeply influenced each other: the cult of the human Jesus with the meditation on his human life which it inspired, and a movement in art and literature which gave dramatic expression to a human sympathy with his sufferings. The drama which influenced Gislebertus's portrayal of the flight into Egypt continued to inspire artists and preachers in the 13th century. If it was the art of the Roman sarcophagus and a knowledge of Byzantine painting and mosaic which enabled Nicola and Giovanni Pisano to portray the drama of real life on their pulpits and Giotto to add a new dimension to the presentation of the Gospel story in the Arena Chapel at Padua, the inspiration of the preacher's art playing on these scenes is also very clear.

Few aspects of popular religion are more obscure than the development of drama. The broad lines indeed are clear; the detail eludes us. Long before 1000 the mass was conceived as drama: learned drama, inspired by the complex symbolism of the great Carolingian liturgist Amalarius and his disciples; and popular drama which saw in the spaces of a Romanesque basilica a vast theatre – the nave as the auditorium, the choir, or the space about the nave altar, as the stage; and which saw also in the very dramatic liturgies of Holy Week and Easter the drama of salvation unfold. To the popular eye this fulfilled a need the obscure symbols of Amalarius could never answer, the need for theatre; a need all the more strongly felt among the faithful because the secular plays were anathema to the Church's hierarchy, and the word 'actor' (*histrio*), was a term of opprobrium and abuse. Yet

the liturgy was theatre indeed; and on special occasions, such as
the procession on Palm Sunday, the drama came out of church and
filled the town – the procession through and beyond the town
gate, and back into town and church, was already well established
in the 10th century and possibly earlier. Established too was the
first simple 'play' of the resurrection. On the first Easter morning
three women came to Jesus's tomb to anoint his body, and were
met by an angel who told them that the tomb was empty. This
scene was dramatically recreated in many churches already in the
10th century; and by the 12th century plays outside the church
representing scenes of the resurrection and the nativity were
evidently spreading over western Europe from a cradle which
seems to have been in the Anglo-Norman realm. The details are
entirely obscure; but those who contemplate the works of
Gislebertus and Giotto with imaginative insight cannot doubt that
they have been led into a theatre. The next step was taken, not in
the liturgy of the mass, but in an alliance between the dramatist
and the preacher.

A fine scholarly tradition attributes the mingling of drama and
religious teaching among 13th-century preachers especially to the
teaching of St Francis. Doubtless the explanation must be sought
very widely in the experience and interests and artistic fashions of
the age; but somewhere in its centre the story of Francis's own
vivid, dramatic lessons may well lie. The Friars' preaching
distilled for the 13th century what was to become a central thread
in the history of religious teaching: the presentation of the human
drama, and especially of the life of Jesus, in vivid, dramatic,
meditation. The roots of this lie among the 12th-century
Cistercians, and especially St Ailred of Rievaulx.

St Ailred and 'Jesus at the age of twelve'

The practice of meditating on the human life of Jesus, step by step,
has become so familiar a part of the devotional tradition of
Western Christendom that it is difficult to imagine Christian
devotion without it. In some sense, indeed, the idea was already
present when the Gospels were written; and they cannot be read
by imaginative folk without evoking a picture of the scene. Few of
the world's stories have inspired so many fine works of art as that
of the appearance to Mary Magdalene in the garden: it can speak 33
directly to us as it spoke to Gislebertus and many another artist.
The great biblical scholar, C. H. Dodd, after a meticulous critical

examination of the language, structure and theology of the passage in the Fourth Gospel, wrote of it thus: 'There is nothing quite like it in the gospels. Is there anything quite like it in all ancient literature?'.

Yet the fashion for regular meditation on the human life of Jesus, and for portraying it in detail, was new. The same age which produced the ceiling at Zillis witnessed the first Cistercian meditations, inspired by St Bernard, and behind him by a great tradition of 11th-century devotion; but led by Bernard's English disciple, St Ailred of Rievaulx.

Thus Ailred to the fellow-Cistercians who asked him to write on *Jesus at the age of twelve:* 'You begged me to suggest to you where the boy Jesus was during those days when his mother was looking for him, where he found shelter, what food he ate, in what company he took pleasure, what business occupied him. I am aware, my son, indeed, I am aware with what familiarity, with what devotion, with what tears you are wont to ask these very questions of Jesus himself in your holy prayers, when you have before the eyes of your heart the sweet likeness of that dear boy, when with a certain spiritual imagination you reproduce the features of that most beautiful face; when you rejoice in the gaze of those most charming and gentle eyes bent upon you . . .'. Ailred turns to Jesus himself and asks the question so many have asked – 'But how is it, my dear Lord, that you did not have compassion on your most Holy Mother as she looked for you, grieved for you, sighed for you?' – and then he deftly turns the question to Jesus's mother – why did she look for him whom she knew to be God; or 'Indeed, my Lady, if you will allow me to say so, why did you lose your dearest son so easily, why did you watch over him with such little care, why were you so late in noticing that he was missing? Would that Jesus himself would deign to communicate to me in what interior and spiritual words he answered you when you sought him so, on fire with such anxiety, that so I might be able to impart to you what I knew and had tasted.' So little by little he turns the thought to the way in which we, in the childhood of our conversion, should model ourselves on Jesus as a child; and then he turns to what Jesus was up to in the three days he was missing. He roundly asserts that it is 'wrong to make any rash assertions' but he does not hesitate to make attractive conjectures.

'Tell me, my dearest Lady, Mother of my Lord, what were your feelings, your surprise, your joy, when you found your dearest son, the boy Jesus, not among boys but among teachers, and beheld the gaze of all eyes bent on him, everyone eagerly listening to him . . .?

' "I found", she says, "him whom my soul loves. I held him fast and would not let him go." ' Not for nothing was Ailred a Cistercian and a disciple of St Bernard; his Mary speaks quite naturally, by a devout analogy, the language of the *Song of Solomon*. 'Hold him fast, dearest Lady, hold fast him whom you love, cast yourself upon his neck, embrace him, kiss him and make up for his absence during three days with increased delight.' And so he concludes his meditation on the literal, historical sense of the story, by considering the closing words in Luke's narrative, and goes on to draw out many complex lessons by suggesting possible allegorical and moral interpretations. At the end Ailred reminds us that he is a monk and a man of learning. But there is copious evidence that the type of pious meditation he is describing entered popular imagination and a wider field of teaching than the Cistercian communities for whom he immediately wrote.

In his *Rule of Life for a Recluse*, Ailred instructed his sister in a manner even more revealing of the modes and aims of meditation in his circle. She is taken step by step through the Passion, made to feel all the horror and delight of the Lord's death and resurrection. She is made to feel with the ladies watching the crucifixion, to observe Joseph of Arimathaea taking the body down from the Cross. 'See how in his most happy arms he embraces that sweet body and clasps it to his breast. . . . Do not fail subsequently to keep Magdalene company, remember to visit with her your Lord's tomb, taking with you the perfumes she has prepared. . . .' And so to an extremely moving interpretation of the appearance of Jesus and of 'noli me tangere'.

When we met the scenes of the nativity in Autun we conjectured a possible source in contemporary drama. But in his study of the life and influences of a 12th-century recluse Henry Mayr-Harting has suggested that the intensely personal presentations of the deposition which appear in the English art of the mid-12th century are linked to such meditations as Ailred's. The problem is set in sharp focus by the paintings of the deposition in the Chapel of the Holy Sepulchre at Winchester. It was the normal practice to deposit the crucifix, crosses and ornaments of the altar in an 'Easter sepulchre' during Lent, and restore them with much pomp, and a liturgical drama, at Easter. The little chapel at Winchester was evidently made in the mid-12th century as a large

Easter sepulchre, to house the Cross and trappings of the altar during Lent; from it their return at Easter was closely linked with the liturgical dramas of that time. On the east wall was painted a very intense and moving representation of Joseph of Arimathaea and Nicodemus taking the body from the Cross and laying it in the tomb, just as Ailred describes the scene, completed by the presence of Jesus's sorrowing mother, who was absent from that stage of the story in the Gospels, and Ailred, but was soon to become an essential element in every such scene. One cannot say whether the drama of this scene owes more to the personal meditations of such as Ailred, or to the dramatic scenes enacted Easter by Easter in church. They belong to a common world of religious sentiment.

As also does the devout recluse of Ailred's treatise. We began this chapter by conjecturing on the way in which instruction in the Bible came to ordinary folk; it will be good to end it with an example of how such instruction could be given. In the same study, Mayr-Harting has drawn out all the remarkable functions a holy man might perform in a village community in 12th-century England, likening him to the holy man revealed in a well-known paper of Peter Brown's concerning late antiquity. He could settle village quarrels, act as a safe deposit for valuables, as a banker, and offer advice on a host of different problems, perform some of the functions ignored by absentee landlords, and if he was a craftsman help others in his crafts. 'Amidst all this it can easily be forgotten', writes Mayr-Harting, 'that recluses in general (doubtless there were some frauds) could have had no standing in the community and performed no useful functions unless they shared genuinely in Christian spirituality and culture and unless their actions were seen to have a solid basis of recognised spiritual achievement behind them. . . . If we ask how recluses shared in the Christian spirituality and culture of their age, we should perhaps put an anterior question: what did they actually spend their day doing? To this, Peter the Venerable gives us a general answer. Prayer, he said, was the special good which repelled all evils, but as it was not possible to pray for long, prayer should be accompanied by reading, meditation and the work of the hands;' – and he goes on to draw out the special interest of Ailred's treatise in this context, and its relation to contemporary art.

Christina of Markyate and the compassion of Jesus

Our most concrete information on this link comes from two lady recluses, Ailred's sister and Christina of Markyate, for whom the St Albans Psalter, containing one of the earliest known depositions of this character, was made. But it is likely enough that in the 12th century male recluses, more readily placed to give instruction to village folk, enjoyed similar books, even if rarely of such exceptional quality. Nor should we assume that the female recluse was wholly cut off from the world. At the end of Christina's *Life* is a moving description of a male visitor who came and talked and ate with Christina and her companion. It is implied that the visitor was Jesus calling on Mary and Martha, and eating with his disciples as Jesus ate with the two at Emmaus; but it also assumed that she would normally speak with a pious pilgrim in this way. This was one, though only one, of many modes of communication, by which ideas and fashions, of every kind, including themes of art and religious sentiment, spread rapidly from one end of Western Christendom to the other.

In a vision recorded in her life just before the pilgrim's visit, Christina meditated on the destiny of one of her friends. And while she meditated she felt as it were a tap on the shoulder, turned and 'saw Jesus standing at the altar in the loving attitude and mien of one who has compassion on sinners' – and beside him her friend; and so received the assurance that he would be saved. But the Jesus of popular piety was not always seen with so compassionate a mien. Contemporary sentiment revelled in the paradox of the human, kindly, compassionate Jesus who was also a stern and strict judge.

VIII

Judgment

'I am afraid of my life. For when I examine myself carefully, it seems to me that my whole life is either sinful or sterile.' Thus St Anselm, in one of his imaginative meditations written in the cloister at Bec, probably between 1070 and 1080. 'Barren soul, what are you doing? Sinful soul, why are you lying still? The day of judgement is coming', 'that great day of the Lord is nigh, it is near and comes quickly, day of wrath and day of mourning . . .'.

Even in Anselm's gloomy piety a more hopeful note is struck in the end, but only after fearful preliminaries. 'Barren tree, where is your fruit? You deserve to be cut down and burnt, cut up and put on the fire. . . . Perhaps you think of some sin as small? Would that the strict judge would regard any sin as small. . . . Barren and useless wood, deserving eternal burning, what reply will you make in that day?' And in another meditation, in which he imagines himself a virgin deflowered – 'Sulphurous flames, flames of hell, eddying darknesses, swirling with terrible sounds. Worms living in the fire, is it not marvellous that such greediness of burning should gnaw you, and that you should be burnt up by the flame of fire? Devils that burn with us, raging with fire and gnashing your teeth in madness, why are you so cruel to those who roll about among you?. . . ' But even for the fornicator there is hope: 'In terror I flee from the dread of your justice to the comfort of your mercy . . .'. And for the ordinary male sinner, 'Who will deliver me out of the hands of God? Where shall I find counsel, where safety? Who is he who is called angel of mighty counsel, who is called Saviour, that I may call upon his name? But it is he himself, he himself is Jesus. . . . Have mercy, Jesus, while the time of mercy lasts, lest in the time of judgement you condemn. . . . O most desired Jesus, admit me to the number of your elect. . . .'

Heaven, hell and purgatory

There can be little doubt that in general estimation the population of heaven greatly increased in the 12th century. It is abundantly clear that in the thought of St Peter Damian in the mid-11th century, or of St Anselm at the end of the century, the chances of salvation were slight for any but monks. Quite a different spirit animates the literature of the 12th century, even if the theme of judgment and the pains of hell lost nothing in the process. Yet all was not gain for sinful man. We are familiar with the pattern firmly established by 1300 in Dante's *Divina Commedia,* of hell, purgatory and heaven – hell the place of eternal torment; purgatory the place of punishment from which all who entered it would rise to heaven after their due reparation had been made, which could include masses and prayers offered on their behalf to heaven; heaven the place of eternal felicity. The doctrine of purgatory had developed in the 11th and 12th centuries; it was in some essentials a novelty. The idea of punishment and purgation, of penance after absolution, went back much further, and earlier Christian literature portrays many of the features of Dante's world. But the clear distinction between purgatory and hell was new.

The older view is most vividly portrayed in the version of the story of the infernal march of Herla or Herlequin or Harlequin in the *Ecclesiastical History* of Orderic Vitalis. Writing in the 1130s, he described an incident of 1091. A Norman parish priest called Walchelin set off on the night of 1 January 'to visit a sick man on the fringes of his parish'. On his way back, alone, in a remote spot, 'he heard a sound like the movement of a great army, and took it to be the household troops of Robert of Bellême' [in Orderic's eyes, the type of the unsavoury robber baron], hurrying to a siege. The moon shone brightly and he saw the road clear ahead. As the sound of disorderly feet came nearer he tried to flee, but a giant with a mace stopped him. . . . 'A great crowd on foot appeared, carrying across their necks and shoulders animals and clothes and every kind of furnishing and household goods that raiders usually seize as plunder. But all lamented bitterly and urged each other to hurry. The priest recognised among them many of his neighbours who had recently died, and heard them bewailing the torments they suffered because of their sins.' Presently came a group carrying biers, and there was frequent change of type and physiognomy; one wretch, tightly trussed, was being goaded by a demon with red-hot spurs. 'Next came a troop of women' riding side-saddle, 'on seats studded with burning nails. . . . Indeed it was for the seductions and obscene delights in which they had wallowed without restraint on earth that they now endured the fire and stench and other agonies too many to enumerate, and gave voice to their sufferings with loud wailing. The priest recognised a number of noble women in this troop, and also saw the horses and mules with empty women's litters belonging to many who were still alive.'

But the scene of torment revealed to him not only those who had lived evil lives, but some men of good repute – one of Orderic's abbots at Saint-Évroult among them – who inspired the author to reflection on the difference between God's judgment and man's. 'God looks into the heart. In the kingdom of eternal blessedness light eternal illumines all things; there true sanctity is won and every delight brings joy to the heirs of the kingdom. Nothing there is disorderly, no trace of guilt enters in, nothing evil or wrong can be found there. So all unseemliness of which base humanity is guilty is burned away in purgatorial fire and the soul is purified by every kind of purgation that the eternal judge deems right. And just as a vessel, cleansed from rust and well-polished, is placed in the treasury, so the soul, purified from the stain of every sin is led to paradise, where it enters into perfect blessedness and the joy that knows no fear or shadow.' Thus Orderic turns this fearful vision or dream or delirium – perhaps the priest had encountered Robert of Bellême's men after all – into a moral tale and exposition of purgatory.

For the tale ends with the priest trying to seize a riderless horse in the hope of keeping it to convince his mortal friends of the truth of what he had seen. But a group of knights come and threaten to carry him off with them. However, one of them forces his release, and tells his story: 'I am William of Glos, the son of Barnon, who was the renowned steward of William of Breteuil . . .'; and he explains that he is tormented for his many sins, above all for usury. 'For I lent my money to a poor man, receiving a mill of his as a pledge, and because he was unable to repay the loan I retained the pledge all my life and disinherited the legitimate heir by leaving it to my heirs. See, I carry a burning mill-shaft in my mouth, which, believe me, seems heavier than the castle of Rouen. Therefore tell my wife Beatrice and my son Roger that they must help me by quickly restoring to the heir the pledge, from which they have received far more than I ever gave. . . .'

The priest was incredulous since William had died long before, and hardly dared think of giving such a message; but the knight gripped him with a hand 'burning like fire', till the priest cried out in anguish: 'Blessed Mary, glorious mother of Christ, help me'. In an instant another knight appeared and William and his companions rode on, 'following the dark host'. 'Do you not recognise me?' said the rescuer, 'I am Robert, son of Ralph the fair, and your brother.' But again the priest was incredulous and fearful of accepting what was said to him. 'I am amazed by your hardness and obstinacy. I brought you up after both our parents died, and loved you more than any living person. I sent you to the schools of France, kept you well provided with clothes and money, and in many other ways furthered your progress . . . ' – and eventually the priest broke down in tears and accepted his identity. 'You deserved by right to die and be carried along with us to share in our punishment, for you rashly tried to seize things that are ours . . . but the Mass which you sang today has saved you from death . . .'. He went on to describe his own death in England and his punishment: 'The arms which we bear are red-hot, and offend us with an appalling stench, weighing us down with intolerable weight, and burning with everlasting fire. . . . When you were ordained in England and sang your first Mass for the faithful departed your father Ralph escaped from his punishments and my shield, which caused me great pain, fell from me. As you see I still carry this sword, but I look in faith for release from this burden within the year.'

We are between two worlds. Here in essence, or embryo, is the developed doctrine of purgatory, and the notion that masses for the soul help to release those enduring punishment there; from this was to grow the whole Chantry movement – of foundations to sing mass for the souls of the dead – and the system of prayers, indulgences and masses. But it is also clear that we are in the world of the First Crusade, not of later Crusades; that the full logic of purgatory and indulgences has not yet been worked out. For the vision is a vision of hell and it seems that some of the figures tormented in the whirling host will be there for ever. The compensation for the dark hopelessness of 10th- and 11th-century eschatology is that the gates of hell were not locked. But already there was another tradition stemming from the Apocalypse which locked the gates of hell. 'And I saw an angel come down from Heaven, having the key of the bottomless pit and a great chain in his hand and he laid hold on the dragon, that old serpent which is

The Last Judgment from the Liber Vitae: top, *St Peter opens the gate of the New Jerusalem;* centre, *he saves a soul;* bottom, *the angel locks the gate of hell.*

the Devil, and Satan, and bound him a thousand years; and cast him into the bottomless pit, and shut him up, and set a seal upon him.' Already by *c.* 1030 this was represented in the *Liber Vitae* of New Minster at Winchester as an angel locking the door with the damned inside enduring torment and being swallowed in the jaws of hell. By the middle of the 12th century the full story is spelt out in the Winchester Psalter.

The day of Judgment

This psalter is one of the most splendid illuminated books of its age. Its contents are not without perplexities, but it seems most likely that its patron was Henry of Blois, Bishop of Winchester, and that it was painted for a house of nuns; certainly it found its way within two or three generations to the library of the nuns of Shaftesbury. It contains among a fascinating and dramatic group of pictures one of the fullest painted Judgment scenes, in which an angel concludes the Judgment by locking the door of hell. 'Ici est enfers e li angels ki enferme les portes' – Here is Hell and the angel who locks the gates. The inscription is in French, very probably because it was designed for use by nuns who even in the age of the Abbess Heloise and of St Hildegarde were not expected to know Latin. The Winchester Psalter is a very high-class example of visual instruction; but no horrors are spared. There is a high proportion of ladies within the infernal jaws, and at least two of them are queens. In the earlier scenes as choice a collection of medieval instruments of torture as were ever gathered in one picture is applied to mainly male victims, while archbishops and monks and kings and other men stand by waiting their turn.

The centre piece of this Judgment scene is a figure of Christ in majesty, half clothed, showing his wound, and below, two angels lifting the cross onto an altar. The Christ of the Judgment in 13th-century sculpture, on numerous tympana over the doors of French cathedrals and abbeys, is commonly shown in similar fashion, half-clothed; in 13th-century examples like that at Chartres the Blessed Virgin and St John stand beside him, as in a Crucifixion, evidently to represent the feelings of pity and the desire for mercy which the scene of Judgment naturally evoked. Terror and pity were combined at Chartres with a notable dignity.

The heaven and hell of Gislebertus

None of the later Judgment scenes surpasses in imagination the tympanum over the western portal at Autun, carved in the early 1130s by Gislebertus – *Gislebertus hoc fecit*. Thus he proudly acknowledges his craftsmanship at the feet of Christ the Judge. Here the figure is clothed, majestic and calm, with his hands outstretched to the right, to the good and to heaven, and to the left, to the sinister side, to the evil and the damned and hell. Inscriptions interpret the scene: 'I alone dispose of all things and crown the just' on his right; 'Those who follow crime I judge and punish' on his left. To either side an angel sounds the trumpet. Under his feet the souls of the dead are rising from the tombs.

Those on the judge's right are thus inscribed: 'Thus shall rise again everyone who does not lead an impious life, and endless light of day shall shine for him.' At first one sees a line of figures, scarcely distinguishable. But as one looks more closely small groups emerge: here husband and wife look at their child rising from a
34   nearby tomb; there a group of small figures cling to an angel who is helping them to rise. Below the judge's left hand the inscription reads: 'Here let fear strike those whom earthly error binds, for their fate is shown by the horror of these figures.' Groups of figures stand in fear and despair; an adulteress is gripped on her breasts by serpents; two enormous hands come down over the
35   head of another terrified figure, to represent hell's stranglehold.

The day of wrath: dies irae

The endless terror of Christian souls at the moment of death, deeply felt by St Anselm in the 11th century, found vivid expression in the famous 13th-century hymn sometimes attributed to St Francis's disciple and biographer, Thomas of Celano, and certainly by a writer of acute and vivid imagination.

dies irae, dies illa
solvet saeclum in favilla . . .

The day of wrath, the day when the world is reduced to ashes; when the Judge is come and everything will be strictly examined: the trumpet sounds through the tombs and forces everyone before the throne. What am I, wretched man, to say then? Whose protection shall I seek, when even a just man may scarcely feel confidence? No appeal is made to the traditional intercessors, to the Blessed Virgin and the saints. In this moment St Anselm, acting perhaps out of character for his age when the aid of saintly intercessors was normally sought, had turned directly to Christ; so did the author of the *Dies irae*, and his intensely personal approach has echoed through the requiem ever since. He builds an argument based on human needs, on his own imperfection, above all on his personal consciousness of an astonishing individuality. The transition is elegantly effected. O king of terrifying majesty who saves those who are to be saved – save *me*, O source of pity. Remember, gracious Jesus, that it is *I* who am the cause of the road you took: do not lose me on that day. It was in search of *me* you sat down weary; *me* you redeemed by enduring the Cross: let not that effort be wasted. You, who forgave Mary [Magdalene] and listened favourably to the thief, give hope to me also. In the medieval West Mary Magdalene was identified with the 'woman who was a sinner', and supposed a converted prostitute; and in Luke's Gospel one of the thieves crucified with Jesus was promised salvation.

My prayers are not worthy, but do *you* – *tu*, the most personal word of address – act mercifully, Good Lord, lest I burn in everlasting fire. Put me in your fold among the sheep; separate me from the goats; cause me to stand on your right side.

The Jubilee of 1300

The theme of Judgment runs through religious ideas to the end of the Middle Ages and beyond. The human spirit cannot sustain such imaginative torments without any relief, and beside the accumulated horror of the great dooms there flourished two modes of escape. First of all, the inexorable judge was also the Jesus of mercy, and numerous human aids to remission existed or were devised. Most characteristic was the indulgence. The indulgence to the Crusaders which promised them the fruits of martyrdom or other suitable rewards led on to other forms of plenary indulgence – that is, of methods to escape the pains of purgatory altogether for Christians who sought such escape in the state of grace. Much more common were the lesser indulgences which came to grow and flourish in the 12th century: first remission of penances, later remission of penalties, for those who contributed to a charity or a building fund or visited a shrine on the saint's chief festival. The remission of penalties was fixed by a curious kind of celestial arithmetic which included days and years of purgatory. These were never intended to be taken literally but only to indicate the scale of the benefit; but human nature being what it is, they soon deceived some of the faithful – and even more profoundly many modern students – into thinking that purgatory could be measured in time.

The whole structure of indulgences is strange to most of us today, and its abuses well known. It had many faces; and most obviously represented a desperate search for relief from the vivid torments portrayed in scenes of judgment. It also reflected a much more acceptable face of medieval religion. One of the plenary indulgences was attached to the Portiuncula, the ancient, tiny church outside Assisi which St Francis made the headquarters of his Order. Precisely how the Portiuncula Indulgence was associated with Francis himself is not clear; but it evidently grew out of the notion of divine mercy which he himself did so much to propagate. This idea was spread about by his disciples and by the lay members of his Third Order, the Order of Penitents, men and women who promised to live a Christian life without taking the full vows of friars.

In the course of the 13th century the Franciscan Order and its satellites were deeply influenced by the apocalyptic, eschatological prophecies of Joachim of Fiore, the millenarist prophet of the 12th century. The second coming of Jesus was widely expected, and special dates were assigned to the future transformation of the world. Some of these ideas led on to heresy, others were harnessed to the work of the Catholic Church and of its hierarchy. The idea of a special year of remission and forgiveness and pardon and indulgences became naturally entwined with a similar doctrine of the ancient Hebrews, described in Leviticus 25: 'A jubilee shall that 50th year be to you . . .; it shall be holy to you . . .' (25:10, 12).

The ideas of jubilee and of plenary indulgence flowed together in the cult of saints such as Francis and Thomas Becket; but the first full statement of the Christian Jubilee came in 1300, when Pope Boniface VIII pronounced the first Roman Jubilee, the first *anno santo*, offering an indulgence not only 'plenam' but 'plenissimam' of the most solemn kind to all who performed certain acts within the year. Like so many of the deeds of Pope Boniface, it was a grand gesture with a strong material purpose enshrined within it. He needed money, and knew well how cults were promoted; he gathered pilgrims by one of the most powerful advertising campaigns of the Middle Ages. The unprecedented crowds caused such congestion in the streets that temporary measures were introduced to regulate the flow. Dante tells us that traffic control was in operation on the bridge over the Tiber at the Castel Sant'Angelo; in his journey to Hell which he ascribed to that very same year 1300, the panders and seducers file endlessly in opposite directions along the first sunken circular road of Malebolge, kept moving by the whips of horned demons (*Inferno*, canto XVIII). The analogy with Boniface's Rome and the papal Jubilee is scarcely veiled. Millenarism, lofty idealism, holiday-making and the lure of gold all played their part; as in the Crusading movement one cannot now distinguish the elements. The modest hopes of 1000 heralded the papal revival of the 11th century and form a prelude to our story; the mingling of millenarist idealism and Mammon in the Jubilee of 1300 presaged the decline of the medieval papacy. It forms a natural coda.

Epilogue – the heaven and hell of Aucassin

But there was also another way to escape from the pains of hell – or at least from the harsh nightmares they might conjure. In the first half of the 13th century an anonymous French poet composed an enchanting parody of a romance, *Aucassin and Nicolette*. Aucassin is heir to a Count, and so cannot possibly marry the beautiful Nicolette who was rescued from the Saracens and is at best a liberated slave. Happily she discovers in the end that she is a king's daughter, and all is well. Long before this, her foster-father reads her lover a lecture on marriage customs.

'Good sir,' said the viscount, 'leave this be. Nicolette is a captive whom I brought back from foreign parts and bought with my money from the Saracens. I stood sponsor to her at her baptism and brought her up as my godchild, and intended providing her one of these days with a young fellow who would have earned her bread for her in honourable service. You have no call to meddle in this; take instead the daughter of a king or a count. Besides which, what do you think you would have gained if you had made her your mistress or taken her to your bed? Precious little, for your soul would sojourn in hell for it till the end of time, for you'd never enter heaven.'

'What would I do in heaven? I have no wish to enter there, unless I have Nicolette, my own sweet love, whom I love so dearly. For to heaven go only such people as I'll tell you of: all those doddering priests and the halt and one-armed dotards who grovel all day and all night in front of the altars and in fusty crypts, and the folk garbed in rags and tatters and old, worn cloaks, who go barefoot and bare-buttocked and who die of hunger and thirst and cold and wretchedness. These are the ones who go to heaven, and I want nothing to do with them. Nay, I would go to hell; for to hell go the pretty clerks and the fine knights killed in tournaments and splendid wars, good soldiers and all free and noble men. I want to go along with these. And there too go the lovely ladies, gently bred and mannered, those who have had two lovers or three besides their lords, and there go gold and silver, and silk and sable, and harpers and minstrels and all the kings of this world. I want to go along with these, provided I have Nicolette, my own sweet love, with me.'

And so the inhabitants of hell, who seemed to be growing less in the 12th century, could increase and multiply once more.

Abbreviations

Brooke and Swaan   C. Brooke and W. Swaan, *The Monastic World*. London 1974

Brooke, *Coming*   R. B. Brooke, *The Coming of the Friars*. London 1975

Brooke, *MCS*   C. Brooke, *Medieval Church and Society*. London 1971

Finucane   R. C. Finucane, *Miracles and Pilgrims: Popular Beliefs in Medieval England*. London 1977

NMT   Nelson's Medieval Texts

OMT   Oxford Medieval Texts

PL   *Patrologiae Cursus Completus, Series Latina*, ed. J.-P. Migne, 221 vols. Paris 1844-64

SCH   *Studies in Church History*

Sumption, *Pilgrimage*   J. Sumption, *Pilgrimage, an image of mediaeval religion*. London 1975

Bibliographical note and references

No general work covers the specific themes of this book. A valuable introduction is R. Manselli, *La religion populaire au moyen âge* (Montreal, Paris, 1975); many topics are considered in J. Sumption, *Pilgrimage, an image of mediaeval religion* (London 1975), with useful bibliography; and the collected essays in E. Delaruelle, *La piété populaire au moyen âge* (Turin 1975); *Popular Belief and Practice: Studies in Church History*, 8 (ed. G. J. Cuming and Derek Baker, Cambridge 1972); C. Brooke, *Medieval Church and Society* (London 1971); A. Vauchez, *La spiritualité du moyen âge occidental* (Paris 1975). For the background, and the wider context, R. W. Southern, *The Making of the Middle Ages* (London 1953), and *Western Society and the Church in the Middle Ages* (Harmondsworth 1970); D. Knowles and D. Obolensky, *The Christian Centuries* II, *The Middle Ages* (London 1969); C. Morris, *The Discovery of the Individual 1050-1200* (London 1972); C. Brooke, *Europe in the Central Middle Ages* (London 1964) and *The Twelfth Century Renaissance* (London 1969). On the papacy see G. Barraclough, *The medieval papacy* (London 1968), and literature cited; W. Ullmann, *A short history of the papacy in the Middle Ages* (London 1972). On the religious orders D. Knowles, *Monastic Order in England* and *Religious Orders in England* (Cambridge 1940, 2nd edn. 1963; and 1948-59); and esp. illustrations in C. Brooke and W. Swaan, *The Monastic World* (London

1974) (Brooke and Swaan). On the relations of popular religion and poverty, L. Little, *Religious poverty and the profit economy* (London 1978); M. Mollat, *Études sur l'histoire de la pauvreté* (2 vols. Paris 1974). For medieval art, see esp. G. Zarnecki, *Art of the Medieval World* (New York 1975); P. Kidson, *The Medieval World* (New York 1967). An important recent study which throws light on some of the intellectual and social context of the theme is A. Murray, *Reason and Society in the Middle Ages* (Oxford 1978).

I Prologue

For Manselli and other general works, see above. The first chronicles of the First Crusade are the *Gesta Francorum*, ed. and trans. R. Hill (NMT 1962; repr. OMT 1980), by a lay knight who was a participant; also participating were Raymond of Agiles, canon of Le Puy and Fulcher of Chartres, both of them clerks. Raymond's work is in *Recueil des historiens des croisades* (Paris, 1841-1906), *Historiens occidentaux*, III; Fulcher's was ed. H. Hagenmeyer (Heidelberg, 1913). See pp. 161-2.

On Matthew Paris, see R. Vaughan, *Matthew Paris* (Cambridge 1958).

The *Libellus* on the life and miracles of St Godric of Finchale was ed. J. Stevenson in the Surtees Society, 1847, and has been studied by Victoria

157

Tudor (unpubl. Durham Ph.D. thesis); cf. Finucane, pp. 126-7.

On magic and superstition, see esp. B. Helbling-Gloor, *Natur und Aberglaube im Policraticus des Johannes von Salisbury* (Geist und Werk der Zeiten, Heft 1, Zurich 1956).

II Relics and pilgrims

The passage from Raoul (Rodulfus) Glaber is in *Les cinq livres de ses histoires*, iii. 4, ed. M. Prou (Paris 1886), p. 62 'ac si mundus . . . passim candidam aecclesiarum vestem indueret'.

Chronicle of Hugh Candidus, a monk of Peterborough, ed. W. T. Mellows (London 1949), esp. pp. 48-65, 77-82; also translated by C. and W. T. Mellows (revised edn. by A. Bell, Peterborough 1966) (we quote from pp. 28-9, 42, slightly adapted). On the arm of St Bartholomew see Eadmer, citation below. The 'invention' of St Ives was discussed by G. H. Doble in *Laudate*, XII (1934), 149-56, based on Goscelin's life in *Acta Sanctorum Bollandiana*, June II, 288-92. On St. Alban and St Albans see *Cathedral and City: St Albans ancient and modern*, ed. R. K. Runcie (London 1977); R. Vaughan, *Matthew Paris* (Cambridge 1958), pp. 198-204. On St Teilo, G. H. Doble, *St Teilo* (Lampeter 1942), repr. in Doble, *Lives of the Welsh Saints*, ed. D. S. Evans (Cardiff 1971); the story is in his *Life* in *The Text of the Book of Llan Dâv*, ed. J. G. Evans and J. Rhys (Oxford 1893), pp. 116-17, and cf. C. Brooke in K. Jackson *et al.*, *Celt and Saxon* (Cambridge 1963), p. 309.

On thefts of relics, see P. J. Geary, *Furta Sacra: thefts of relics in the central Middle Ages* (Princeton 1978); on the humiliation of saints and relics, see Geary in *Annales*, 1979, pp. 27-42. On St Hugh of Lincoln see *Magna Vita S. Hugonis*, ed. D. Douie and H. Farmer (NMT 1961-2), II, 169-70. Guibert's treatise 'The relics of the Saints' is printed in *PL* CLVI, 607-80, see esp.

cols. 621, 622, 624-6; and cf. C. Morris in *Studies in Church History*, VIII (1971), 55-60; K. Guth, *Guibert von Nogent und die hochmittelalterliche Kritik an der Reliquienverehrung* (Ottobeuren 1970). For Eadmer, see his *Life of St Anselm*, ed. and trans. R. W. Southern (NMT 1962; repr. OMT 1972); *Historia Novorum*, ed. M. Rule, Rolls Series 1884; trans. G. Bosanquet (London 1964); and esp. R. W. Southern, *St Anselm and his biographer* (Cambridge 1963); the passage on p. 15 is based on *Historia Novorum*, ed. Rule pp. 107-10; trans. Bosanquet, p. 111-14. The chest at Bury is described by Jocelin of Brakelond, *Chronicle*, ed. and trans. H. E. Butler (NMT 1949), pp. 9-10.

On travel to Rome, see John of Salisbury, *Letters* I, ed. W. J. Millor, H. E. Butler and C. N. L. Brooke (NMT 1955), pp. xxix-xxxv; R. L. Poole in *Studies in Chronology and History*, ed. A. L. Poole (Oxford 1934), pp. 263-4.

On Santiago de Compostela and the cult of St James, see Sumption, *Pilgrimage*, pp. 115-16, 119-20 etc., and refs. on pp. 324-5; *Le guide du pèlerin de Saint-Jacques de Compostelle . . .*, ed. and French transl. J. Vielliard (Macon 1938, 4th edn. 1969; esp. pp. 8-9, 12-15, 18-21, 24-5, 36-41, 54-7, 84-5, 94-5. References are to 1st edn.) There are fine illustrations, with copious annotation, on the churches, shrines, reliquaries etc. of the pilgrimage routes in V. and H. Hell, *The great pilgrimage of the Middle Ages: the road to St James of Compostela* (Eng. trans., London 1966). On Compostela in the 12th century, R. A. Fletcher, *The episcopate in the kingdom of León in the 12th century* (Oxford 1978), esp. pp. 53-61. On pilgrim churches see K. J. Conant, *Carolingian and Romanesque Architecture 800-1200* (Harmondsworth 1959), pp. 91-103. For criticisms of pilgrimage see G. Constable in *Studia Gratiana*, XIX (1976), 123-46. On Conques, Sumption, pp. 51-2, 158-9; *Rouergue roman* (Zodiaque

1963), pp. 27-184; P. J. Geary, *Furta sacra,* pp. 70-6, 169-74. The passage from Walter Daniel's *Life of Ailred of Rievaulx* is from ed. and trans. F. M. Powicke (NMT 1950), pp. 12-13.

On St Francis and animals see esp. E. A. Armstrong, *St Francis: Nature Mystic* (Berkeley–Los Angeles–London 1973).

III The saints

Ailred's 'Jesus at the age of twelve' is translated in *The Works of Aelred of Rievaulx,* I, Cistercian Fathers Series, no. 2. (Spencer Mass. 1971), pp. 3-39 (see below, p. 166). On the cult of St Anne and the English origins of the Feast of the Conception, see A. Wilmart, *Auteurs spirituels et textes dévots du moyen âge latin* (Paris 1932), esp. chaps. IV, XII, XIII, XV; E. Bishop, *Liturgica Historica* (Oxford 1918), chap. X; R. W. Southern, *St Anselm and his biographer* (Cambridge 1963), pp. 290-96; D. Knowles, *Monastic Order in England* (Cambridge 1940; 2nd edn. 1963), pp. 510-14, who refers both to St Bernard's attack and to Peter of Celle's reference to the English mists (p. 513).

The dedications of English religious houses are noted in D. Knowles and R. N. Hadcock, *Medieval Religious Houses, England and Wales* (edn. of London 1971): the point on p. 31 was first made to us by Miss Barbara SoRelle. On the Servites, see F. A. dal Pino, *I Frati Servi di S. Maria dall'origini all'approvazione (1233 ca. – 1304),* 2 vols. in 3 (Louvain, 1972). On the miracles of the Virgin and the story from Chiusa, see esp. R. W. Southern in *Mediaeval and Renaissance Studies,* IV (London 1958), pp. 176-216, esp. 190-91; cf. J. C. Jennings in ibid. VI (1968), 84-93; on her coronation, G. Zarnecki in *Journal of the Warburg and Courtauld Institutes,* XIII (1950), 1-12; P. Verdier, *Le couronnement de la Vierge* (Montreal 1981).

On early dedications in Britain, see W. Levison, *England and the Continent in the 8th Century* (Oxford 1946), pp. 259-65; in Italy, C. Violante and C. D. Fonseca, 'Ubicazione e dedicazione delle cattedrali dalle origini al periodo romanico nelle città dell'Italia centrosettentrionale' in *Il Romanico Pistoiese . . . Atti del 1 Convegno internaz. di studi medioevali di storia e d'arte* (Pistoia 1964), 303-46. For general information on English dedications, there is still value in F. Arnold-Foster, *Studies in church dedications* (3 vols. London 1899); F. Bond, *Dedications and patron saints of English Churches* (London 1914).

On the use of relics in the consecration of altars, see Sumption, *Pilgrimage,* p. 29 and references on p. 309. On the relics of St Nicholas, see Orderic Vitalis, *Ecclesiastical History,* ed. and trans. Marjorie Chibnall, IV (OMT 1973), 54-71 and refs.; on the church of St Nicholas Acon in London, C. Brooke and G. Keir, *London 800-1216* (London 1975), p. 138.

On the cult of St Michael, see references in C. Brooke and W. Swaan, *The Monastic World* (London 1974), pp. 210-11, 255, chap. 13, n.8; and esp. *Millénaire monastique du Mont Saint-Michel* (4 vols, ed. J. Laporte et al. Paris 1966-71), III.

On Winchester Cathedral, see R. Willis, 'The architectural history of Winchester Cathedral', in *Proceedings at the Annual Meeting of the Archaeological Institute of Great Britain and Ireland at Winchester, September 1845:* repr. with paper by C. Brooke, 'The Normans as Cathedral Builders' (Friends of Winchester Cathedral, 1980); cf. Brooke, *MCS* (London 1971), pp. 176-7; N. Pevsner in *Archaeological Journal,* CXVI (1959) 133ff. For its early history see M. Biddle and D. Keene in F. Barlow, M. Biddle et al. *Winchester Studies* I (Oxford 1976), pp. 306-13 (more fully in *Winchester Studies* IV, ed. M. and B. Kjølbye Biddle, forthcoming). The extracts on St Swithun are from *Ælfric's Lives of the Saints,* ed. W. W. Skeat, I (Early English Texts Soc. 1881, repr. 1966), pp. 442-5, 450-51, 466-7 (slightly adapted).

On Conques and Vézelay, see pp. 158-9, 163. On Saint-Bénigne, Dijon, see references in Brooke and Swaan, *The Monastic World*, p. 260, especially to B. de Vregille, 'Aldebald the Scribe of Cluny and the Bible of Abbot William of Dijon' in *Cluniac Monasticism in the Central Middle Ages*, ed. Noreen Hunt (London 1971), chap. 6; K. J. Conant, *Carolingian and Romanesque Architecture 800-1200* (Harmondsworth 1959), pp. 85-6, with plan.

On Suger see E. Panofsky, *Abbot Suger on the abbey church of Saint-Denis* (Princeton 1946); on Canterbury, Brooke, *MCS*, pp. 169-74 and references; also esp. R. Willis, *The architectural history of Canterbury Cathedral* (London 1845). The quotation from John of Salisbury is in his *Letters*, II, ed. W. J. Millor and C. N. L. Brooke (OMT 1979), pp. 735, 737 (no. 305). On the translation of St Thomas of Canterbury, *Materials for the History of Thomas Becket . . .*, IV, ed. J. C. Robertson (Rolls Series 1879), pp. 264, 427.

On Westminster Abbey, see esp. *The King's Works*, ed. H. M. Colvin, I (London 1963), pp. 130-57 and refs.

On the cult and miracles of St Thomas of Canterbury, R. Foreville, *Thomas Becket dans la tradition historique et hagiographique* (Variorum Reprints, London 1981); Finucane, esp. pp. 121-6; E. A. Abbott, *St Thomas of Canterbury* (2 vols. London 1898); and the recent book by Sister Benedicta Ward *Miracles and the Medieval Mind* (London 1982). The texts are in *Materials . . . for Thomas Becket*, I (1875), 529, 282-3, 397-402; John of Salisbury, *Letters*, II, no. 325. On the Becket of history, see esp. D. Knowles, *Thomas Becket* (London 1970) and in Knowles, *The Historian and Character and other Essays* (Cambridge 1963), chap. 6.

On the cult of the living saint, see R. B. Brooke in *Latin Biography*, ed.

T. A. Dorey (London 1967), pp. 177-98; R. W. Southern, *St Anselm and his biographer* (Cambridge 1963); Eadmer, *Life of St Anselm*, ed. and trans. R. W. Southern (NMT 1962; repr. OMT 1972); for examples of Francis's devotion to the Blessed Virgin, see *Scripta Leonis . . .*, ed. and trans. R. B. Brooke (OMT 1970), pp. 102-3, 252-3.

On the analogies of divine and secular love in the 12th century, see J. Leclercq, *Monks and love in 12th-century France* (Oxford 1979).

IV What is Popular Religion?

For general literature, see above; on the papal reform and its background, see literature cited in C. Brooke, *Europe in the Central Middle Ages*, pp. 237-8, esp. G. Tellenbach, *Church, State and Christian Society at the Time of the Investiture Contest* (trans. R. F. Bennett, Oxford 1940); W. Ullmann, *The Growth of Papal Government in the Middle Ages* (London 1955, 3rd edn. 1970); see also now Ian Robinson, *Authority and Resistance in the Investiture Contest* (Manchester 1978). Among older works Z. N. Brooke's chapters in *Cambridge Medieval History*, V, and A. Fliche, *La réforme grégorienne*, I-III (Louvain–Paris 1924-37) are still useful. On Christianity and war, and the Crusades, see H.-E. Mayer, *The Crusades*, trans. J. Gillingham (Oxford 1972); and the classical study by C. Erdmann, *The origin of the Idea of Crusade* (trans. M. W. Baldwin and W. Goffart, Princeton 1977, with a useful new introduction); E. O. Blake, 'The formation of the "Crusade Idea"', *Journal of Ecclesiastical History*, XXI (1970), 11-31; E. D. Hehl, *Kirche und Krieg im 12. Jahrhundert* (Stuttgart 1980).

On Becket at Vézelay, *The Letters of John of Salisbury*, II, ed. W. J. Millor and C. N. L. Brooke (OMT 1979), pp. 112-15; on the version of the constitutions of Clarendon see esp. *Councils and Synods*, I, ed. D.

Whitelock, M. Brett and C. N. L. Brooke (Oxford 1981), pt. ii, pp. 875-6. On St Bernard at Vézelay, A. A. Cherest in *Mon. Vizeliacensia* (see p. 163), pp. 66-7, 420.

The quotation from King Alfred is from his version of Boethius, *Consolations of Philosophy*, c.xvii, as trans. in *English Historical Documents*, I, ed. D. Whitelock (1st edn., London 1955), p. 846. Cf. G. Duby, *The Three Orders: Feudal Society Imagined* (Eng. trans. by A. Goldhammer, Chicago and London 1980), esp. pp. 99-102.

On the religious orders see Brooke and Swaan, and suggestions for further reading cited there; for fuller details, G. Constable, *Medieval Monasticism: a select bibliography* (Toronto 1976). For Orderic Vitalis, see his *Ecclesiastical History*, ed. and trans. Marjorie Chibnall (OMT 1968-80), esp. VI, 552-3; cf. Brooke and Swaan, p. 122. The *Regularis Concordia* was ed. and trans. T. Symons (NMT 1953): see esp. pp. 1-2. For the edict of 1009 see *Councils and Synods . . .*, I, ed. D. Whitelock, M. Brett and C. N. L. Brooke (Oxford 1981), i, 373-82, esp. pp. 379-82.

On the Patarene movement in Milan, see R. I. Moore, *The Origins of European Dissent* (London 1977), pp. 55-61, 296, with bibliography; H. E. J. Cowdrey in *Trans. Royal Hist. Soc.* 5th ser. XVIII (1968), 25-48; and the classic study of C. Violante, 'I laici nel movimento patarino', repr. in his *Studi sulla cristianità medioevale* (Milan 1972), pp. 145-246. On the pope and Rome the quotation is from C. Brooke and G. Keir, *London 800-1216: the Shaping of a City* (London 1975), pp. 5-6; cf. ibid. pp. 66-82 for a brief general account of the urban renaissance; on the Italian cities, see D. Waley, *The Italian City-Republics* (London 1969; revised edition 1978); J. K. Hyde, *Society and Politics in Medieval Italy* (London 1973). On Moslem Spain, see E. Lévi-Provençal, *Histoire de l'Espagne musulmane*, esp. III (Paris 1967); R. Menéndez Pidal,

The Cid and his Spain (London 1934).

For Odo of Cluny's Life of St Gerald, see G. Sitwell, *Odo of Cluny* (London 1958); see esp. pp. 100-01; and cf. D. Baker in *Studies in Church History*, VIII (1972), pp. 43-53. On William the Conqueror and the papal banner, see C. Morton in *Latomus: Revue d'Études Latines*, XXXIV (1975), 362-82. On Adela and Stephen of Blois, and the First Crusade, see Orderic Vitalis, *Ecclesiastical History*, ed. and trans. M. Chibnall, V (OMT 1975), pp. 324-5.

On the *Song of Roland* as a crusading epic see Brooke, *Europe in the Central Middle Ages*, pp. 358-64. On the Rolandslied, F. Urbanek, 'The Rolandslied by Pfaffe Conrad . . .', *Euphorion*, LXV (1971), 219-44.

The relationship of popular religious beliefs and practices and official theology has been much discussed, and disputed – see pp. 9-12; R. Manselli, *La religion populaire au moyen âge* (Montreal, Paris 1975), chap. I (the quotation on p. 61 is from p. 27). On purgatory, see below, p. 166.

Guibert de Nogent makes Urban II refer to death on Crusade as martyrdom in *Recueil des historiens des Croisades, Historiens Occidentaux*, IV (Paris 1879), p. 138 (we owe this reference to an unpublished paper by Professor C. Morris). St Bernard is quoted from letter 458, the *De laude novae militiae*, and letter 64 (ed. J. Leclercq and H. M. Rochais, *Opera S. Bernardi*, III (Rome 1963), 214-15, VII (1974), 157-8, VIII (1977), 434-7; *Letters*, trans. B. S. James, London 1953, nos. 392, 67). The *Song of Roland* is quoted from the translation of Dorothy L. Sayers (Penguin Classics, 1957), lines 1127-38. For the Turkish heads at Antioch, William of Tyre, *A History of Deeds done beyond the Sea*, trans. and ed. E. A. Babcock and A. C. Krey (New York 1943), p. 228 (cf. Nicaea, p. 157).

The narratives of the First Crusade cited are in *Gesta Francorum et aliorum Hierosolimitanorum*, ed. and trans.

Rosalind Hill (NMT 1962; repr. OMT 1980); *The Alexiad of Anna Comnena*, trans. E. R. A. Sewter (Penguin Classics 1969).

For Waldo's Profession of Faith see R. B. Brooke, *The Coming of the Friars* (London 1975), Documents no. 12, pp. 148-50 (cf. pp. 71-4); C. Thouzellier, *Catharisme et Valdéisme en Languedoc à la fin du XIIe et au début du XIIIe siècle* (2nd edn., Louvain–Paris, 1969), esp. pp. 27-30. On heresy, below, p. 163.

V Popular and unpopular religion

On churches as historical evidence, on their function and furnishing, see C. Brooke, 'Religious sentiment and church design in the later Middle Ages', in Brooke, *MCS*, chap. 8; and 'Church design and the needs of patrons and builders in the 11th and 12th centuries', in the proceedings of the Warsaw Colloquium of 1978, forthcoming in *Misc. Historiae Ecclesiasticae*, on which some of what follows is based. For monastic sites, complexes and architecture, see Brooke and Swaan; W. Braunfels, *Monasteries of Western Europe* (Eng. trans. London 1972).

On Peter of Bruis, see Brooke, *Coming*, pp. 63-6, 140-42; this includes (p. 142) a translation from the passage in Peter the Venerable's *Contra Petrobrusianos*, ed. J. V. Fearns, *Corpus Christianorum, Continuatio Mediaeualis*, X (Turnhout 1968), pp. 5-6, which describes the burning of the heresiarch. On San Romerio, E. Poeschel, *Die Kunstdenkmäler des Kantons Graubünden*, VI (1945), 20-25; Willy Zeller, *Kunst und Kultur in Graubünden* (Berne, n.d.), p. 224 (we owe these references to Frau B. Hesse). For the Carceri above Assisi, see Brooke and Swaan, plate 306; for other surviving hermitages, A. Prandi and Jean Hubert in *L'eremitismo in Occidente nei secoli XI e XII* (Miscellanea del Centro di Studi Medioevali, IV, Milan 1965 = Settimana . . .

Mendola, 1962), pp. 435-61, 462-90. On Wulfric of Haselbury, see H. Mayr-Harting in *History*, LX (1975), 337-52.

The history of European dioceses and parishes has been studied in a recent *Settimana di Studio del Centro Italiano di Studi sull'alto medievo* at Spoleto, no. XXVII, 1980, forthcoming, and for the English sees, C. N. L. Brooke, 'Rural ecclesiastical institutions in England: the search for their origins', ibid., with references e.g. for St Just and Kirkby Ireleth, to N. Pevsner, *The Buildings of England: Cornwall*, 2nd edn. by E. Radcliffe (Harmondsworth 1970), pp. 183-4 and plate 11; *Victoria History of Lancashire*, VIII, 387-92. See also F. Barlow, *The English Church 1000-1066* (2nd edn. London 1979). On Sant'-Ambrogio, Brooke and Swaan, pp. 219-23, 259. On Atcham, ibid. p. 122 and plate 201; Orderic Vitalis, *Ecclesiastical History*, ed. and trans. M. Chibnall, VI (OMT 1978), pp. 552-3. On the churches of London, C. Brooke and G. Keir, *London 800-1216: the Shaping of a City* (London 1975), chap. 6.

On the transition from Romanesque to Gothic, see E. Panofsky, *Abbot Suger on the Abbey Church of Saint-Denis* (Princeton 1946); O. von Simson, *The Gothic Cathedral* (New York 1956); J. Harvey in *Antiquaries Journal*, XLVIII (1968), 87-99; P. Frankl, *Gothic Architecture* (Harmondsworth 1962); W. Swaan, *The Gothic Cathedral* (London 1969); E. Mâle, *L'Art religieux du XIIe siècle en France* (6th edn. Paris 1953).

On Santiago, see p. 158; on Laon, Amiens and Wells, W. Swaan, *The Gothic Cathedral*, pp. 105-9, 134-42, 188-96, and other books cited above. Much interesting detail on Amiens is gathered in H. Kraus, *Gold was their Mortar* (London etc. 1979), pp. 39-59, 223-32; for the grant of 1145 (p. 120) Thierry, *Recueil des monuments inédits . . .*, I, Amiens (Paris 1850), 55-7. For the furnishing and visual effect of churches see above, and for San Clemente and Ely esp. Brooke, *MCS*, pp. 166-8 and plate II.

Our account of Vézelay is based on R. B. Brooke, 'Abbots and monks, pilgrims and townsfolk: the example of Vézelay', a paper for the Warsaw Colloquium of 1978, forthcoming in *Misc. Historiae Ecclesiasticae*; see F. Salin, *La Madeleine de Vézelay: Étude iconographique* par Jean Adhemar (Melun 1948); V. Saxer, *Le culte de Marie Madeleine en Occident des origines à la fin du moyen âge* (2 vols. Auxerre–Paris 1959 (the quotation on p. 92 is from Saxer, I, 70)); *Monumenta Vizeliacensia*, ed. R. B. C. Huygens, *Corpus Christianorum, Continuatio Mediaeualis*, XLI (Turnhout 1976). For Count William of Nevers see ibid., pp. 419-23; *Magna Vita S. Hugonis*, ed. and trans. D. L. Douie and H. Farmer (NMT 1961-2), I, 32-3, II, 55-6, where he is called Gerard. The account of his relation to Louis VII and his retirement to the Chartreuse leaves no doubt of the identification with Count William II. The phrase 'naked to follow the naked Christ' was a favourite proverb of the age: for some examples, see M. Bernards in *Wissenschaft und Weisheit: Augustinisch-Franziskanische Theologie und Philosophie in der Gegenwart*, XIV (Düsseldorf, 1951), 148-51.

On dissent and heresy, see R. I. Moore, *The Origins of European Dissent* (London 1977), esp. chapter VII on the arrival of the Cathars, and *The Birth of Popular Heresy* (London 1975); M. D. Lambert, *Medieval Heresy* (London 1977); J. Le Goff (ed.), *Hérésies et sociétés dans l'Europe préindustrielle* (Paris and The Hague 1968); Brooke, *Coming*, chap. 4 and documents 9-15, esp. pp. 69-71 for Arnold of Brescia, and pp. 146-7 for John of Salisbury's account of him (from *Historia Pontificalis*, ed. and trans. M. Chibnall, NMT 1956, pp. 62-5). For Gottfried von Strassburg's *Tristan*, see A. T. Hatto's translation in Penguin Classics (1960). The quotation from

the *Lay of the Reflection* is from the translation by P. Matarasso in *Aucassin and Nicolette and other tales* (Penguin Classics 1971), p. 72; that from the Archpoet from Helen Waddell, *Mediaeval Latin Lyrics* (4th edn., London 1933), pp. 172-3, 176-7, with the Latin text corrected from *Die Gedichte des Archipoeta*, ed. H. Watenphul and H. Krefeld (Heidelberg 1958), pp. 74-5. On Wolfram, see esp. H. Sacker, *An introduction to Wolfram's Parzival* (Cambridge 1963); M. F. Richey, *Studies of Wolfram von Eschenbach* (Edinburgh 1957); C. Brooke in *The Layman in Christian History*, ed. S. C. Neill and H.-R. Weber (London 1963), pp. 123-6. See Brooke, *Coming*, pp. 63-6, 140-42 for Peter of Bruis. For heretics in England in 1165-6 see *Councils and Synods*, I, ii, 920-25. For the Cathar ritual of the early 13th century, see *Rituel cathare*, ed. C. Thouzellier (Sources chrétiennes, no. 236, Paris 1977) – with Latin text and French translation; the passage cited is on pp. 254-61; cf. pp. 22-6 and charts *ad fin.* for comparison with the slightly later Provençal version, which is translated in W. L. Wakefield and A. P. Evans, *Heresies of the High Middle Ages* (Columbia Records of Civilisation, New York 1969), pp. 483-94. The Cathar denunciation of the Roman Church is quoted from J. R. Strayer, *The Albigensian Crusades* (New York 1971), p. 22. The closing quotation from Peter the Venerable, *Contra Petrobrusianos*, is from Brooke, *Coming*, pp. 141-2 (based on J. V. Fearns' edition: see above).

VI The laity and the Church

On baptism, see *Dictionnaire de Théologie Catholique*, II, s.v. Baptême, esp. coll. 250-96. On Baptisteries, see E. Cattaneo, 'Il Battistero in Italia dopo il mille', pp. 171-95 of *Miscellanea Gilles Gerard Meersseman*, I (= *Italia Sacra* 15, Padua 1970); C. Brooke, 'The medieval town as an ecclesiastical centre' in *European Towns and their Archaeology and early History*, ed. M. W. Barley (London 1977), pp. 459-74, esp. 460-61, 465-7. On St Wulfstan, see *The Vita Wulfstani of William of Malmesbury*, ed. R. R. Darlington (Camden 3rd Series 40, 1928; the passages in the text are our own translation from pp. 36-8, 40-41, 43-4, on confirmation, the tree at Longney, and the Bristol slave-trade respectively; there is a full translation by J. H. F. Peile, Oxford 1934). On English fonts (p. 107), see F. Bond, *Fonts and Font Covers* (London 1908); on the Liège font, W. Oakeshott, *Classical inspiration in medieval art* (London 1959), pp. 87-9.

For 13th-century synodal statutes etc. see *Councils and Synods*, II, ed. F. M. Powicke and C. R. Cheney (Oxford 1964), i, 30-32, 67-70; ii, 1405, Index s.v. Baptism. The quotations on pp. 106, 107-8, are from ibid. II, i, 141, 298-9, 297; that on p. 107 (Laws of Athelstan) from *Councils and Synods*, I, ed. D. Whitelock *et al.* (Oxford 1981), i, 50-51.

On cemeteries in towns, and the practice of burial in church, see Brooke and Keir, *London 800-1216*, p. 130 and n.3. On the Office for the Dead, E. Bishop, 'On the origin of the Prymer', *Liturgica Historica* (Oxford 1918), pp. 211-37; D. Sicard, *La liturgie de la mort* (Münster 1978). On chantries, K. Wood-Legh, *Perpetual Chantries in Britain* (Cambridge 1965); T. S. R. Boase, *Death in the Middle Ages* (London 1972).

On marriage, see *Family and Marriage in Medieval Europe: a working bibliography*, ed. M. M. Sheehan and K. D. Scardelatto (Vancouver 1976); G. Duby, *Medieval Marriage* (Baltimore–London 1978); C. Brooke, 'Aspects of marriage law in the eleventh and twelfth centuries', in *Proceedings of the Fifth International Congress of Medieval Canon Law* (Rome 1980), pp. 163-74; 'Marriage and Society in the Twelfth Century', in *Marriage and Society*, ed. B. Outh-

waite (London 1981), pp. 17-34. On the betrothal of Christina, see *The Life of Christina of Markyate*, ed. and trans. C. H. Talbot (Oxford 1959), esp. pp. 44-55; on the marriage of Parzival and Condwiramurs, Brooke, 'Marriage and Society', pp. 33-4 and references, esp. to M. Schumacher, *Die Auffassung der Ehe in den Dichtungen Wolframs von Eschenbach* (Heidelberg 1967); M. F. Richey, *The story of Parzival and the Graal* (Oxford 1935), pp. 62-71. On annulment in the late Middle Ages, R. H. Helmholz, *Marriage Litigation in Medieval England* (Cambridge 1974), esp. chaps. ii-iii. On the liturgy of marriage, see J.-B. Molin and P. Mutembe, *Le rituel du mariage en France du XIIe au XVIe siècle* (Paris 1974).

On the eucharist, see Gary Macy's dissertation on the history of eucharistic theology in this period (Cambridge 1978), esp. chap. 3; P. Browe, *Die Pflichtkommunion im Mittelalter* (Münster 1940); and the writings of E. Dumoutet cited by Macy. That layfolk shall communicate at least once a year was laid down in *4th Lateran Council*, canon 21; see R. Foreville, *Latran I, II, III et Latran IV* (Paris 1965), pp. 357-8. On Henry III's attendance at mass, Nicholas Trivet or Trevet, *Annales*, ed. T. Hog (English Hist. Soc., London 1845), p. 280; continuation of Matthew Paris, *Chronica maiora*, edn. of Zurich 1589, p. 977; trans. J. A. Giles, III (London 1854), p. 382. On the history of the elevation of the host, see Brooke, *MCS*, p. 164; V. L. Kennedy in *Mediaeval Studies*, VI (1944), 121-50; and other references in Macy. Cf. *Lay Folks' Mass Book* (cited Brooke, *MCS*, pp. 163-4), ed. T. F. Simmons (Early English Text Society 1879); Brooke, *MCS*, p. 164, for the story of the magistrate in the rood loft.

On confession, *Dict. de Théologie Catholique*, III, s.v. Confession; C. Morris, *The Discovery of the Individual 1050-1200* (London 1972), pp. 70-75; on its earlier history, A. Teetaert, *La confession aux laïques dans l'Église latine* (Paris–Bruges 1926). On Amiens, see p. 162. For Siena, see J. White, *Duccio* (London 1979).

On preaching there is a brief summary and note of the earlier literature in *New Catholic Encyclopedia*, XI (New York 1967), 691-3; for recent studies on vernacular homilies, see K. Greenfield, 'Changing emphases in English vernacular homiletic literature, 960-1225', *Journal of Medieval History*, VII (1981), 283-97. The Salisbury visitation is in *The Register of St Osmund*, ed. W. H. R. Jones (2 vols., Rolls Series 1883-4), I, 304-14, esp. p. 305. Bishop Richard Poore's injunctions are in *Councils and Synods . . .*, II (p. 164), i, 57-96.

On Lambert le Bègue, see R. I. Moore, *The Origins of European Dissent* (London 1977), pp. 191-5, based on P. Fredericq, *Corpus documentorum inquisitionis haereticae pravitatis Neerlandicae*, II (Ghent–The Hague 1896), pp. 9-36.

On Montaillou, Emmanuel le Roy Ladurie, *Montaillou* (Eng. trans. by B. Bray, London 1978). On Manx crosses, A. M. Cubban, *The Art of the Manx Crosses* (Douglas 1971); D. M. Wilson in *Saga-Book of the Viking Society for Northern Research*, XVIII, 1-2 (1970-71), 1-18; and for their wider context, Wilson and O. Klindt-Jensen, *Viking Art* (London 1966).

On St Francis, see Brooke, *Coming,* esp. chap. 2 and works there cited; for the best of the early stories about him, see *Scripta Leonis, Rufini et Angeli . . .*, ed. and trans. R. B. Brooke (OMT 1970); the quotations on pp. 128-9, are from cc. 19, 114, pp. 118-23, 286-9; cf. Brooke, *Coming,* pp. 18-19. On St Clare, R. and C. Brooke in *Medieval Women*, ed. D. Baker (Studies in Church History, Subsidia I, Oxford 1978), pp. 275-87. On the Church and commerce, Lester Little, *Religious Poverty and the Profit Economy in Medieval Europe* (London 1978), and refs. esp. on p. 252; J. Gilchrist, *The Church and Economic Activity . . .* (New York 1969).

On the Beguines, see Southern, *Western Society and the Church* (p. 157), pp. 318-31; E. W. McDonnell, *The Béguines and Beghards in medieval culture* (New Brunswick 1954). On female religious and Marie of Oignies, B. M. Bolton in *SCH*, X (1973), 77-97 and *Medieval Women*, ed. Baker, pp. 253-73, with refs. on p. 253 n.1. On Jacques de Vitry, see Brooke, *Coming,* pp. 203-4 and refs.; also J. F. Hinnebusch, *The Historia Occidentalis of Jacques de Vitry* (Freiburg 1972).

VII The Bible

Fundamental is B. Smalley, *The Study of the Bible in the Middle Ages* (2nd edn. Oxford 1952).

On the vernacular Bible, M. Deanesly, *The Lollard Bible* (Cambridge 1920); M. J. Wilks in *Studies in Church History*, XI (1975), ed. D. Baker, pp. 147-61, with useful bibliography esp. in p. 147 n.1.

Gregory the Great's references to pictures as books for the unlearned are in his *Registrum*, ix. 208, xi. 10 ('quod legentibus scriptura, hoc idiotis praestat pictura . . .'), ed. L. M. Hartmann, *Monumenta Germaniae Historica, Epist.* II-III (Berlin 1899), II, 195, 270.

On Christian iconography, see esp. E. Mâle, *L'art religieux du XIIe siècle en France* (4th edn. Paris 1940); id., *The Gothic Image: Religious Art in France in the 13th century* (trans. D. Nussey, London 1913; Fontana 1961); *Lexikon der christlichen Ikonographie* (8 vols., ed. E. Kirschbaum, G. Bondmann, W. Braunfels, *et al.*, Freiburg 1968-76). On the use of the Bible in art see the vivid summary in Sir Ernst Gombrich, *Ends and Means* (London 1976), pp. 32-4.

On Saint-Savin and Winchester, see O. Demus, *Romanesque Mural Painting* (London 1970), 101-4, 420-23, 509-11; cf. G. Henderson in *Journ. British Arch. Ass.*, 3rd ser., XXVI (1963),

11-26; on Bernard of Tiron, Brooke, *Coming*, pp. 49-57. On the coronation service, *The Coronation Service of H.M. Queen Elizabeth II*, ed. E. C. Ratcliff (London etc., 1953), pp. 9-10, 43.

There is a full photographic record and interpretation of the wooden ceiling at Zillis in E. Murbach and P. Heman, *Zillis: die romanische Bilderdecke der Kirche St Martin* (Zurich 1967). For the view that Mark 16:8 represents the original end of the Gospel (which is not generally accepted, however), see R. H. Lightfoot, *The Gospel Message of St Mark* (Oxford 1950), chap. VII.

The quotation from the *Dream of the Rood* (p. 139) is from R. K. Gordon, *Anglo-Saxon Poetry* (Everyman edn. of 1954), pp. 235-8; from R. W. Southern on pp. 139-40, *Making of the Middle Ages* (London 1953), pp. 237-8. On liturgy and drama, see O. B. Hardison, Jr., *Christian Rite and Christian Drama* (Baltimore 1965). The quotation from C. H. Dodd (pp. 141-2) is from *Studies in the Gospels: essays in memory of R. H. Lightfoot* (ed. D. E. Nineham, Oxford 1955, p. 20) and repeated in his *Historical Tradition in the Fourth Gospel* (Cambridge 1963), p. 148: for a 12th century 'Noli me tangere' see D. Grivot and G. Zarnecki, *Gislebertus* (London 1961), p. 71 and pls. 21, 21a. For Ailred, *The Works of Aelred of Rievaulx* (Cistercian Fathers Series, 2, Spencer Mass. 1971), pp. 4-12 *(Jesus at the age of twelve)*, p. 91 *(Rule of Life for a Recluse)*. Henry Mayr-Harting's study of the 12th-century recluse Wulfric of Haselbury is in *History*, LX (1975), 337-52, esp. 350-52; we quote from pp. 349-50. Peter Brown's paper is 'The rise and function of the Holy Man in Late Antiquity', *Journal of Roman Studies*, LXI (1971), 80-101; see now his *The Cult of the saints* (Chicago–London 1981). Christina's vision, and the visit of the pilgrim, are from *The Life of Christina of Markyate*, ed.

33

and trans. C. H. Talbot (Oxford 1959), pp. 180-85.

VIII Judgment

We comment principally on five texts, two paintings and one sculpture. The texts: *Prayers and Meditations of St Anselm*, trans. Benedicta Ward (Harmondsworth 1973), pp. 221-9; *The Ecclesiastical History of Orderic Vitalis*, ed. and trans. M. Chibnall, IV (OMT 1973), 236-51; the *Dies Irae*, cited from F. J. E. Raby, *A History of Christian Latin Poetry* (Oxford 1927; 2nd edn. 1953), pp. 448-9; cf. K. Vellekoop, *Dies Irae Dies Illa* (Bithoven 1978); Dante's *Divina Commedia*; and, at the end, *Aucassin and Nicolette*, trans. Pauline Matarasso (Penguin Classics 1971), pp. 28-9. The paintings (introduced by the passage from Revelation 20:1-3) are from the *Liber Vitae . . . of New Minster and Hyde Abbey Winchester* (British Library Stowe MS 944, fos. 6ᵛ-7; cf. the edition by Walter de Gray Birch, Hampshire Record Soc. 1892); and the *Winchester Psalter* (see the full edition by F. Wormald, London 1973; the original is British Library Cotton MS Nero C. iv, fos. 31-9). On Gislebertus, see the classic study of D. Grivot and G. Zarnecki, *Gislebertus, Sculptor of Autun* (London 1961).

On purgatory, see J. Le Goff, *La naissance du purgatoire* (Paris 1981); cf. review by Sir Richard Southern in *Times Literary Supplement*, 18 June 1982, pp. 651-2; on the doctrine see also R. Ombres, 'The doctrine of Purgatory according to St Thomas Aquinas', *Downside Review*, October 1981, pp. 279-87. On the liturgy, see D. Sicard, *La liturgie de la mort* (Münster 1978). On Joachim and medieval prophecy, M. Reeves, *The influence of Prophecy in the later Middle Ages* (Oxford 1969). On the history of the jubilees, R. Foreville, *Le jubilé de S. Thomas Becket* (Paris 1958), esp. chap. II.

List of Illustrations

PLATES (between pages 64 and 81)

1 The reliquary of Sainte-Foy, Conques, 9th and 10th centuries, with head from a late antique bust: Conques, Treasury: see J. Taralon, *Treasures of the Churches of France* (London 1966), pp. 291-3 and pls 201-2, cf. p. 23. Photo: Hirmer.

2 The Abbey Church of Sainte-Foy, Conques (Aveyron). Photo: Jean Roubier.

3 Rievaulx Abbey (Yorkshire): see D. Knowles and J. K. S. St Joseph, *Monastic Sites from the Air* (Cambridge 1952), pp. 82-5. Photo: Cambridge University Collection: Copyright reserved.

4 The Coronation of the Virgin: a capital from Reading Abbey, found in Borough Marsh, now the property of the Reading Museum: see G. Zarnecki in *Journal of the Warburg and Courtauld Institutes*, XIII (1950), 1-12, esp. pp. 1-6 and pl. 1a. Photo: G. Zarnecki.

5 A miracle of St Thomas Becket, from a 12th-century window in the Trinity Chapel in Canterbury Cathedral. See M. H. Caviness, *The early Stained Glass of Canterbury Cathedral* (Princeton 1977), pp. 146-50, 164 (n.IV.16) and pl. 159(16) and *Corpus Vitrearum . . . Christ Church Cathedral, Canterbury* (London 1981), p. 185 and pls 268, 268a (n.IV.8). The representation of the cure of Ethel-dreda of Canterbury is based on Benedict of Peterborough, *Miracula* in *Materials for the history of Thomas Becket . . .*, II, ed. J. C. Robertson, Rolls Series 1876, p. 54. Photo: Sonia Halliday and Laura Lushington.

6 Speyer, the Jewish bath-house, ante-chamber. Dated *c.* 1109-26 by G. Stein in *Judenhof und Judenbad in Speyer am Rhein*, Grosse Baudenkmäler, Heft 238 (2nd edn Berlin 1974), p. 7. Photo: Helga Schmidt-Glassner.

7 Autun Cathedral, capital by Gislebertus: the fall of Simon Magus. See D. Grivot and G. Zarnecki, *Gislebertus, Sculptor of Autun* (London 1961), p. 75 and pls 35, 38a-b. Photo: Jean Roubier.

8 The Church of San Romerio: see E. Poeschel, *Die Kunstdenkmäler des Kantons Graubünden*, VI (1945), 20-25; above, p. 164. Photo: Die kantonale Denkmalpflege Graubünden, Switzerland.

9 Wells Cathedral, nave. See W. Swaan, *The Gothic Cathedral*, pp. 188-96 and pls 217-23. Photo: Martin Hürlimann.

10 Saint-Gilles Abbey Church, the west front. See C. Brooke and W. Swaan, *The Monastic World* (London 1974), pp. 99-101, 262, and pls 158-62. Photo: Wim Swaan.

11 Amiens Cathedral, interior of nave: see W. Swaan, *The Gothic Cathedral* (London 1969), pp. 134-41 and pls 140-43, 151-4. Photo: Wim Swaan.

12 Liège, Saint-Barthélemy, font (originally for Notre-Dame-des-Fonts); see W. Oakeshott, *Classical inspiration in medieval art* (London 1959), pp. 87-9; G. Zarnecki, *Art of the Medieval World* (New York 1975), p. 318 and pls 321-2. Photo: R. & C. Brooke.

13 Wells Cathedral, south transept, capitals of the last quarter of the 12th century. Photo: Courtauld Institute.

14 San Zeno, Verona, crypt and choir: see C. Brooke and W. Swaan, *The Monastic World*, pp. 95-8 and pl. 153. Photo: Wim Swaan.

15 San Zeno, Verona, bronze bas relief on west door. Cf. Brooke and Swaan, *Monastic World*, pp. 95-8 and pls 147-8, 151-7. Photo: Wim Swaan.

16 Vézelay Abbey Church, interior: see p. 165. Photo: A. F. Kersting.

17 Malmesbury Abbey Church, the outer doorway of the south porch, *c.* 1160-70; above the bench within figures of the apostles can just be seen. See G. Zarnecki, *Later English Romanesque Sculpture* (London 1953), pp. 40-43; T. S. R. Boase, *English Art 1100-1216*, pp. 208-9. Photo: Edwin Smith.

18 Amiens Cathedral, St Nicholas's Chapel, exterior. Woad-sellers with sack of wool, late 13th century. See H. Kraus, *Gold was the Mortar* (London etc. 1979), pp. 47-9, 226. Photo: Jean Roubier.

19 A northern font: the baptism of Jesus at Castle Frome, Herefordshire, 12th century. See T. S. R. Boase, *English Art 1100-1216* (Oxford 1953), pp. 80-82. Photo: National Monuments Record.

20 Amiens Cathedral, the rose window in the south transept. See W. Swaan, *The Gothic Cathedral,* pp. 137, 139 and pl. 154. Photo: Wim Swaan.

21 Pisa, Duomo, pulpit by Giovanni Pisano, 1302-11. See M. Ayrton, *Giovanni Pisano, Sculptor* (London 1969), pp. 157-84, 206, 223-7 and pls 155-79. Photo: I. Bessi.

22 Duccio, Maestà, Siena, Museo dell'Opera del Duomo, 1308-11. See J. White, *Duccio* (London 1979), esp. chap. 6. Photo: Grassi.

23 Siena, Palazzo Pubblico, detail from Ambrogio Lorenzetti's allegorical fresco of good government, completed 1339. See N. Rubinstein in *Journal of the Warburg and Courtauld Institutes,* XXI (1958), 179-207, esp. pp. 179-89; for this detail, p. 182. Photo: Alinari.

24 Saint-Bénigne, Dijon, tympanum, showing the Last Supper, 12th century. See W. Sauerländer, *Gothic Sculpture in France, 1140-1270* (London 1972), pp. 389ff., and pl. 23. Photo: Wim Swaan.

25 London, Lambeth Palace Library, MS 3, fo. 132: the death of Saul. Photo: Courtauld Institute.

26 Saint-Savin-sur-Gartempe, Noah's ark from the Pentateuch on the nave ceiling, end of 11th century. See O. Demus, *Romanesque Mural Painting* (London 1970), pp. 47, 420-23 and pls 125-42, etc. Photo: Hirmer.

27 Lincoln Cathedral, bas relief of Noah's ark from the frieze on the west front, mid-12th century. See G. Zarnecki, *Later English Romanesque Sculpture,* pp. 20-27, 56-8, and *Romanesque Sculpture at Lincoln Cathedral* (Lincoln Minster Pamphlets, 2nd ser., 2), esp. pp. 4-5. Photo: Courtauld Institute.

28 Autun, chapter house, capital of the Flight into Egypt, formerly in the choir. See D. Grivot and G. Zarnecki, *Gislebertus*, pp. 67, 160, 162 and pls 5a–c. Photo: Jean Roubier.

29 Zillis, St Martin, nave ceiling, 12th century. See E. Murbach and P. Heman, *Zillis: die romanische Bilderdecke der Kirche St Martin* (Zurich 1967). Photo: Peter Heman.

30 Zillis: fishy monster with elephant's trunk. See Murbach and Heman, *Zillis*, p. 32 and pl. G–I 43★ Photo: Peter Heman.

31 Zillis: Joseph on the flight into Egypt. See Murbach and Heman, *Zillis*, p. 34 and pl. F–VI 81★. Photo: Peter Heman.

32 Zillis: the Gadarene swine. See Murbach and Heman, *Zillis*, p. 36 and pl. K–V 108★. Photo: Peter Heman.

33 Autun, nave capital by Gislebertus: Christ's appearance to Mary Magdalene. See Grivot and Zarnecki, *Gislebertus*, pp. 71, 159, 160, 162 and pls 21a–b. Photo: Jean Roubier.

34 Autun, tympanum over west door, Resurrection of the Dead by Gislebertus, detail. See Grivot and Zarnecki, *Gislebertus*, p. 26 and pl. B etc. The inscription reads '[Quisque resurg]et ita quem non trahit impia vita . . .' (see p. 152). Photo: Jean Roubier.

35 Autun, tympanum over west door, Last Judgment, detail. See Grivot and Zarnecki, *Gislebertus*, p. 26 and pls P and R. The inscription reads '[Terreat hic terror quos terreus allig]at error, Nam fore sic verum not[at hic horror specierum]' (see p. 152). Photo: Jean Roubier.

IN-TEXT ILLUSTRATIONS

p. 28 The Last Judgment, tympanum over west door, Conques, Abbey Church of Sainte-Foy (Aveyron). See *Rouergue roman* (Zodiaque 1963), pp. 49–50 and pls 3–19 and facing p. 34. Drawing by Ian Mackenzie-Kerr.

p. 36 Plan of Winchester Cathedral.

p. 49 John of Wallingford, monk of St Albans in the mid-13th century: drawing by Matthew Paris. See R. Vaughan, *Matthew Paris* (Cambridge 1958), p. 220, and in *Trans. of the Cambridge Bibliog. Soc.* I (1949–53), esp. p. 392. London, British Library, Cotton MS Julius D.vii, fo. 42ᵛ.

p. 85 Drawing by Villard de Honnecourt of the south-west tower of Laon Cathedral, *c.* 1235. From Villard's album, Bibliothèque Nationale, Paris, MS fr. 19093, fo. 10ʳ.

p. 87 Plan of St Augustine's Abbey, Canterbury, before the Norman Conquest, after A. W. Clapham, *English Romanesque Architecture before the Norman Conquest* (Oxford 1930), p. 150, fig. 49, revised by H. M. and J. Taylor, *Anglo-Saxon Architecture,* I (Cambridge 1965), 136.

p. 91 Building in progress: a 13th-century impression of the building of

St Alban's Abbey, by Matthew Paris: cf. Vaughan, *Matthew Paris,* pp. 219, 221, 227-8. From the Life of St Alban, Trinity College, Dublin, MS E.i.40, fo. 60ʳ.

p. 134 The death of Judas Maccabaeus (1 Macc. 9:19) by the Master of the Apocrypha Legends in the Winchester Bible. See W. Oakeshott, *The Artists of the Winchester Bible* (London 1945), p. 5 and pl. xv, and *The Two Winchester Bibles* (Oxford 1981), esp. p. 144 and pl. 151.

p. 137 Christ visits Martha and Mary at Bethany, from a late 13th-century *Bible moralisée,* written in France. British Library, Add. MS 18719, fo. 25.

p. 150 The Last Judgment from the *Liber Vitae* of New Minster, Winchester, *c.* 1030. See F. Wormald, *English Drawings of the 10th and 11th centuries* (London 1952), pp. 72-3. British Library, Stowe MS 944, fo. 7ʳ.

Index

Italic numerals refer to the numbers of plates.

Aachen, 50
Aaron's rod, 19
Abel, *15*
Abelard, Peter, 94
Abraham, 135
Adam, 135
Adela, Countess of Blois, 161
Aelfheah, St, Archbishop of Canterbury, 40
Aelfsige, Abbot of Peterborough, 14-15, 19
Aethelred II, the Unready, King of England, 51
Aethelwold, St, Bishop of Winchester, 19, 36-7
Aidan, St, 19
Ailred, St, monk and Abbot of Rievaulx, and treatises of, 29-31, 141-5, 159, 166; *Life* of, 29-30; his sister, 145
Alban, St, 15-16, 158
Albigensian Crusade, 102; *and see* Cathars
Aldhelm, St, 19
Alexander, Bishop of Lincoln, 19
Alexander II, Pope (Anselm of Lucca), 54
Alexander III, Pope, 46, 113
Alexius I, Comnenus, Byzantine Emperor, 58
Alfonso VIII, King of Castile, 109
Alfred, King of Wessex, 19, 47-8, 161
Alps, Alpine pastures, 64
Amalarius, 140
Ambrose, St, Archbishop of Milan (Ambrogio), 53, 81, *and see* Milan
Amiens, city and cathedral, 84-6, 120-21, 162; *11, 18, 20*; Chemin de l'Eau 120; Hôtel du Noir Chevalier, 121;

Church of St Martin aux Waides, 121
Andrew, St, 19
Angers, 18
Anna Comnena, 61
Anne, St, 31
Anselm, Abbot of Bury, 32
Anselm, St, monk and Abbot of Bec, Archbishop of Canterbury, 20, 40, 44, 95-6, 146-7, 152; as monk of Bec, 139-40
Anselm of Lucca, *see* Alexander II
anti-clericalism, 94, 98
Antioch, 60, 161
Apulia, 15
Aragon, 24
Archpoet, 96, 163
Ariald, 54
Arian heretic, 131
Arnaud, Abbot of Vézelay, 93
Arnold of Brescia, 94-5, 163
Assisi, 95, 129; Basilica of St Francis, 84, 132; Carceri, 64, 162; Portiuncula and indulgence, 153-4; San Damiano, 139
astrology, 13
Atcham (near Shrewsbury), 82, 162
Athelstan, King of Wessex, Laws of, 107, 164
Aucassin, and poem *Aucassin and Nicolette*, 155
Augustine, St, Archbishop of Canterbury, 39, 40
Augustine, St, Bishop of Hippo, 81; Rule of, 128
Autun Cathedral, 87, 119; sculpture of Gislebertus in, 93, 132, 136-7, 143, 151-2; *7, 28, 33-5*
Avignon, 95

Babel, Tower of, 135
Babylon (for Rome), 101
Bamberg, Bishop of, 97
baptism, 97-8, 104-7, 163; and heretics, 62, 103
baptisteries, 81, 104-5, 107, 119
Bari, cult and church of St Nicholas, 34
Bartholomew, St, 15, 20, 158
Bath, Wife of, 113
Bathsheba, Queen, 136
Bayeux Tapestry, 133, 135
Bec, Abbey, 139, 146
Bede, 26
Beguines, 129, 165
Benedict, St, 30, 133; relics, 16; Rule of, 16, 48, 128
Benevento, 15; Bishop of, 15
Bénigne, Benignus, St, 39-40, 44
Bernard, St, Abbot of Clairvaux, 44, 128; and architecture, 86; and Arnold of Brescia, 94-5; and the Bishop of Lincoln, 61; and the Crusade(s), 47, 58, 60, 161; and St Mary, 31, 143, 159; and meditation on the life of Jesus, 142; his sermons on the Song of Solomon, 133
Bernard, St, Prior of Saint-Savin and Abbot of Tiron, 135, 165
Bernard, Treasurer of Compostela Cathedral, 24
Bernardino, St, 64
Berthold of Regensburg, O.F.M., 25
Bethlehem, 138
Bible, the, 11, 127, 130-45, 165-6; in art, 133-9, 165; *Bible moralisée*, 137; vernacular versions 125, 130-31; Books of: Genesis, 136; the Pentateuch

at Saint-Savin, 134-6; Judges, 136; Kings, 133, 136; Song of Solomon, 133; Mark, 139; Acts, 125, 131
bishops, 104-7
blasphemers, 95-7
Blois, Count of, *see* Stephen
Boethius, 161
Bogomils, 99
Bohemia, 19
Boniface, St, Archbishop of Mainz, 81, 154
Bonn, 99
Bonneval, *see* Saint-Florentin
Bosnia, 99
Bosphorus, 59
Bourges, 132
Brand, Abbot of Peterborough, 19-20
Bristol, 106, 164
Bulgaria, 99
Buoncontro da Montefeltro, 108
Burgos, Las Huelgas Abbey, 109
Burgundy, 46
burial, 107-10, 164
Burthred, 111
Bury St Edmunds, Abbey church, 21, 90, 158; Abbot of, 32
Byzantine Empire, Byzantium, 'East Rome', 13, 58; Byzantine art, 13, 140; princess, *see* Anna Comnena

Cain, 135; *15*
Cambridge University, 124
Campaldino, Battle of, 108
Cana, marriage at, 138
Canossa, 54
Canterbury, Archbishop of, 41, *and see* Anselm, Dunstan, Lanfranc, Thomas Becket; Cathedral, 20, 40-44, 107; *5*; relics at, 15; St Augustine's Abbey, 87
Capetian dynasty in France and Hugh Capet, 50
Carpasius, St, 26
Castile, King and Queen of, 109; travel in, 23-4
Castle Frome (Herefordshire), *19*
Cathars, Albigensians, 99-103, 126, 127, 163
cathedrals and the laity, 119-22
cemeteries, 109, 164
Champagne, 99

chantries, 110, 164
Charlemagne, 24, 50, 97
Chartres, Abbey of Saint-Père, 43-4; Cathedral, 87, 120, 132, 151; and St Mary, 32; city, 43-4, 132
Chartreuse, La Grande, 29, 93-4, 163
Chaucer, 22, 113
chess, 94
Chiusa, *see* Sagra di San Michele
Christina of Markyate, and her *Life*, 111- 13, 145, 164, 166
Christmas crib, 31
church(es) as historical evidence, 11, 162; site, 63-4, 81-3; style, design and furnishing, 27, 61, 83-91; and year 1000, 14
church courts, 22
Cistercian Order, 49; devotion to Jesus and Mary, 31, 141-3; Cistercian sites, 29; *and see* Sweetheart Abbey
Clare, St, 129, 165
Clarendon, Constitutions of, 46, 160
Cluny Abbey and monks of, 59, 92-3
Cnut, 15
Coleman, monk of Worcester, 106
Cologne, Archbishop of, 96; Cathedral, 84; Beguines in, 129; heretics in, 99
Compostela, Santiago de, Saint James of, and pilgrimage to, 21-5, 28, 33, 39, 84, 119, 158; Cathedral, 24, 84-6
Condwiramurs, 114-15, 164
confession, and penance, 51, 62, 106, 118, 164-5
confirmation, 62, 105-7, 164
Conques, Sainte-Foy, town, Abbey and cult, 26-9, 39, 44, 46, 84, 158-9; *1, 2*
consolamentum, 100
Constance Cathedral, 57
Constantinople, 18, 99
Cordova, Caliphate of, 56
coronation(s), coronation service, 136, 166
Corvey Abbey, 19
Cross, True, relics of, 14
Crusades, 12, 56-61, 98; and martyrdom, 59, 161; First Crusade, 10, 58-61, 149, 157, 161; Second, 47; doctrine of,

57-9, 153
Crucifixion, 151

Dagon, 136
Danes in England, Danish invasions and kings, 15, 20, 50-51, 81
Dante, *Commedia,* 147, 154; *Inferno,* 104-5, 154; *Purgatorio,* 108, 126-7; Dante and Florence, 123
David, King, 136
dedications, 33-5, 159
Denmark, Crucifixions in, 140; King of, 20
Dervorguilla de Balliol, 109
devil(s), 29, 36, 52, 101, 108, 138, 146-51
Diego, Bishop of Osma, 97
Dies irae, requiem hymn, 152-3
Dijon, Saint-Bénigne, saint and Abbey, 39-40, 44, 158; *24*
dissent, 94-7, 163
Dominic, St, 97; Dominican Friars, Order of Preachers, 97
Dorchester (Oxfordshire), 81
drama, 117, 132-3, 135, 137, 140-41, 143
dreams, 35-6; *Dream of the Rood,* 139
Duccio, 122; *22*
Duddon, River and valley, 82
Dunstan, St, Archbishop of Canterbury, 40
Durham, Bishop of, 111; Cathedral, 87

Eadmer, monk of Christ Church, Canterbury, 20-21, 44, 95, 158
Eadsige, 36
East Rome, *see* Byzantine Empire
Edgar, King of England, 36, 51
Edward, St, King and Martyr, 19
Edward the Confessor, King of England, 41-2
Egwin, St, of Evesham, 19
Egypt, Flight into, 137, 140; *28, 31*
Eleanor, Queen of Castile, 109
Eleanor of Aquitaine, Queen of England, 109
Ely Abbey, 16; Cathedral, 89, 163
Emma, Queen, 14-15
Emmaus, 137, 145
Emperors, Holy Roman, im-

perial authority, 47, 50, 54
England, 22, 82-3, 120; Bible in, 130; heretics in, 99; English kingdom(s), monarchy, 41-2, 50-51, 54
Erlembald, 54
Etheldreda, St, 88
Ethelred II, King of England, the Unready, 19
eucharist, 32, 62, 115-17, 125, 164
Eve, 135
Exuperius, St, 18

Faith (Foy), St, 26-9, 39, 44; *1*
Falstaff, 108
fire, 90
Flanders, cloth, 120; heretics in, 99-100
Fleury (Saint-Benoît-sur-Loire), 16
Florence, 32, 122, 123; Baptistery, 104; San Miniato, 89
Florentin, St, 14, 33
fonts, 104-5, 107, 164; *12, 19*
Foy, *see* Conques, Faith
France, French, 14, 15, 23, 24, 82, 89-90; Arnold of Brescia in, 94; Île de, 132; French language, 117, 151; monarchy, 50, 54
Francis, St, 31, 49, 126-8, 129, 139, 152-4, 160, 165; as living saint, 44-5; and drama, 141; and heretics, 102; and St Mary, 32; and nature, 30; and wealth, 95
Franciscan Order, 154, *and see* friars
Frederick I, Barbarossa, Emperor, 96
friars, 49, 129; and drama, 140-41; and preaching, 124-5

Gadarene swine, 138; *32*
Galicia, 23, 24
Galilee, 22
Gascony, 23-4
George, St, 35
Gerald of Aurillac, St, 56-7, 161
Germany, 19, 27, 130-31; Beguines in, 129; German kingdom, 50, 53, 54, *and see* Emperors
Gesta Francorum, 10, 61
Giles, St, 23
Giotto, 140-41
Giovanni Pisano, 121, 140; *21*

Gislebertus (Gilbert), sculptor of Autun, 93, 136, 137, 140-41, 151-2; *7, 28, 33-5*
Glastonbury Abbey, 84
Gloucester and Abbey, 105-6
Godric of Finchale, St, 13, 158
Goliath, 136
Gothic art and architecture, 13, 83-7, 132, 162; in France, 83-7; in England, 84, 86; in Italy, 84
Gothic language, Gospels in, 131
Gottfried von Strassburg, 96, 163
Graubünden, 134, 138
Greek, Greek Orthodox Christians, 54; *and see* Byzantine Empire
Gregory I, the Great, St, Pope, 131, 165
Gregory VII (Hildebrand), Pope, 27, 52-5 *passim*, 58
Gregory IX, Pope, *see* Hugolino
Grimbald, St, 19
Guibert, Abbot of Nogent, 17-18, 60, 161
Guido, Archbishop of Milan, 53-4
Gurnemanz, 114

Haedde, Bishop of Winchester, 35
Harlequin, *see* Herla
Harold II, King of England, 20
Hastings, Battle of, 57
heathen practices, 51
heaven, 11, 59, 60, 147-52
Hebrews, ancient, and Jubilee, 154
Helisen, 111
hell, 11, 29, 59, 94, 101, 146-55
Heloise, 151
Henry III, Emperor, 52, 57
Henry IV, Emperor, 27, 52, 54, 58
Henry II, King of England, 41, 46, 100, 109
Henry III, King of England, 41, 116, 164
Henry of Blois, Bishop of Winchester, 151
Henry of Lausanne, 99
heresy, heretics, 62, 63-4, 99-103, 162, 163
Hereward the Wake, 20
Herla, Herlequin or Harlequin, 147-9

hermit(s), hermitage, 26, 29, 64, 143-4
Herodias, 93
hierarchy of earth and heaven, 38-9
Hildebrand, *see* Gregory VII
Hildegarde, St, 151
Homer, 27
Honorius III, Pope, 117
Hugh, St, of Avalon, Bishop of Lincoln, 17, 93, 158
Hugh Candidus, monk of Peterborough, 19-21
Hugh Capet, King of France, 50
Hugh of Poitou, monk of Vézelay, 92-3
Hugolino, Cardinal, later Pope Gregory IX, 128
Hungary, 81
Huntingdon, 111

indulgence(s), 59-60, 153-4
Innocent III, Pope, 95, 102
Inquisition, inquisitors, 102, 125-6
Ireland, slave trade to, 106
Islam, Moslems, 54, 56-8, 98; Islamic art and architecture, 13, 87
Isle of Man, *see* Man
Israel, kings of, 136
Italy, 15, 34, 127; baptisteries in, 104, 119; churches in, 81, 82, 88-90, 119; heretics in, 100; Norman kingdom, 54; Italian cities, 55-6, 119, 161
Ives, St, 15, 158

Jacques de Vitry, Bishop of Acre, later Cardinal Bishop, 129, 165
James, St, cult of, 21-5, 33, 39, 158
Jarrow, 26
Jeremiah, Archdeacon, 117
Jerusalem, and the Crusades, 13, 22, 58-9, 61; the Heavenly Jerusalem, 61, 150; the Holy Sepulchre, 32; the Entry into, 138; the Cleansing of the Temple, 138
Jesus, the human life of, 31, 45, 137-45; and judgment, 145-6, 153; Passion and crucifixion, 139-40; relics of, 18
Jews, Jewry, 56, 96, 98; *and see* Speyer
Jezebel, 93

Joachim of Fiore, 154, 166
Jocelin of Brakelond, monk of Bury, 158
John, St, *Apocalypse* of, 101; the Apostle, 52, 151
John the Baptist, St, 18, 40, 104, 107
John of Salisbury, 40–41, 94, 136, 163; as Bishop of Chartres, 43–4
Joseph (Patriarch), 136
Joseph, St, 113, 137; *31*
Joseph of Arimathaea, 143
Jubilee(s), 12, 153–5, 166
Judaea, 92; Judah, Kings of, 136
Judaism, 98, *and see* Jews
Judgment, the Last, 28–9, 108, 146–55, 166; *34-5*

kings, kingship, 47, 50–51, 54
Kirkby Ireleth, 82, 162
knighthood, 57
Knights, Hospitallers and Templars, 49

Lambert le Bègue, 125, 129, 131, 165
Lambeth Bible, *25*
Lanfranc, Archbishop of Canterbury, 40
Languedoc, 100, 102
Laon Cathedral, 84–5, 162
Last Supper, 138
Latin language, 124, 151
Laws, Old English, 107
Lay Folks' Mass Book, 116–17
Lay of the Reflection, 96, 163
Lazarus, St, 138
Leo I, the Great, St, Pope, 52
Leo IX, St, Pope, 52
León-Castile, King–Emperor of, 56; *and see* Castile
Léonard, St, 23
Le Puy, canon of, 157
Liège, 125, 129; Bishop of, 125; Church of Saint-Barthélemy, font in, 84, 107, 164; *12*
Limousin, the, 43
Lincoln, Bishop of (Alexander), 61; Cathedral and see, 81; *27*
Lombards, 16; Lombard kings of Italy, 54
London, St Paul's Cathedral, 28, 42; other churches, 82–3, 162; St Faith, 28; St Nicholas Acon, 34, 159; *and see* Westminster

Longney (on Severn, Gloucestershire), 106, 164
Lorca, 24
Lorenzetti, Ambrogio, 122–3; *23*
Louis VII, King of France, 93–4, 95, 163
love, courtly, 96
Low Countries, Beguines in, 129
Lucca, 90
Luke, St, 143
Luther, Martin, 130
Lyon, 62, 131

Magdeburg, 81
Magi, Adoration of, 137
magic, 13, 61
Mainz, Archbishop of, 81; Cathedral, 84
Malebolge, 104, 154
Malmesbury Abbey, 20; *17*
Man, Isle of, and Manx crosses, 126, 165
Marie, Mary, of Oignies, 129, 165
Mark, St, cult of, 33; Gospel of, 139
Markyate, 112, *and see* Christina
marriage, 110–15, 164; and heretics, and Waldo, 62, 101, 103
Martha, St, 145
Martin, St, 42, 138
Martin, Abbot of Peterborough, 19
Martini, Simone, 122
martyrdom, and crusades, 59–60
Mary, St, Blessed Virgin Mary, 12, 31–4, 101, 149; Annunciation, 127; Conception, 31; Coronation, 33; *4*; cult of, 22, 31–4, 39, 44, 48; dedications to, 33–4; and the human Jesus, 44–5, 142–3; marriage of, 133; as mediator, 152; miracles of, 32, 159; relics, 18, 19, 22; her sorrows, 144
and Amiens, 120–21; and Chartres, 22, 151; in Dante, 108; and Siena, 122; and Waldo, 62
Mary, St, of Bethany (identified with Mary Magdalene in the Middle Ages), 145
Mary Magdalene, St, 17, 39,

44, 92–3, 141, 143, 152–3; *33*
Mary I, Queen of England, 117
Matthew Paris, 10, 157
Maurice, St, 35
Maximian, Emperor, throne of, 134
Michael, St, 34–5, 88, 159
Milan, Cathedral, 81; Sant'-Ambrogio, 40, 81, 162; 11th-century reform and *Patarini*, 53–4, 95, 161
miracles, 40–44; of St Mary Magdalene, 92–3; of St Swithun, 35–6; *and see* Mary, St, Thomas Becket, St
missions, missionaries, 97
Montaillou, 102, 125–6, 165
Monte Cassino Abbey, 16
Mont Saint-Michel, Le, Abbey, 34, 105
Moses, 136
Moslem, *see* Islam
Myra, 34

Nathan, 136
Navarrese, 24
Nazareth, 138
Nevers, Counts of, 93–4
Nicholas, St, 34, 159
Nicholas II, Pope, 54
Nicholas, son of Mainer, 120
Nicodemus, 144
Nicola Pisano, 121, 140
Nicolette, 155
Noah, 135, 136; *26-7*
Noblat, St Léonard de, 23
Nogent, *see* Guibert
Normandy, 14, 50; Duke of (Robert), 58
Normans, 37–8, 119; Norman Conquest (of England), 57, 133; Norman kingdom of South Italy and Sicily, 54
Norse in England, 81, 82
Norway, King of, 97

Odense, 15–16
Odo, St, Abbot of Cluny, 56–7, 161
Odo, Bishop of Bayeux, 18
Olaf, St, King of Norway, 97
Old English, Bible in, 131
Orderic Vitalis, 50, 82, 147–9, 161
Osma, Bishop of, 97
Oswald, St, King of Northumbria, 17, 19–20
Otto, Bishop of Bamberg, 97

Ottonian architecture, 27
Oxford, 99; Balliol College, 109; University 124

Padua, 128; Arena Chapel, 140-41
Paris, 22, 128 *and see* Saint-Denis
parishes, parish churches, 82-3, 90
Parzival, 114-15, 164
Paschal II, Pope, 96
Patarene movement, *Patarini,* in Milan, 53-4, 161
Paul, St, 33, 42, 44; relics, 19, 33
peace, Peace of God, 56-7
penance, 118, *and see* confession
Perugia, 127
Peter, St, 44, 52, 55, 101, 150; cult of, 22, 33, 39-40, 42; relics of, 19, 33; tomb of, 53
Peter, Abbot of (Moutier-la-) Celle, 159
Peter Damian, St, 54, 147
Peter of Bruis, 63, 99, 103, 131, 162-3
Peter the Hermit, 12, 58-9
Peter the Venerable, Abbot of Cluny, formerly monk of Vézelay, 93, 103, 144, 162-3
Peterborough Abbey, 14, 17, 19-21, 33, 134, 158
Petrobrusians, 99, 103
Philip, canon of Lincoln, 61
pilgrims, pilgrimage(s), 11, 13, 21-9, 61, 63, 84, 92-3, 158; and Christina of Markyate, 145, 166; compared to courtly love, 96; the pilgrim guide, 22-5; *and also* Compostela, Conques, Vézelay
Pisa, 104, 121; *21*
Pisano, Giovanni and Nicola, 121, 140; *21*
Poland, 31, 81
Pomeranians, 97
Ponthieu, 42
popular religion defined, 9-12, 61-2
porch(es), church, 113; *17*
Portugal, 31
Poschiavo, 64
poverty, 125, 127-8; Lady Poverty, 128
preaching, 107, 123-5, 132, 133, 135, 165; and drama, 140-41; Preachers, *see* Dominic

Provençal, version of Cathar ritual, 163
Provence, 23
purgatory, 59, 101, 110, 147-9, 166
Pyrenees, 102, 126

Quickly, Mistress, 108

Rainald of Dassel, Archbishop of Cologne, 96
Ralph, father of William and Walchelin, 149
Ranulf Flambard, Bishop of Durham, 111
Raoul Glaber, 14, 52, 160
Ravenna, Church of San Vitale, 39
Raymond of Agiles, 157
Reading Abbey, 33; *4*
recluse, *see* hermit
Regularis Concordia, 51, 161
relics, 11, 13, 14-29, 51, 53, 61, 158-9; of St Faith, 26-9; of St James, 22-5; of St Mary, 18, 19, 22; of St Mary Magdalene, 92-3; of St Swithun, 35-9; relic churches, 39-40; Guibert's treatise on, 17-18
Rembrandt, 136
Remi, Remigius, St, 64
Rheims, Archbishop of, 41; and St Remi, 64
Rhine, 81; Rhineland, 46, 59, 99
Rhône, 23, 63
Richard Poore, Bishop of Salisbury, 124
Rie, River, 29
Rievaulx Abbey, 29-30; *3*
Robert of Bellême, 147-8
Robert, son of Ralph, 149
Roland, Song of, 58-60, 161; *Rolandslied,* 58, 161
Romanesque art and architecture, 63, 83-7, 140, 162-3
Rome
ancient, 86-7; Roman Emperors, 54, Empire, 110; provinces, 81
architecture, Roman, 63
Church(es) of Rome, Basilica of San Clemente, 88, 163; of St Peter and of St Paul, 39; cult of St Peter, 22, 33; Roman martyrs, 19, 33, 39, 53, 81, 135; titular churches, 82

Church, Papacy and Popes, 50; authority of Pope, 47, 52-6; Curia, 22, 55; and St Francis, 128; Lateran Councils, III, 62; IV, 107, 115, 118, 164; papal banner, 57, 161; and Crusade indulgence, 59; papal jubilee, 154; papal reform, 52-6; Pope as Vicar of Christ, 55; relations with Arnold of Brescia, 95; with city of Rome, 55-6; with Emperor, 50, 54; with England, 35; with Milan, 53-4
City, and Pope, 55-6, 161; St Francis in, 95; sack of (1084), 88; travel to, 158; Castel Sant'Angelo, 154
Romerio, San, 64, 82, 162; *8*
Rood, Dream of the, 139, 166
Rouen, 148
Rouergue, the, 26, 29

sacraments, 62, 104-18 *passim*
Sagra di San Michele (near Turin), Chiusa Abbey, 32, 35, 159
saint(s), cult of, 11, chaps II-III, 159-60; and nature, 29-30; *and see* relics
St Albans Abbey, 10, 15-16, 91, 158; Abbot, 16; Psalter, 145
Saint-Benoît-sur-Loire, Fleury, Abbey, 16
Saint-Denis (Paris), 33, 40, 83-4
Saint-Évroult Abbey, 50; abbots of, 148
Saint-Florentin, Abbey (Bonneval) and saint, 14, 33
Saint-Gilles, Abbey and town, 23, 63, 87, 103; *10*
St-Just-in-Roseland, 82, 162
Saint-Maximin (Provence), 92
St Michael's Mount, 34
Saint-Savin-sur-Gartempe, Abbey, 134-6, 165; *26*
Salian dynasty, 27
Salisbury, diocese, 124, 165; Dean of, 124
Samaritan woman, 138
Samson, 136
San Romerio, 64, 82, 162; *8*
Santiago, *see* Compostela
Satan, and the Cathars, 100, 102; *and see* devil(s)
Saul, *25*

Scandinavia, Scandinavians, 22, 81, 97
Scotland, 31, 81, 109
screens in churches, 83, 88-90
Selva, 64
Serlo, Abbot of Gloucester, 105-6
Servites, Order of, 32, 159
Shaftesbury, 19
Shakespeare, 10
Sicily, 13, 31, 57-8, 98
Siena, city, Cathedral and Palazzo Pubblico, 122-3; *22-3*; Stalloreggi Gate, 122
Simon Magus, and simony, 52; *7*
Sinai, Mount, 61
slaves, slave trade, 106, 164
Soissons, Abbey of Saint-Médard, 17-18
Solomon, King, 136
Solomon, Song of, 133, 143
Somme, River, 120
Sonning (Berkshire, dioc. Salisbury), 124
Sorde, 24
Spain, 13, 56, 97, 98; and St James, 22-5
Speyer, Cathedral, 27; Jewish bath-house, 59; *6*
Stephen, Count of Blois, 58, 161
Suger, Abbot of Saint-Denis, 40, 83-4, 86, 93, 133, 160
superstition, 11, 13, 61
Sutton Hoo, 108
Sweetheart Abbey, 109
Swithun, St, cult and relics of, 19, 35-9, 42, 159
Switzerland, 64

Teilo, St, 16, 158
Thomas Becket, St, Archbishop of Canterbury, as chancellor, 41; as archbishop, and cult and miracles, 22,

40-44, 154, 160; *5*; at Vézelay, 46, 119, 160
Thomas of Celano, 152
Tiber, River, 154
Tiron Abbey, 135
tolerance, 10-11, 98
Toulouse, 63, 102
Tours, 42, 84
Trajan, Emperor, 127
Turks, Seljuk, 58, 161
Turold, Abbot of Malmesbury and Peterborough, 20
Turpin, Archbishop, 60
Tuscany, Tuscan churches, 91

Umbria, 127
unction, extreme, 62, 115
Urban II, Pope, 12, 58-60

Venice, 33, 61
Verona, San Zeno Abbey, 40, 89; *14, 15*
Vézelay, Abbey, shrine and cult of St Mary Magdalene, 23, 24, 39, 46-7, 88, 91-4, 119, 120, 160-61, 163; *16*; sculpture, 132
Vikings, 81
Viollet-le-Duc, 83

Waldensians, Waldo, 62, 99, 131, 162
Walkelin, Bishop of Winchester, 38
Wearmouth, Monkwearmouth, 26
weavers, and heresy, 100
Weingarten Crucifixion, 139
Wells Cathedral, 84, 86, 162; *9, 13*
Wenceslas, St, 19
Westminster Abbey, 41-2, 160
Whitehaven, 81
William I, the Conqueror, King of England, 16, 20, 50, 58, 161

William II, Rufus, King of England, 95-6
William, Archbishop of Tyre, 60, 161
William, Count of Nevers (II), 93-4, 163
William of Breteuil, 148
William of Canterbury, 42-3
William of Glos, and Beatrice his wife and Roger his son, 148
William of Malmesbury, 105, 106
Winchcombe (Gloucestershire), 36
Winchester, Bishop of, 151; Cathedral and Old Minster, St Peter and St Paul, *alias* St Swithun's, 35-9, 42, 159; Chapel of the Holy Sepulchre, 143; Winchester Psalter, 150-51, 166; New Minster (later Hyde Abbey), *Liber Vitae* of, 150
witchcraft, 11, 61
Wolfram von Eschenbach, 12, 163; *Parzival*, 98, 114-15; *Willehalm*, 10-11, 98
Worcester, Bishop of, 105-8; see of, 81
Wulfric of Haselbury, 64, 162, 166
Wulfstan, Archbishop of York, 51
Wulfstan, St, Bishop of Worcester, 105-7

York, (arch)diocese, 81, 117

Zadok, 136
Zeno, St, 40
Zillis (Graubünden, Switzerland), 134, 136-8, 142, 166; *29-32*
Zurich, 138

Merriam-Webster's Intermediate Dictionary

Merriam-Webster, Incorporated
Springfield, Massachusetts, U.S.A.

A GENUINE MERRIAM-WEBSTER

The name *Webster* alone is no guarantee of excellence. It is used by a number of publishers and may serve mainly to mislead an unwary buyer.

Merriam-Webster™ is the name you should look for when you consider the purchase of dictionaries or other fine reference books. It carries the reputation of a company that has been publishing since 1831 and is your assurance of quality and authority.

Library of Congress Cataloging-in-Publication Data

Merriam-Webster's intermediate dictionary.
    p. cm.
    Summary: Provides definitions, pronunciation, etymology, part of speech designation, and other appropriate information. Intended for use by students in grades six to eight.
    ISBN 0-87779-579-7
    1. English language—Dictionaries, Juvenile [1. English language—Dictionaries.] I. Title: Intermediate dictionary. II. Merriam-Webster, Inc.

PE1628.5.M44 2004
423—dc22
                                         2004045792

Merriam-Webster's Intermediate Dictionary principal copyright 1986

Made in the United States of America

12345TT:QWV0504

Contents

Preface   7a

Using Your Dictionary   9a

Abbreviations Used in This Dictionary   17a

Pronunciation Symbols   18a

A Dictionary of the English Language   **1**

Abbreviations and Symbols for Chemical Elements   939

Biographical, Biblical, and Mythological Names   945

Geographical Names   961

Signs and Symbols   995

A Handbook of Style   999

Preface

Merriam-Webster's Intermediate Dictionary is part of a series of dictionaries prepared especially for elementary and secondary students. It is preceded by *Merriam-Webster's Elementary Dictionary* and followed by *Merriam-Webster's School Dictionary. Merriam-Webster's Intermediate Dictionary* is intended for use primarily by students in middle school and junior high school. The range of vocabulary covered is suited to the needs of older students, but the definitions have been written in everyday language that will be clear to younger students.

The dictionary has been written and edited by Merriam-Webster's permanent staff of trained and experienced lexicographers. They have included words chiefly on the basis of their occurrence in textbooks and other materials in all subjects. The editors have also had access to the many millions of examples of English words used in context that form the extensive Merriam-Webster citation files and that underlie the entire family of Merriam-Webster dictionaries, including *Webster's Third New International Dictionary* and *Merriam-Webster's Collegiate Dictionary.*

By basing their work on this broad body of evidence, the editors have ensured that the current general vocabulary of English has received its proper share of attention, while also giving the language of special subjects—such as mathematics, science, social studies, and computers—the full coverage that today's students need.

Merriam-Webster's Intermediate Dictionary will give students all of the information they need about how words are spelled, how they are pronounced, and what they mean. In addition, it also has some features found in more advanced dictionaries. For example, word history paragraphs at many entries, each followed by a traditional dictionary etymology, introduce the fascinating study of where words come from and build dictionary skills in understanding etymologies. Synonym paragraphs introduce students to the small but important differences in meaning that make one word more appropriate than another in a particular context.

Over a thousand illustrations of animals, plants, vehicles, musical instruments, articles of clothing, and many other kinds of things supplement and enrich the information given in definitions. Special tables throughout the book answer questions about such matters as the name of a chemical element, the relation of a U.S. measure to its metric equivalent, or the diameter of a planet in our solar system.

In the back of the dictionary there are separate sections giving information about common abbreviations; names of figures from history, mythology, and the Bible; names of places; and signs and symbols.

Merriam-Webster's Intermediate Dictionary can become a very valuable book for students facing the special challenges of developing language skills and basic knowledge across a broad range of topics. The more a student uses the dictionary, the more useful it becomes. However, using a dictionary is not always an easy and obvious matter. To assist students in building necessary dictionary skills, this dictionary includes an introductory section called "Using Your Dictionary." Students should read this section carefully and become thoroughly familiar with what it tells them about the variety of type styles, symbols, special words, and abbreviations used in this dictionary. By doing this, students will be sure to get the most from their dictionary.

Using Your Dictionary

Dictionary Entries

The entries in the dictionary are all the words printed in **boldface** type. The **main entries** are the entries that are listed in alphabetical order at the far left in a column. Most main entries are provided with a pronunciation, a part-of-speech label, and a definition.

Most main entries are single words, but some are not. A main entry can also be a prefix like **¹a-**, a suffix like **-ability**, a combining form like **bio-**, a combination of words like **abominable snow-man** and **about–face**, a combination of letters like **IOU**, or a combination of a numeral and a letter like **3-D**.

Run-on Entries

At the end of many entries are additional bold-face words and sometimes boldface phrases introduced with a dash. These are known as **run-on entries**. These words and compounds are derived from the main-entry word in different ways. They may come about through a shift in function (as the noun *implant* comes from the verb *implant*) or they may be formed by the addition of suffixes (as the adverb *closely* and the noun *closeness* come from the adjective *close*). The derived words are run on without definitions when their meanings are easy to figure out. But if the meaning of the run-on word is not easy to figure out from the meaning of the base word and the meaning of any added suffix, we always enter it as a main entry with a definition.

The boldface phrases run on at the end of many entries are common idioms whose meanings are more than the sum of the meanings of the individual words. These phrases are generally entered under the first major element (for example, a noun or verb or sometimes an adjective or adverb, rather than a preposition or article).

For example, the phrases *on board, in any case,* and *to date* will appear at the entries **board, case,** and **date,** respectively. *Break camp, cast lots,* and *now and then* will appear respectively under **break, cast,** and **now.**

Order of Entries

Throughout the dictionary, main entries are alphabetized by first letter, then second letter, and so on, regardless of any spaces or hyphens that may appear in them. When a main entry contains a numeral, consider the numeral as though it were a spelled-out word and you will find it at its alphabetical place. For example, **4–H** appears between **four–footed** and **four–in–hand.** Likewise, when a word is usually spelled with an abbreviation, such as **St. Bernard**, consider the spelled-out form (in this case **Saint**) and you will find it at its alphabetical place between **Saint Andrew's cross** and **sainted.**

When main entries are spelled exactly alike but have different functions in a sentence (such as noun and verb) or have different origins, they are called **homographs**. Each homograph is indicated by a small raised numeral at the very beginning of the word. For example, **¹account** and **²account** are entered as separate homographs because they have different functions (the first is a noun, the second is a verb). The entries **¹calf** and **²calf** are separate homographs because they have different origins (the first from an Old English word, the second from a Norse word). In general, homographs are listed and numbered in the order in which they came into the language. The word *calf* meaning a young cow came into the language before the word *calf* meaning a part of the leg.

When main entries are spelled alike except that one of them is capitalized, the one not capitalized is listed first. For example, **frank** is listed before **Frank.**

When main entries are compounds, such as **layoff, lay off, lay–up,** and **lay up,** the solid form is entered first, then the hyphenated form, and then the open form with a space between the parts. Thus, **layoff** comes before **lay off,** and **lay–up** comes before **lay up.**

Guide Words

At the top of each page are two large boldface words separated by a dot. These are called **guide words.** They show the alphabetical range of the entries on that page, and you can use them to help you find a word quickly. For example, if you are looking up the word *aplomb*, flip through the pages looking at the guide words. Stop when you come to the guide words between which the word *aplomb* alphabetically falls. The page having the guide words **apartment • apparently** (page 35) is the page you want. If you stop at the preceding page (page 34), the guide words **antiparticle** • **apartheid** tell you that you are not yet where you want to be. If you stop at the following page (page 36), the guide words **apparition** • **apposition** tell you that you have gone too far.

The guide words are usually that first and last main entries on the page, but there are exceptions. Actually, the guide words are the first and last entries alphabetically on the page, and this includes all the boldface entries, not just the main entries. A guide word is most often a main entry, but it may also be a variant spelling, an inflected form, or a run-on entry.

Look, for example, at the guide words on page 66. The first guide word, **bed**, is also the first main entry. But the second guide word is **beeves**, while the last main entry is **beetle**. Beeves is actually a boldface inflected form at the main entry **beef**, but it is alphabetically the last entry on the page and so is the proper guide word.

Like main entries, guide words are always in alphabetical order from page to page throughout the book. Once in a while, this presents a problem where the alphabetically last entry on a page—the one that would normally be chosen as the second guide word—is actually later in alphabetical order than the first guide word on the next page. When this happens, a different second guide word must be chosen, one that does not disturb the alphabetical order of the guide words from page to page.

Look, for example, at pages 73 and 74. Notice that the first guide word on page 74 is **billboard**, because it is the alphabetically first entry on the page. Now look at page 73: you notice that the alphabetically last entry on the page is the run-on entry **billed**, at **¹bill**, yet it is not the second guide word. The second guide word is **bill**, which is in alphabetical order with **billboard** on the next page. If **billed** were used as the second guide word, alphabetical order would be broken, so it is ignored.

Variant Spellings

A number of main entries have a second and sometimes a third spelling also shown in boldface. These alternate spellings are called **variants**.

Variants that are separated by the word *or* are equal variants. This means that either spelling is equally acceptable with the other in current English. Equal variants are usually listed in alphabetical order.

bob·by socks *or* **bob·by sox**

However, if one of the equal variants is used

slightly more frequently, that one is entered first even though it may not fall alphabetically first.

pol·ly·wog *or* **pol·li·wog**

Variants that are separated by the word *also* are not equal variants, and the one listed before the word *also* is quite a bit more common than the one that follows the word *also*. So, at the entry

glam·or·ous *also* **glam·our·ous**

the first spelling is used more often than the second, but both spellings are considered acceptable.

Occasionally both *or* and *also* are used to separate a number of variants at a single entry. The example below indicates that neither **bogy** nor **bogie** is as commonly used as **bogey**, but all three are considered acceptable.

bo·gey *also* **bo·gy** *or* **bo·gie**

Some variants are entered separately at their own alphabetical places. These are followed by the italicized words *variant of* and a cross-reference in small capital letters to the more common spelling or form.

lichee *variant of* LYCHEE

despatch *chiefly British variant of* DISPATCH

Variants that are standard in American English are given at the main entry and are entered again at their own alphabetical places only if they fall one column or more away from the main entry. Variants that are restricted in some way (as by being chiefly British or dialect) are found only at their own alphabetical places.

When one variant is more common for a particular meaning than for other meanings, it is given before the definition with an indication of how common it is.

¹disk *or* **disc** . . . 2 : a thin circular object: as **a** *usually disc* : a phonograph record

¹nick·el . . . 2 a *also* **nick·le** : the U.S. five-cent piece made of nickel and copper

If the variant is shown in boldface at the beginning of the entry, as **disc** is, it appears in italic before the definition. If it is not shown at the beginning of the entry, as **nickle** is not, it appears in boldface before the definition.

Centered Dots and Hyphenation

This dictionary shows you how to divide words for two distinct purposes: for end-of-line division by the use of **centered dots** in the entry word, and second, for syllabification by the use of **hyphens** in the pronunciations.

The boldface centered dots in entries indicate the acceptable places to put a hyphen when the word is divided at the end of a line. For example, the dots in the entry **in·ter·con·ti·nen·tal** indicate that the word may be broken at the end of a line as follows:

in-
tercontinental

or

inter-
continental

or

intercon-
tinental

or

interconti-
nental

or

intercontinen-
tal

It is customary to avoid dividing a word so that a single letter is left at the end of one line or the beginning of the next line. For this reason this dictionary does not show any division in such words as **eject, away,** and **lily.**

It is very important to understand that the dots that show end-of-line division do *not* always separate the syllables of a word. Syllables are shown only in the pronunciation, explained in the next section.

In the case of homographs, the divisions are usually indicated only in the first homograph. The divisions shown in the first homograph apply to all the following homographs.

¹**mas·ter** . . . *n*

²**master** *adj*

³**master** *vb*

A word in a compound made up of two or more separate words is divided only when no individual entry exists for that word.

Dew·ey decimal classification . . . *n*

diabetes mel·li·tus . . . *n*

ha·be·as cor·pus . . . *n*

There are no separate entries for *Dewey, mellitus, habeas,* or *corpus.*

This dictionary also uses a special double hyphen ⸗ at the end of a line when the word being broken is usually spelled with a hyphen at that point. For example, at the entry **duckbill** on page 241 the word in italics is broken at the end of the

first line with a double hyphen so as to show that the word is spelled *duck-billed platypus* and not *duckbilled platypus.*

Pronunciation

It is often difficult to tell how a word is pronounced from its spelling. For example, in *bat, late, any,* and *above* the letter *a* stands for a different sound in each word. In addition, there are many words that are pronounced in more than one way, even though there may be only one accepted spelling.

In order to represent the sounds of spoken English in a written form, a special set of pronunciation symbols is used. Each symbol stands for only one sound and each sound is represented by only one symbol.

The pronunciation of most entry words is shown immediately following the boldface entry. To make it clear that pronunciation symbols are being used and not regular letters, the symbols are always shown between slant lines \ \.

A complete list of pronunciation symbols used in this dictionary appears on page 18a. A shorter list of symbols you may need to be reminded of is printed at the bottom of the right column on odd⸗ numbered pages throughout the dictionary. After most of the symbols in the chart are words containing the sound of that symbol. The boldface letters in these words are the letters which have the same sound as the symbol.

For example, following the symbol **j** are the words **j**ob, **g**em, e**dge**. The boldface **j** in **j**ob, the **g** in **g**em, and the **dge** in e**dge** are all pronounced \j\.

At the beginning of the list of pronunciation symbols is the symbol ə, called a **schwa** \ˈshwä\. This symbol often represents the sound of an unstressed vowel (as the first and last vowels in *America*), but it may also represent the sound of a stressed vowel (as the first vowel of *brother*).

Hyphens are used in the pronunciation to indicate the syllables of a word.

noisy \ˈnȯi-zē\ (2 syllables)

no·tice·able \ˈnōt-ə-sə-bəl\ (4 syllables)

Of course, the syllables of words are not separated when we speak. One sound follows right after another without pause. It is obvious in the example *noticeable* above that the number and position of hyphens are not the same as the number and position of dots in the entry word. Only the hyphens show syllables; the dots mark acceptable places to divide the word at the end of a line.

Some syllables are spoken with greater force or stress than others. In this dictionary the primary (strongest) stress is shown by a high-set vertical mark \'\ placed immediately *before* the stressed syllable. Secondary (slightly weaker) stress is shown by a low-set vertical mark \ˌ\ also placed immediately *before* the stressed syllable. In the word *notify*, for example, the first syllable receives primary stress and the last syllable receives secondary stress. The middle syllable receives weak stress and is not marked in the dictionary. All of this is shown in the pronunciation \'nōt-ə-ˌfī\.

Many words can be pronounced in more than one way. Variant pronunciations are separated by commas, and sometimes groups of variants are separated by semicolons. When the word *also* separates variant pronunciations, the one following the *also* is not as common as the one preceding it. All the variant pronunciations shown in this dictionary are quite acceptable and are used by educated speakers of English.

Sometimes when a variant pronunciation is shown, only part of the pronunciation of the word changes. When that happens, only the part that changes may be shown. To get the full pronunciation, add the part that changes to the part that stays the same.

> **ec·o·nom·ic** \ˌek-ə-'näm-ik, ˌē-kə-\
>
> **¹ei·ther** \'ē-thər *also* 'ī-\
>
> **ex·pi·ra·to·ry** \ik-'spī-rə-ˌtōr-ē, ek-, -ˌtȯr-; 'ek-sp(ə-)rə-\

If a variant is used mostly in a particular region of the U.S. or a part of the English-speaking world outside the U.S., that location is identified.

> **¹sure** \'shu̇(ə)r, *especially Southern* 'shō(ə)r\
>
> **¹sched·ule** \'skej-ü(ə)l, -əl, *Canadian also* 'shej-, *British usually* 'shed-yü(ə)l\

When a pronunciation symbol is enclosed in parentheses, that sound may or may not be pronounced.

> **¹ear** \'i(ə)r\

The parentheses at **¹ear** indicate that *ear* may be pronounced \'ir\ or \'iər\.

If an incomplete pronunciation is given for an entry word, the missing portion may be found at a preceding entry.

> **cat·bird** \'kat-ˌbərd\
>
> **cat·boat** \-ˌbōt\

Thus, the full pronunciation of *catboat* is \'kat-ˌbōt\. In the case of homographs, if the pronunciation is the same for each homograph, the pronunciation is given only for the first.

> **¹cheer** \'chi(ə)r\ *n*
>
> **²cheer** *vb*
>
> **¹her·ald** \'her-əld\ *n*
>
> **²herald** *vb*

Many entries for compounds made up of two or more separate words will also have missing pronunciations. Look at the entries for the separate words to determine the pronunciation. If one of the words has no entry of its own, however, the pronunciation of that word will be shown at the entry for the compound.

> **monarch butterfly** *n*
>
> **hog·nose snake** \ˌhȯg-ˌnōz-, ˌhäg-\ *n*

Some undefined run-on entries show no pronunciation. In these cases, the pronunciation of the run-on is the pronunciation of the main entry plus the pronunciation of the suffix, which may be found at its own alphabetical place.

> **bossy** \'bȯ-sē\ *adj* . . . — **boss·i·ness** *n*

Thus, the pronunciation of **bossiness** is \'bȯ-sē-nəs\; it is not shown because it is simply \'bȯ-sē\ plus \nəs\.

The Functions of Words

Words are used in many different ways in a sentence. A word may serve as the name of something, or be used to indicate an action or to describe a thing or the way something happens. The several different grammatical functions of words are known as parts of speech. This dictionary identifies the function of most entry words with one of the eight traditional part-of-speech labels, abbreviated, italicized, and placed after the boldface entry itself or after the pronunciation, when one is given.

> **bur·glar** . . . *n* (noun)
>
> **cease** . . . *vb* (verb)
>
> **de·li·cious** . . . *adj* (adjective)
>
> **fair·ly** . . . *adv* (adverb)
>
> **you** . . . *pron* (pronoun)
>
> **in·to** . . . *prep* (preposition)
>
> **or** . . . *conj* (conjunction)
>
> **ouch** . . . *interj* (interjection)

When a noun is always used in the plural, the label *n pl* is used. A noun so labeled always takes a plural verb.

> **munch·ies** . . . *n pl*

Sometimes an entry word that is spelled as a

plural may take either a singular or a plural verb, depending on its use. For example, although the word *acrobatics* is plural in form, it may be singular in such uses as "Acrobatics is a strenuous activity" or plural in "You make these acrobatics look easy." To indicate such uses, the word *acrobatics* is given the label *n sing or pl*.

In addition to the traditional part-of-speech labels, there are a number of other functional labels used in this dictionary.

> **may** . . . *helping verb*
>
> **me·thinks** . . . *impersonal verb*
>
> **avast** . . . *imperative verb*
>
> **an** . . . *indefinite article*
>
> **the** . . . *definite article*
>
> **Fris·bee** . . . *trademark*
>
> **Re·al·tor** . . . *collective mark*
>
> **NC–17** . . . *certification mark*
>
> **-gram** . . . *n combining form*
>
> **-ous** . . . *adj suffix*
>
> **non-** . . . *prefix*
>
> **-nd** . . . *symbol*

Inflected Forms

The plural forms of nouns, the past tense, past participle, and present participle forms of verbs, and the comparative and superlative forms of adjectives and adverbs are known as **inflected forms**. In most instances, these forms are regular (that is, they are formed by the addition of *-s* or *-es* to nouns, *-ed* and *-ing* to verbs, and *-er* and *-est* to adjectives and adverbs). These regular inflected forms are not shown in this dictionary. Irregular inflected forms, such as those that involve a change in the spelling of the root word or a doubling of a final letter, are shown in boldface.

Just as with variants of main entries, variants of inflected forms are equal when they are separated by *or*. If they are out of alphabetical order, the one shown first is slightly more common. Variants separated by *also* are not equal, however, and the one shown first is considerably more common than the other. Even so, both variants are acceptable.

An effort is usually made to save space in showing inflected forms by showing only the last part for words of more than two syllables. The form is usually cut back to the point that corresponds to the last indicated end-of-line division in the main entry.

> **can·di·da·cy** . . . *n, pl* **-cies**
>
> **or·ga·nize** . . . *vb* **-nized; -niz·ing**

Inflected forms whose own alphabetical places are more than one column away from the main entry are given separate entry there with a cross-reference in small capital letters to the main entry.

> **geese** *plural of* GOOSE
>
> **brought** *past and past participle of* BRING

PLURALS OF NOUNS

Nouns that form their plurals simply by the addition of *-s* or *-es* are not shown unless there is a chance that they may be mistaken or misspelled.

> **mon·key** . . . *n, pl* **monkeys** (not *monkies*)
>
> **mon·goose** . . . *n, pl* **mon·goos·es** (not *mongeese*)

Nouns that form their plurals in any other way than by the addition of *-s* or *-es* to an unchanged base have such plurals shown.

> **cad·dy** . . . *n, pl* **caddies** (*-y* changes to *-i-*)
>
> **child** . . . *n, pl* **chil·dren** (irregular ending)
>
> **knife** . . . *n, pl* **knives** (*-f-* changes to *-v-*)
>
> **oa·sis** . . . *n, pl* **oa·ses** (Greek plural)
>
> **se·ta** . . . *n, pl* **se·tae** (Latin plural)
>
> **ser·aph** . . . *n, pl* **ser·a·phim** . . . (Hebrew plural)
>
> **deer** . . . *n, pl* **deer** (no change at all)

Most compound nouns form their plural by pluralizing the final element. Such plurals are not shown when the final element is a recognizable word entered at its own place (such as *blueberry* and *eyetooth*). Plurals for compounds that pluralize any but the last element are shown.

> **mother–in–law** . . . *n, pl* **mothers–in–law**
>
> **postmaster general** *n, pl* **postmasters general**

Plurals are also given for all entries that have variant plural forms.

> **¹in·dex** . . . *n, pl* **in·dex·es** . . . *or* **in·di·ces**
>
> **mon·si·gnor** . . . *n, pl* **monsignors** *or* **mon·si·gno·ri**
>
> **ban·jo** . . . *n, pl* **banjos** *also* **banjoes**

Irregular plural forms are also entered at their own alphabetical place in this dictionary when they fall more than one column away from the singular entry. You will find the plural form **feet**, for example, entered at its own alphabetical place between **feeling** and **feetfirst** because it falls more than a column away from the singular **foot**. However, the irregular plural **oxen** is not shown at its own place because it does not fall more than a column away from **ox**. Irregular plurals that are shown at their own alphabetical place have a cross-reference in small capital letters to the singular form.

> **lice** *plural of* LOUSE
>
> **media** *plural of* MEDIUM

FORMS OF VERBS

Some inflected forms of a verb are especially important because they are used to form all of the verb tenses. These forms are the present tense, past tense, past participle, and present participle. Most verbs in English form the past tense and past participle by the addition of *-ed* to the base form, which is also the present tense form. They form the present participle by the addition of *-ing* to the base form. These verbs are considered to be regular, and their inflected forms are not shown in this dictionary.

Inflected forms are shown if they are created in any other way, even if it is no more than a matter of dropping a final *-e* before the ending is added. Variants of inflected forms are always shown. When the past participle has the same form as the past tense, only one form is shown.

> ¹**blow** . . . *vb* **blew** . . . ; **blown** . . . ; **blow·ing**
>
> ¹**fade** . . . *vb* **fad·ed; fad·ing**
>
> ¹**chop** . . . *vb* **chopped; chop·ping**
>
> ²**bias** *vb* **bi·ased** *or* **bi·assed; bi·as·ing** *or* **bi·as·sing**
>
> ²**picnic** *vb* **pic·nicked; pic·nick·ing**
>
> ¹**fry** . . . *vb* **fried; fry·ing**

FORMS OF ADJECTIVES AND ADVERBS

Most adjectives and adverbs form their comparative and superlative forms with the words *more* or *most* or with the addition of *-er* and *-est* to the simple form. These adjectives and adverbs are considered regular, and such forms are not shown in this dictionary. Any other spelling changes (such as the changing of *-y* to *-i-*, the doubling of the final consonant, or the dropping of *-e*) are shown. All variant forms are shown. To save space, superlative forms are often cut back to the ending **-est.**

> ¹**good** . . . *adj* **bet·ter** . . . ; **best**
>
> **mad** . . . *adj* **mad·der; mad·dest**
>
> ²**dandy** *adj* **dan·di·er; -est**
>
> ³**fine** *adj* **fin·er; fin·est**
>
> ¹**ear·ly** . . . *adv* **ear·li·er; -est**
>
> ²**much** *adv* **more; most**
>
> **spry** . . . *adj* **spri·er** *or* **spry·er** . . . ; **spri·est** *or* **spry·est**

Definitions

A definition is the statement of the meaning of an entry word. In this dictionary each definition is introduced by a boldface colon.

> ³**fan** *n* : an enthusiastic follower or admirer
>
> **op·ti·mis·tic** . . . *adj* : showing optimism : expecting everything to come out all right : HOPEFUL

Often, instead of a statement or in addition to it, one or more cross-references to synonyms are given in small capital letters.

> **law·mak·er** . . . *n* : LEGISLATOR
>
> **mer·i·to·ri·ous** . . . *adj* : deserving reward or honor : PRAISEWORTHY

This tells you that the meaning of *lawmaker* and the meaning of *legislator* are the same, and the meaning of *meritorious* and the meaning of *praiseworthy* are the same.

When an entry word has more than one sense, the appropriate number precedes each sense.

> **hoax** . . . *n* **1** : an act intended to trick or deceive **2** : something false passed off or accepted as genuine

Sometimes a particular relationship between two meanings is shown by the use of an italic label. Two labels are used: *esp* (for *especially*) and *also*. The divider *esp* is used to introduce the most common meaning that is included in the general definition just before it. The divider *also* is used to introduce a meaning that is closely related to the meaning given just before it but is not as common.

> **opus** . . . *n* . . . : ¹WORK 7; *esp* : a musical composition or set of compositions
>
> **demi·tasse** . . . *n* : a small cup of black coffee; *also* : the cup used to serve it

A numbered sense can be further divided into subsenses preceded by small boldface letters. Sometimes an unnumbered sense is divided into lettered subsenses.

> **erode** . . . *vb* . . . **1 a** : to destroy gradually by chemical means : CORRODE **b** : to wear away by or as if by the action of water, wind, or glacial ice **2** : to undergo erosion
>
> ²**scope** *n* : any of various instruments for viewing: as **a** : MICROSCOPE **b** : ¹TELESCOPE **c** : OSCILLOSCOPE

In this dictionary, the definitions of senses of a word are generally listed in historical order, just as homographs are. This means that sense 1 was used in English before sense 2, sense 2 before sense 3, and so forth. It does not mean, however, that sense 3 necessarily developed from sense 2. It may have done so, or sense 2 and sense 3 may have developed independently from sense 1. Sometimes it is possible to see that one sense developed out of another just by the way their definitions are worded.

¹branch . . . *n*   **1** : a natural division of a plant stem (as a bough growing from a trunk or twig from a bough)   **2** : something extending from a main line or source ⟨river *branch*⟩ ⟨a railroad *branch*⟩   **3** : a separate or subordinate division or part of a central system ⟨executive *branch* of the government⟩ ⟨a *branch* of a bank⟩

In the above entry, phrases are provided within angle brackets ⟨   ⟩ to illustrate common ways of using the entry word in the indicated sense. These phrases are called **verbal illustrations**.

Sometimes, in addition to or in place of a definition, you will find a cross-reference to a table in which other similar terms are listed or a cross-reference that sends you to another entry for related information.

Leo . . . *n* . . .   **2 a** : the fifth sign of the zodiac — see ZODIAC table

Dan·iel . . . *n* — see BIBLE table

digital computer *n* : a computer that operates with numbers expressed as digits (as in the binary system) — compare ANALOG COMPUTER

Capitalization

When an entry word is usually capitalized in ordinary writing, it is entered in this dictionary with a capital letter. Other entries begin with a lowercase letter. A few such entries also have an italic label *often cap*. This label indicates that the word is capitalized about as often as not.

    Oc·to·ber . . . *n*

    back·ground . . . *n*

    an·gli·cize . . . *vb* . . . *often cap*

Some words have special meanings when capitalized that they do not have when they are written without a capital letter. This dictionary shows the use of the capital with such entries by putting the label *cap* or *often cap* at the appropriate sense.

re·nais·sance . . . *n*   **1** *cap* : the period of European history between the 14th and 17th centuries marked by a flourishing of art and literature inspired by ancient times and by the beginnings of modern science   **2** *often cap* : a movement or period of great activity (as in literature, science, and the arts)

Occasionally, some words that are almost always capitalized in their usual meanings have special meanings in which they are not capitalized. In this dictionary the labels *not cap* or *often not cap* are given at the proper sense.

DJ . . . *n, often not cap* : DISC JOCKEY

²Roman *adj*   **1** : of or relating to Rome or the Romans or the empire of which Rome was the original capital   **2 a** . . . **b** . . . **3** *not cap* : of or relating to a type style with upright characters (as in "these definitions")

Special Usage Labels and Guide Phrases

For many entries italic labels identify the kind of context in which the word or a sense of the word is usually found. Some of the most commonly used labels in this dictionary are the following:

archaic (once standard but now used only in special contexts)

slang (very informal usage not usually found in formal writing)

substandard (not normally used by educated speakers and writers)

nonstandard (sometimes used by well-educated people but not always considered appropriate for good usage)

British (common only in Great Britain or the British Commonwealth countries)

Scottish (common only in Scotland)

dialect (common only in one or more regions of the U.S.)

Regional labels like the last three in the list above are often preceded by the word *chiefly*. This modifier indicates that the word or meaning is most common in the named region but has some use outside of it.

The following examples illustrate the use of such special usage labels:

¹fain . . . *adj*   **1** *archaic* : GLAD, HAPPY

lid . . . *n* . . . **3** *slang* : HAT

learn . . . *vb* . . . **4** *substandard* : to cause to learn : TEACH

¹lay . . . *vb* . . . **4** *nonstandard* : ¹LIE

³chap *n, chiefly British* : ¹FELLOW 4a

auld . . . *adj, chiefly Scottish* : OLD

craw·dad . . . *n, dialect* : CRAYFISH 1

At a few entries an italicized **guide phrase** may be provided before a definition to identify the reference of a special meaning.

¹bounce . . . *vb* . . . **5** *of a check* : to be returned by a bank . . .

Usage Notes

For some entries, a note beginning with a phrase such as "used as," "used in," or "used to" may be added to a definition. This **usage note** is set off by a dash.

> **le·ga·to** . . . *adv or adj* : in a manner that is smooth and connected — used as a direction in music

> **²cave** *vb* . . . : to fall or cause to fall in or down : COL-LAPSE — usually used with *in*

> **¹chamber** . . . *n* . . . 3 . . . b : a room where a judge conducts business out of court — usually used in plural

When a word has a special use that cannot easily or clearly be explained in a definition, a usage note may take the place of a definition.

> **ouch** . . . *interj* — used to express sudden pain

> **²let** *vb* . . . 3 . . . b — used to introduce a request

Synonym Paragraphs

At selected entries, the boldface italic word *synonyms* introduces a paragraph of explanation at the end of the definition. This *synonym paragraph* explains and illustrates with examples the relation of words that are similar in meaning to the main entry. Following is one such paragraph:

> **¹de·cline** . . . *vb* . . . 5 . . .
> *synonyms* DECLINE, REFUSE, REJECT mean to express unwillingness to go along with a demand or request. DECLINE suggests a polite negative response ⟨*decline* an invitation to a party⟩. REFUSE suggests a forceful or absolute denial ⟨*refused* to see him at all⟩. REJECT may suggest an unwillingness even to consider a demand or request ⟨*rejected* her plan before she had finished speaking⟩.

Notice that the words being discussed are listed at the beginning of the paragraph in small capital letters, followed by a statement of the meaning which they have in common. Next something is said about the special element of meaning each word has that makes it different from the other words in the list. A verbal illustration follows showing the special meaning of the word in action.

At the main entries for these words (except the first word) you will find a cross-reference to this synonym paragraph. This cross-reference is also introduced by the boldface italic word *synonyms* following the definition.

> **¹re·fuse** . . . *vb* . . . 3 . . . *synonyms* see DECLINE

> **¹re·ject** . . . *vb* . . . 4 . . . *synonyms* see DECLINE

Etymologies

At many entries, the origin of the entry word is shown by tracing it or its parts back to the earliest known forms and meanings. Such informa-

tion is called an **etymology**. In this dictionary the etymologies are shown within square brackets [ ] generally just after the definition.

Names of languages in etymologies are given in full rather than abbreviated. No attempt has been made to distinguish the major historical periods of languages other than English. The appearance of the phrase "derived from" before a new language name and form indicates that one or more minor stages of development have been omitted for clarity and simplicity. Language forms within etymologies are given in italics, and their meanings are placed inside quotation marks. If no language name appears before a form, the language is the last one named. Thus, in the etymology of **abbreviate**, *abbreviare* and *brevis* are Latin words and *ad-* is a Latin prefix.

> **li·co·rice** . . . *n* . . . [Middle English *licorice* "licorice," from early French *licoris* (same meaning), from Latin *liquiritia* (same meaning), derived from Greek *glykyr-rhiza*, literally "sweet root"]

> **ab·bre·vi·ate** . . . *vb* . . . [Middle English *abbreviaten* "abbreviate," from Latin *abbreviatus* "made short," from *abbreviare* "to shorten," from earlier *ad-* "to" and *brevis* "short" — related to ABRIDGE, BRIEF]

Sometimes an etymology explains how the word came to be applied to something.

> **red–let·ter** . . . *adj* : worth remembering especially in a happy or joyful way ⟨a *red-letter* day⟩ [from the practice of marking holy days in red letters in church calendars]

When a word comes from the name of a person, the name of a place, or some other proper name, this fact is often given in the etymology.

> **sax·o·phone** . . . *n* [named for Antoine "Adolph" *Sax* 1814–1894 a Belgian maker of musical instruments]

> **pan·de·mo·ni·um** . . . *n* . . . [from *Pandemonium*, name of the place of demons in *Paradise Lost* by John Milton, from Greek *pan-* "all, every, completely" and Greek *daimon* "evil spirit, demon"]

> **Wal·dorf salad** . . . *n* . . . [named for the *Waldorf*-Astoria Hotel in New York City]

To some extent words exist in families, just as people do. Particularly with borrowings into English from Latin and Greek, many words may be derived from a single ancestor. Sometimes the connection is evident when you see the words together, as in the case of *final, define, finish,* and *infinity*. Sometimes, however, the connection may have been blurred somewhat by changes in spelling, pronunciation, and meaning over the centuries, as in the case of *nautical, nausea,* and *noise*. Such connections between words are interesting in themselves, and they can also be helpful to you in learning new words. Your attention is drawn to such connections in etymologies by a note that begins "—related to" and continues with one or more cross-references in small capital letters to the related entries. Each of the entries named will have its own etymology and a similar note.

¹cross . . . *n* . . . [Old English *cros,* probably from an early Norse or an early Irish word derived from Latin *crux* "cross" — related to CRUCIAL, CRUISE, CRUSADE, CRUX, EXCRUCIATING]

cru·cial . . . *adj* . . . [from French *crucial* "having the form of a cross, being or involving a crisis," from Latin *cruc-, crux* "cross, trouble, torture" — related to CROSS, CRUCIFY, CRUX]

cruise . . . *vb* . . . [from Dutch *kruisen* "to cruise, move crosswise," from early Dutch *crūce* "cross," from Latin *crux* "cross" — related to CROSS, CRUCIAL]

¹cru·sade . . . *n* . . . [derived from early French *croisade* and Spanish *cruzada,* both meaning literally "an expedition of persons marked with or bearing the sign of the cross" and both derived from Latin *cruc-, crux* "cross" — related to CROSS]

crux . . . *n* . . . [from Latin *crux* "cross, torture, trouble" — related to CROSS, CRUCIAL, CRUCIFY]

ex·cru·ci·at·ing . . . *adj* . . . [derived from Latin *excruciatus,* past participle of *excruciare* "to torture," from *ex-* "out of, from" and *cruciare* "to torment, crucify," from *cruc-, crux* "cross" — related to CROSS, CRUCIAL, CRUCIFY]

Word Histories

Some of the many English words that have interesting histories are provided with a *Word History* paragraph. Such a paragraph follows the definition and is followed by the etymology.

can·di·date . . . *n* . . .

Word History In ancient Rome it was the custom for a person who wanted to be elected to public office to wear a toga that had been rubbed with chalk to make it white. The Latin word for "dressed in white" was *candidatus.* In time this word came to be used for the person himself, or the candidate. The Latin word *candidatus* came from *candidus,* meaning "bright, shining white." This in turn came from *candēre,* a verb meaning "to shine, be bright." Latin *candēre* has given us two other English words: *candid,* which at first meant "white, free from prejudice" but now usually means "honest, natural," and *candle,* the mass of wax with a wick that is burned to give off a bright light. [from Latin *candidatus* "candidate," from *candidatus* (adjective) "dressed in white," from *candidus* "shining white," from *candēre* "to be bright, shine" —related to CANDID, CANDLE]

Lists of Undefined Words

Lists of words appear without definitions at the following prefix entries in this dictionary:

non-	re-
over-	un-

The meanings of the listed compounds formed with these prefixes are easily understandable from the meaning of the prefix and the meaning of the base word. Compounds that are not easily understandable in this way are entered at their own place with definitions. For example, **nonobjective** is entered and defined at its own place because its meaning is not easily understandable as the sum of the meanings of **non-** and **objective**.

Abbreviations Used in This Dictionary

A.D.	anno Domini		**n pl**	noun plural
adj	adjective		**NW**	northwest, northwestern
adv	adverb		**pl**	plural
a.m.	ante meridiem		**p.m.**	post meridiem
B.C.	before Christ		**prep**	preposition
C	Celsius, centigrade		**pron**	pronoun
cap	capitalized		**S**	south, southern
conj	conjunction		**SE**	southeast, southeastern
constr	construction		**sing**	singular
E	east, eastern		**SSE**	south-southeast
ENE	east-northeast		**SSW**	south-southwest
ESE	east-southeast		**SW**	southwest, southwestern
esp	especially		**U.S.**	United States
F	Fahrenheit		**U.S.S.R.**	Union of Soviet Socialist Republics
interj	interjection		**usu**	usually
n	noun		**vb**	verb
N	north, northern		**W**	west, western
NE	northeast, northeastern		**WNW**	west-northwest
NNE	north-northeast		**WSW**	west-southwest
NNW	north-northwest			

Pronunciation Symbols

ə	....	(called *schwa* \'shwä\) banana, collide, abut; in stressed syllables as in humdrum, mother, abut
ᵊ	....	used before \l\, \n\, and \m\, as in battle, mitten, and one pronunciation of open \'ōp-ᵊm\
ər	....	further, merger
a	....	ax, map
ā	....	age, vacation, day
ä	....	father, cot, cart
ȧ	....	used for a sound between \a\ and \ä\, as in an eastern New England pronunciation of aunt, half
au̇	....	out, now
b	....	baby, rib
ch	....	chin, match, nature \'nā-chər\
d	....	did, ladder
e	....	less
ē	....	seaweed, any, serial, cereal
f	....	fifty, cuff, phone
g	....	gift, pig, bigger
h	....	hat, ahead
hw	....	whale as pronounced by those who do not pronounce *whale* and *wail* the same
i	....	trip
ī	....	life, buy, my
j	....	job, gem, edge
k	....	kin, cook, chasm
k̲	....	used for a rasping sound between \k\ and \h\, as in German ich, Buch, one pronunciation of loch, chutzpah
l	....	lily, pool, mortal
m	....	murmur
n	....	nine, cotton
ŋ	....	sing, singer, finger, ink
ō	....	low, bone, cooperate
ȯ	....	moth, law, sort, all

œ	....	French bœuf, German Hölle
œ̄	....	French feu, German Hölhe
ȯi	....	coin, destroy
p	....	pepper, lip
r	....	rarity
s	....	spice, less
sh	....	shy, dish, machine, mission, special
t	....	tight, latter
th	....	thin, ether
t̲h̲	....	this, either
ü	....	boot, rule
u̇	....	foot, pull
ᵫ	....	German füllen, hübsch
ᵫ̄	....	French rue, German fühlen
v	....	give, vivid
w	....	we, away
y	....	you, yet
yü	....	few, union, mule, youth
yu̇	....	furious
z	....	zone, raise
zh	....	vision, beige
\ \	....	slant lines used in pairs to mark the beginning and end of a pronunciation: \'pen\
'	....	mark at the beginning of a syllable that has primary (strongest) stress: \'pen-ə-ˌtrāt\
ˌ	....	mark at the beginning of a syllable that has secondary (next-strongest) stress: \'pen-ə-ˌtrāt\
-	....	mark of syllable division in pronunciations [the mark of end-of-line division in boldface entry words is a centered dot · and the position of the two kinds of division often does not agree, as in build·ing \'bil-diŋ\, spe·cial \'spesh-əl\, ca·ter \'kāt-ər\]
( )	....	parentheses indicate that what is between is present in some utterances but not in others: at fac·to·ry, \'fak-t(ə-)rē\ = \'fak-tə-rē, 'fak-trē\ or \'fak-trē, 'fak-tə-rē\

A

¹a \'ā\ *n, pl* **a's** *or* **as** *often cap* **1** : the first letter of the English alphabet **2** : a musical note referred to by the letter A : the sixth tone of a C-major scale **3** : a grade rating a student's work as superior

²a \ə, (')ā\ *indefinite article* **1** : someone or something unspecified ⟨*a* man in the street⟩ ⟨*a* dozen⟩ **2** : the same : ONE ⟨two of *a* kind⟩ ⟨birds of *a* feather⟩ **3** : of whatever kind : ANY ⟨*a* person who is sick can't work well⟩ — used in all senses before words beginning with a consonant sound; compare AN [Old English *ān* "one"]

³a \ə, (')ā\ *prep* : in each : to each : for each ⟨twice *a* week⟩ ⟨one *a* piece⟩ [Old English *a-, an, on* "on"]

¹a- \ə\ *prefix* **1** : on : in : at ⟨abed⟩ **2** : in a specified state or condition ⟨afire⟩ **3** : in a specified manner ⟨aloud⟩ **4** : in the act or process of ⟨gone *a*-hunting⟩ [Old English *a-* "on, in, at"]

²a- \(')ā\ *or* **an-** \(')an\ *prefix* : not : without ⟨asexual⟩ — *a-* before consonants other than *h* and sometimes before *h*, *an-* before vowels and usually before *h* ⟨anhydrate⟩ [Greek *a-, an-* "not"]

aard·vark \'ärd-ˌvärk\ *n* : a large burrowing African mammal that feeds on insects and especially termites with its long sticky tongue [from obsolete Afrikaans, literally "earth pig"]

ab- *prefix* : from : away : departing from ⟨abnormal⟩ [Latin *ab-* "from, away"]

aardvark

ab·a·ca \ˌab-ə-'kä, 'ab-ə-ˌkä\ *n* : a strong fiber that comes from a banana plant native to the Philippines — called also *Manila hemp*

aback \ə-'bak\ *adv* **1** *archaic* : ²BACK 1, BACKWARD **2** : by surprise : UNAWARES ⟨taken *aback* by the turn of events⟩

aba·cus \'ab-ə-kəs, ə-'bak-əs\ *n, pl* **aba·ci** \'ab-ə-ˌsī, -ˌkē; ə-'bak-ˌī\ *or* **aba·cus·es** : an instrument for making calculations by sliding counters along rods or in grooves

abacus

¹abaft \ə-'baft\ *adv* : toward the stern : at the stern

²abaft *prep* : to the rear of; *esp* : toward the stern from

ab·a·lo·ne \ˌab-ə-'lō-nē, 'ab-ə-ˌ\ *n* : a mollusk with a flattened slightly spiral shell that has holes along the edge and is lined with mother-of-pearl

¹aban·don \ə-'ban-dən\ *vb* **1** : to give up completely **2** : to withdraw from often in the face of danger ⟨*abandon* ship⟩ **3** : to withdraw protection, support, or help from ⟨*abandoned* the dog⟩ **4** : to give oneself up to an emotion — **abandoner** *n* — **aban·don·ment** \-mənt\ *n*

synonyms ABANDON, DESERT, FORSAKE mean to leave without intending to return. ABANDON suggests that the person or thing left behind is helpless or needs protection ⟨the baby was *abandoned* on the steps of the church⟩. DESERT suggests the breaking of a promise, duty, or relationship ⟨*deserted* the cause when there was trouble⟩ ⟨mining towns that were *deserted* after the gold rush⟩. FORSAKE stresses leaving behind something known or loved well ⟨could not *forsake* her friends⟩.

²abandon *n* : a complete yielding to natural impulses; *esp* : ENTHUSIASM 1, EXUBERANCE

aban·doned \ə-'ban-dənd\ *adj* **1** : that has been deserted : left empty or unused ⟨an *abandoned* house⟩ **2** : completely free from restraint ⟨*abandoned* laughter⟩

abase \ə-'bās\ *vb* **abased; abas·ing** : to lower in rank or position : HUMBLE, DEGRADE — **abase·ment** \-mənt\ *n*

abash \ə-'bash\ *vb* : to destroy the self-control or self-confidence of *synonyms* see EMBARRASS — **abash·ment** \-mənt\ *n*

abate \ə-'bāt\ *vb* **abat·ed; abat·ing** : to make or become less ⟨the wind *abated*⟩ ⟨*abated* their prices⟩ — **abat·er** *n*

abate·ment \ə-'bāt-mənt\ *n* **1** : the act or process of abating **2** : an amount abated (as from a tax)

ab·at·toir \'ab-ə-ˌtwär\ *n* : SLAUGHTERHOUSE

ab·bess \'ab-əs\ *n* : the head of a convent of nuns

ab·bey \'ab-ē\ *n, pl* **abbeys** **1 a** : MONASTERY **b** : CONVENT **2** : a church that once belonged to an abbey ⟨Westminster *Abbey*⟩

ab·bot \'ab-ət\ *n* : the head of a monastery for men

ab·bre·vi·ate \ə-'brē-vē-ˌāt\ *vb* **-at·ed; -at·ing** : to make briefer : SHORTEN; *esp* : to reduce (as a word) to a shorter form intended to stand for the whole [Middle English *abbreviaten* "abbreviate," from Latin *abbreviatus* "made short," from *abbreviare* "to shorten," from earlier *ad-* "to" and *brevis* "short" — related to ABRIDGE, BRIEF]

ab·bre·vi·a·tion \ə-ˌbrē-vē-'ā-shən\ *n* **1** : the act or result of abbreviating : ABRIDGMENT **2** : a shortened form of a written word or phrase used in place of the whole

Ab·di·as \ab-'dī-əs\ *n* : OBADIAH

ab·di·cate \'ab-di-ˌkāt\ *vb* **-cat·ed; -cat·ing** : to formally give up sovereign power, office, or responsibility — **ab·di·ca·tion** \ˌab-di-'kā-shən\ *n*

ab·do·men \'ab-də-mən, ab-'dō-mən\ *n* **1 a** : the part of the body between the chest and the hips **b** : the body cavity containing the chief digestive organs — called also *abdominal cavity* **2** : the hind portion of the body behind the thorax in an arthropod — see INSECT illustration — **ab·dom·i·nal** \ab-'däm-ən-ᵊl, -nᵊl\ *adj* — **ab·dom·i·nal·ly** \-ē\ *adv*

ab·duct \ab-'dəkt\ *vb* **1** : to carry (a person) off by force **2** : to draw (a part of the body) away from a middle plane or line that divides the body or a bodily part into right and left halves — **ab·duc·tion** \-'dək-shən\ *n*

ab·duc·tor \ab-'dək-tər\ *n* : one that abducts; *esp* : a muscle that draws a body part (as an arm or finger) away from a plane or a line that divides the body or a hand or foot into right and left halves

abeam \ə-'bēm\ *adv or adj* : at right angles to a ship or plane's length

abed \ə-'bed\ *adv or adj* : in bed

Ab·er·deen An·gus \ˌab-ər-ˌdē-'naŋ-gəs\ *n* : ANGUS

ab·er·rant \ə-'ber-ənt, 'ab-ə-rənt\ *adj* : being different from the usual or natural type

ab·er·ra·tion \ˌab-ə-'rā-shən\ *n* **1** : the act of differing especially from a moral standard or normal state **2** : unsoundness or disorder of the mind **3** : a small regularly occurring change of apparent position in heavenly bodies

\ə\ **abut**	\au̇\ **out**	\i\ **tip**	\ȯ\ **saw**	\u̇\ **foot**
\ər\ **further**	\ch\ **chin**	\ī\ **life**	\ȯi\ **coin**	\y\ **yet**
\a\ **mat**	\e\ **pet**	\j\ **job**	\th\ **thin**	\yü\ **few**
\ā\ **take**	\ē\ **easy**	\ŋ\ **sing**	\th\ **this**	\yu̇\ **cure**
\ä\ **cot, cart**	\g\ **go**	\ō\ **bone**	\ü\ **food**	\zh\ **vision**

due to the combined effect of the motion of light and the motion of the observer

abet \ə-'bet\ *vb* **abet·ted; abet·ting** : to actively encourage or aid — **abet·ment** \-mənt\ *n* — **abet·tor** *also* **abet·ter** \-'bet-ər\ *n*

abey·ance \ə-'bā-ən(t)s\ *n* : a temporary interruption of activity ⟨plans held in *abeyance*⟩ — **abey·ant** \-ənt\ *adj*

ab·hor \əb-'hò(ə)r, ab-\ *vb* **ab·horred; ab·hor·ring** : to shrink from in disgust **synonyms** see HATE — **ab·hor·rence** \-'hòr-ən(t)s, -'här-\ *n* — **ab·hor·rer** \-'hòr-ər\ *n*

ab·hor·rent \əb-'hòr-ənt, -'här-, ab-\ *adj* **1** : causing or deserving strong dislike **2** : not agreeable : CONTRARY ⟨a notion *abhorrent* to their beliefs⟩ — **ab·hor·rent·ly** *adv*

abide \ə-'bīd\ *vb* **abode** \-'bōd\ *or* **abid·ed; abid·ing 1** : to wait for **2** : to bear patiently : TOLERATE **3** : ¹LAST 1, ENDURE ⟨an *abiding* friendship⟩ **4** : to live or continue in a place : DWELL — **abid·ance** \ə-'bīd-ən(t)s\ *n* — **abid·er** *n* — **abide by** : to accept the terms of : be obedient to ⟨*abide by* the rules⟩

abil·i·ty \ə-'bil-ət-ē\ *n, pl* **-ties 1 a** : the quality or state of being able : power to do something **b** : competence in doing : SKILL **2** : natural or learned skill
  synonyms ABILITY, APTITUDE, TALENT mean the capacity for doing or achieving something. ABILITY suggests having from birth the power to do a thing especially well ⟨always has had the *ability* to run fast⟩. APTITUDE suggests a quickness to learn and a natural liking usually for a field or activity ⟨people with a natural *aptitude* for computers⟩. TALENT suggests a great ability to create things and one that needs to be developed ⟨you should work on your *talent* for writing short stories⟩.

-abil·i·ty *also* **-ibil·i·ty** \ə-'bil-ət-ē\ *n suffix, pl* **-ties** : ability, fitness, or likeliness to act or be acted on in (such) a way ⟨read*ability*⟩ [derived from Latin *-abilitas, -ibilitas* "-ability"]

ab·ject \'ab-,jekt\ *adj* : very low in spirit or hope : WRETCHED ⟨*abject* misery⟩ ⟨an *abject* coward⟩ — **ab·ject·ly** \'ab-,jek-(t)lē, ab-'jek-\ *adv* — **ab·ject·ness** \-,jek(t)-nəs, -'jek(t)-\ *n*

ab·jure \ab-'jù(ə)r\ *vb* **ab·jured; ab·jur·ing** : to give up, abandon, or reject solemnly ⟨*abjure* allegiance⟩

ab·late \a-'blāt\ *vb* **ab·lat·ed; ab·lat·ing** : to remove or become removed by cutting, wearing away, evaporating, or vaporizing

ab·la·tion \a-'blā-shən\ *n* : the process of ablating: as **a** : surgical cutting and removal **b** : removal of a part (as the outside of a nose cone) by melting or vaporization

ablaze \ə-'blāz\ *adj* **1** : being on fire **2** : radiant with light or bright color

able \'ā-bəl\ *adj* **abler** \-b(ə-)lər\; **ablest** \-b(ə-)ləst\ **1 a** : having enough power, skill, or resources to do something ⟨*able* to swim⟩ **b** : not prevented ⟨*able* to vote⟩ **2** : SKILLFUL, COMPETENT ⟨an *able* editor⟩ [Middle English *able* "able," from early French *able* (same meaning), from Latin *habilis* "easily managed, skillful," from *habēre* "to have"]

-able *also* **-ible** \ə-bəl\ *adj suffix* **1** : capable of, fit for, or worthy of being ⟨collect*ible*⟩ **2** : tending, given, or likely to ⟨perish*able*⟩ ⟨agree*able*⟩ [derived from Latin *-abilis, -ibilis* "-able"]

able–bod·ied \,ā-bəl-'bäd-ēd\ *adj* : having a healthy strong body : physically fit

abloom \ə-'blüm\ *adj* : being in bloom

ab·lu·tion \ə-'blü-shən, a-'blü-\ *n* : washing oneself especially as a religious rite

ably \'ā-blē\ *adv* : in an able manner

ABM \,ā-(,)bē-'em\ *n* : ANTIBALLISTIC MISSILE

ab·ne·gate \'ab-ni-,gāt\ *vb* **-gat·ed; -gat·ing 1** : to give up a right or privilege ⟨*abnegate* her power⟩ **2** : to deny to oneself : RENOUNCE ⟨*abnegating* outdated beliefs⟩ — **ab·ne·ga·tion** \,ab-ni-'gā-shən\ *n*

ab·nor·mal \(')ab-'nòr-məl\ *adj* : differing from the normal or average : UNUSUAL — **ab·nor·mal·ly** \-mə-lē\ *adv*

ab·nor·mal·i·ty \,ab-nər-'mal-ət-ē, -(,)nòr-\ *n, pl* **-ties 1** : the state of being abnormal **2** : something abnormal

¹**aboard** \ə-'bōrd, -'bòrd\ *adv* : on, onto, or within a vehicle (as a car, ship, or airplane)

²**aboard** *prep* : on or into especially as a passenger ⟨go *aboard* ship⟩

abode \ə-'bōd\ *n* : the place where one stays or lives

abol·ish \ə-'bäl-ish\ *vb* : to do away with completely : put an end to — **abol·ish·able** \-ə-bəl\ *adj* — **abol·ish·er** *n* — **abol·ish·ment** \-mənt\ *n*

ab·o·li·tion \,ab-ə-'lish-ən\ *n* **1** : the act of abolishing : the state of being abolished **2** : the abolishing of slavery — **ab·o·li·tion·ary** \-'lish-ə-,ner-ē\ *adj*

ab·o·li·tion·ist \,ab-ə-'lish-(ə-)nəst\ *n* : a person who is in favor of abolishing especially slavery — **ab·o·li·tion·ism** \-'lish-ə-,niz-əm\ *n*

A–bomb \'ā-,bäm\ *n* : ATOMIC BOMB

abom·i·na·ble \ə-'bäm-(ə-)nə-bəl\ *adj* **1** : deserving or causing disgust : HATEFUL, DETESTABLE ⟨*abominable* behavior⟩ **2** : quite disagreeable ⟨*abominable* weather⟩ — **abom·i·na·bly** \-blē\ *adv*

abominable snow·man \-'snō-mən, -,man\ *n, often cap A&S* : a creature somewhat resembling a human being or ape that is thought to exist in the Himalayas and is usually held to be a bear

abom·i·nate \ə-'bäm-ə-,nāt\ *vb* **-nat·ed; -nat·ing** : HATE, LOATHE — **abom·i·na·tor** \-,nāt-ər\ *n*

abom·i·na·tion \ə-,bäm-ə-'nā-shən\ *n* **1** : something detestable **2** : extreme disgust and hatred : LOATHING

ab·orig·i·nal \,ab-ə-'rij-nəl, -ən-²l\ *adj* **1** : being the first of its kind in a region : INDIGENOUS **2** : of, relating to, or being aborigines — **ab·orig·i·nal·ly** \-'lish-ə-\ *adv*

ab·orig·i·ne \,ab-ə-'rij-ə-(,)nē\ *n* **1** : a member of the original people to live in an area : NATIVE **2** *often cap* : a member of any of the native people of Australia [from Latin *aborigines* "original inhabitants," from *ab origine* "from the beginning," from *origin-, origo* "beginning, source," from *oriri* "to rise" — related to ORIGIN]

abort \ə-'bòrt\ *vb* **1** : to bring forth premature or stillborn offspring **2** : to become checked in development **3** : to put an end to before completion ⟨*abort* a project⟩

abor·tion \ə-'bòr-shən\ *n* **1** : a premature birth whether natural or caused artificially that occurs before the fetus can survive **2** : failure of a project or action to reach full development; *also* : a result of such failure

abor·tion·ist \ə-'bòr-sh(ə-)nəst\ *n* : one who produces abortions

abor·tive \ə-'bòrt-iv\ *adj* **1** : failing to achieve the desired conclusion or result : UNSUCCESSFUL ⟨an *abortive* attempt to escape⟩ **2** : imperfectly formed or developed : RUDIMENTARY — **abor·tive·ly** *adv* — **abor·tive·ness** *n*

abound \ə-'baund\ *vb* **1** : to be present in large numbers or in great quantity ⟨wildlife *abounds*⟩ **2** : to be filled or abundantly supplied ⟨a stream *abounding* in fish⟩

¹**about** \ə-'baut\ *adv* **1** : on all sides : AROUND ⟨wander *about*⟩ ⟨people standing *about*⟩ **2 a** : reasonably close to : APPROXIMATELY, NEARLY ⟨*about* three years⟩ ⟨*about* ready to go⟩ **b** : on the verge of ⟨is *about* to go home⟩ **3** : in the opposite direction ⟨face *about*⟩

²**about** *prep* **1** : on every side of : AROUND ⟨houses *about* the lake⟩ **2 a** : ²NEAR **b** : in the possession of ⟨had no pencil *about* her⟩ **c** : in the control of ⟨keeps her wits *about* her⟩ **3** : in the act or process of doing ⟨do it well while you're *about* it⟩ **4** : having to do with : CONCERNING ⟨tell me *about* it⟩ ⟨a book *about* birds⟩ **5** : over or in different parts of ⟨traveled *about* the country⟩

about–face \ə-'baut-'fās\ *n* **1** : a reversal of direction **2** : a reversal of attitude or point of view — **about–face** *vb*

¹**above** \ə-'bəv\ *adv* **1** : in or to a higher place : OVERHEAD

2 : higher on the same or a preceding page 3 : in or to a higher rank or number

²**above** *prep* 1 : in or to a higher place than : OVER 2 : superior to ⟨a captain is *above* a lieutenant⟩ ⟨*above* criticism⟩ 3 : too proud or honorable to stoop to ⟨*above* such mean tricks⟩ 4 : exceeding in number, quantity, or size : more than ⟨*above* the average⟩ 5 : as distinct from and in addition to ⟨heard the bell *above* the roar of the crowd⟩

³**above** *adj* : written above

above·board \ə-'bəv-ˌbōrd, -ˌbȯrd\ *adv or adj* : without concealment or deceit

above·ground \ə-'bəv-ˌgraund\ *adj* : located or happening on or above the surface of the ground ⟨an *aboveground* swimming pool⟩

ab·ra·ca·dab·ra \ˌab-rə-kə-'dab-rə\ *n* 1 : a magical charm or word 2 : unintelligible language : JARGON

abrade \ə-'brād\ *vb* **abrad·ed; abrad·ing** 1 : to rub or wear away especially by friction 2 : to irritate or roughen by rubbing — **abrad·er** *n*

abra·sion \ə-'brā-zhən\ *n* 1 : a rubbing, grinding, or wearing away by friction 2 : a place where the surface has been rubbed or scraped off ⟨an *abrasion* on her knee⟩

¹**abra·sive** \ə-'brā-siv, -ziv\ *adj* : having the effect of abrading — **abra·sive·ly** *adv* — **abra·sive·ness** *n*

²**abrasive** *n* : a substance (as sand) used for grinding, smoothing, or polishing

abreast \ə-'brest\ *adv or adj* 1 : side by side with bodies in line ⟨lined up three *abreast*⟩ 2 : up to a standard or level especially of knowledge ⟨keep *abreast* of the times⟩

abridge \ə-'brij\ *vb* **abridged; abridg·ing** 1 : to make less : DIMINISH ⟨forbidden to *abridge* the rights of citizens⟩ 2 : to shorten in duration or extent 3 : to shorten by omission of words : CONDENSE [Middle English *abregen* "deprive, reduce," from early French *abreger* (same meaning), from Latin *abbreviare* "to shorten" — related to ABBREVIATE] — **abridg·er** *n*

abridg·ment *or* **abridge·ment** \ə-'brij-mənt\ *n* 1 a : the action of abridging b : the state of being abridged 2 : a shortened form of a written work

abroad \ə-'brȯd\ *adv or adj* 1 : over a wide area 2 : away from one's home ⟨doesn't go *abroad* at night⟩ 3 : in or to foreign countries ⟨travel *abroad*⟩ 4 : in wide circulation ⟨rumors were *abroad*⟩

ab·ro·gate \'ab-rə-ˌgāt\ *vb* **-gat·ed; -gat·ing** : to do away with or cancel by authority ⟨*abrogate* a law⟩ — **ab·ro·ga·tion** \ˌab-rə-'gā-shən\ *n*

abrupt \ə-'brəpt\ *adj* 1 a : SUDDEN 1a ⟨an *abrupt* change in the weather⟩ b : rudely brief : CURT ⟨an *abrupt* manner⟩ 2 : ¹STEEP 1 ⟨the high *abrupt* bank of a stream⟩ — **abrupt·ly** \ə-'brup-(t)lē\ *adv* — **abrupt·ness** \ə-'brəpt-nəs\ *n*

Word History If a person is rudely brief in speech or manner or stops you before you finish talking, you could say that that person is abrupt. If a road ends suddenly, you could say that the road comes to an abrupt end. In both of these cases you might think of something that is abrupt as "breaking off." *Abrupt* comes from the Latin word *abruptus,* meaning "broken off, ending suddenly." That word is formed (with the addition of the prefix *ab-,* meaning "from") from the Latin word *rumpere,* meaning "to break." Latin *rumpere* has given us several other English words that carry the idea of breaking: *interrupt, rupture,* and *corrupt.* [from Latin *abruptus* "abrupt," derived from *abrumpere* "to break off," from *ab-* "from" and *rumpere* "to break" — related to CORRUPT, INTERRUPT, RUPTURE]

ab·scess \'ab-ˌses\ *n* : a collection of pus surrounded by inflamed tissue at some point in the body — **ab·scessed** \-ˌsest\ *adj*

ab·scis·sa \ab-'sis-ə\ *n* : the number in an ordered pair of numbers (as *x* in (*x, y*)) that gives the location of a point

along the x-axis — called also *x-coordinate*; compare ORDINATE

ab·scis·sion \ab-'sizh-ən\ *n* 1 : the act or process of cutting off 2 : the natural separation of flowers, fruit, or leaves from plants

ab·scond \ab-'skänd, əb-\ *vb* : to leave secretly and hide oneself — **ab·scond·er** *n*

ab·sence \'ab-sən(t)s\ *n* 1 : the state of being absent 2 : the time that one is absent 3 : ²WANT 1a, LACK ⟨*absence* of detail⟩

abscissa: *A* is the abscissa of point *P*

¹**ab·sent** \'ab-sənt\ *adj* 1 : not present or attending : MISSING 2 : not existing ⟨enthusiasm was *absent*⟩ 3 : lost in thought : PREOCCUPIED — **ab·sent·ly** *adv*

²**ab·sent** \ab-'sent\ *vb* : to keep (oneself) away

ab·sen·tee \ˌab-sən-'tē\ *n* : a person who is absent — **ab·sentee** *adj*

ab·sent·mind·ed \ˌab-sənt-'mīn-dəd\ *adj* : lost in thought and unaware of one's surroundings or actions — **ab·sent·mind·ed·ly** *adv* — **ab·sent·mind·ed·ness** *n*

ab·so·lute \'ab-sə-ˌlüt, ˌab-sə-'lüt\ *adj* 1 a : free from imperfection : PERFECT b : free or nearly free from mixture : PURE ⟨*absolute* alcohol⟩ 2 : free from restraint or limitation ⟨*absolute* power⟩ ⟨an *absolute* monarch⟩ 3 : having no exceptions ⟨an *absolute* requirement⟩ ⟨*absolute* freedom⟩ 4 : free from doubt : CERTAIN ⟨*absolute* proof⟩ 5 a : independent of standards of measurement that reflect individual choice : ACTUAL ⟨*absolute* brightness of a star⟩ ⟨*absolute* motion⟩ b : relating to or coming from the basic units of length, mass, and time ⟨*absolute* electric units⟩ c : relating to the absolute temperature scale ⟨10° *absolute*⟩ — **ab·so·lute·ness** \-ˌlüt-nəs, -'lüt-\ *n*

ab·so·lute·ly \'ab-sə-ˌlüt-lē, ˌab-sə-'lüt-\ *adv* : in an absolute way : completely or definitely ⟨you are *absolutely* right⟩

absolute temperature *n* : temperature measured on a scale that has absolute zero as the zero point

absolute value *n* : a nonnegative number that is equal to a given number with any negative sign removed ⟨the *absolute value* of -3 is 3⟩

absolute zero *n* : a hypothetical temperature that has never been reached, represents no heat at all, and is equal to approximately −273.15°C or −459.67°F

ab·so·lu·tion \ˌab-sə-'lü-shən\ *n* : the act of absolving; *esp* : a forgiving of sins

ab·solve \əb-'zälv, -'sälv, -'zȯlv, -'sȯlv\ *vb* **ab·solved; ab·solv·ing** : to set free from an obligation or punishment — **ab·solv·er** *n*

ab·sorb \əb-'sȯrb, -'zȯrb\ *vb* 1 : to take in or suck or swallow up ⟨a sponge *absorbs* water⟩ ⟨plant roots *absorb* water⟩ 2 : to hold the interest of : ENGROSS ⟨*absorbed* in thought⟩ 3 a : to receive without giving back ⟨a sound-*absorbing* surface⟩ b : to transform (radiant energy) into a different form usually with a resulting rise in temperature ⟨the earth *absorbs* the sun's rays⟩ — **ab·sorb·abil·i·ty** \əb-ˌsȯr-bə-'bil-ət-ē, -ˌzȯr-\ *n* — **ab·sorb·able** \əb-'sȯr-bə-bəl, -'zȯr-\ *adj* — **ab·sorb·er** *n*

ab·sor·bent \əb-'sȯr-bənt, -'zȯr-\ *adj* : able to absorb ⟨as

\ə\	abut	\au̇\	out	\i\	tip	\o̅\	saw	\u̇\	foot
\ər\	further	\ch\	chin	\ī\	life	\o̅i\	coin	\y\	yet
\a\	mat	\e\	pet	\j\	job	\th\	thin	\yü\	few
\ā\	take	\ē\	easy	\ŋ\	sing	\th\	this	\yu̇\	cure
\ä\	cot, cart	\g\	go	\ō\	bone	\ü\	food	\zh\	vision

absorbent as a sponge⟩ — **ab·sor·ben·cy** \əb-'sör-bən-sē, -'zör-\ *n* — **absorbent** *n*

ab·sorp·tion \əb-'sörp-shən, -'zörp-\ *n* **1** : the process of absorbing or being absorbed: as **a** : the passing of digested food through the wall of the intestines into the blood or lymph **b** : the stopping and taking in especially of radiant energy or sound waves **2** : entire occupation of the mind — **ab·sorp·tive** \-'sörp-tiv, -'zörp-\ *adj*

ab·stain \əb-'stān\ *vb* : to keep oneself from doing something ⟨*abstain* from voting⟩ — **ab·stain·er** *n*

ab·ste·mi·ous \ab-'stē-mē-əs\ *adj* : not eating and drinking much — **ab·ste·mi·ous·ly** *adv*

ab·sten·tion \əb-'sten-chən, ab-\ *n* : the act or practice of abstaining; *esp* : a formal refusal to vote ⟨3 ayes, 5 nays, and 2 *abstentions*⟩

ab·sti·nence \'ab-stə-nən(t)s\ *n* **1** : an abstaining from giving in to an appetite or from eating some foods **2 a** : habitual abstaining from drinking alcoholic beverages **b** : abstention from sexual intercourse — **ab·sti·nent** \-nənt\ *adj* — **ab·sti·nent·ly** *adv*

¹**ab·stract** \ab-'strakt, 'ab-ˌstrakt\ *adj* **1** : expressing a quality or idea without reference to an actual person or thing ⟨*"honesty"* is an *abstract* word⟩ **2** : difficult to understand : HARD ⟨*abstract* problems⟩ **3** : using elements of form (as color, line, or texture) with little or no attempt at creating a realistic picture ⟨*abstract* art⟩ [from Latin *abstractus* "abstract," from earlier *abstrahere* "to draw away," from *abs-, ab-* "from, away" and *trahere* "to draw" — related to ATTRACT, ¹TRACE, ³TRACE] — **ab·stract·ly** \ab-'strak-(t)lē, 'ab-ˌstrak-\ *adv* — **ab·stract·ness** \ab-'strak(t)-nəs, 'ab-ˌstrak(t)-\ *n*

²**ab·stract** \'ab-ˌstrakt\ *n* : a brief statement of the main points or facts : SUMMARY

³**ab·stract** \ab-'strakt, 'ab-ˌstrakt, *in sense 3 usually* 'ab-ˌstrakt\ *vb* **1** : to take out : REMOVE ⟨*abstract* a diamond from a pile of sand⟩ **2** : to consider apart from a particular instance ⟨*abstract* the idea of roundness from a ball⟩ **3** : to make an abstract of : SUMMARIZE **4** : to draw away the attention of — **ab·strac·tor** *or* **ab·stract·er** \-'straktər, -ˌstrak-\ *n*

ab·stract·ed \ab-'strak-təd, 'ab-ˌstrak-\ *adj* : PREOCCUPIED 1, ABSENTMINDED — **ab·stract·ed·ly** *adv* — **abstract·ed·ness** *n*

ab·strac·tion \ab-'strak-shən\ *n* **1 a** : the act or process of abstracting : the state of being abstracted **b** : an abstract idea or term **2** : an artistic composition or creation having designs that do not represent actual objects — **ab·strac·tive** \-'strak-tiv\ *adj*

ab·struse \əb-'strüs, ab-\ *adj* : hard to understand — **ab·struse·ly** *adv* — **ab·struse·ness** *n*

ab·surd \əb-'sərd, -'zərd\ *adj* : completely unreasonable or untrue : RIDICULOUS — **ab·sur·di·ty** \-'sərd-ət-ē, -'zərd-\ *n* — **ab·surd·ly** *adv* — **ab·surd·ness** *n*

abun·dance \ə-'bən-dən(t)s\ *n* **1** : a large quantity : PLENTY **2** : WEALTH 1

abun·dant \ə-'bən-dənt\ *adj* : existing in or possessing abundance : ABOUNDING *synonyms* see PLENTIFUL — **abun·dant·ly** *adv*

¹**abuse** \ə-'byüz\ *vb* **abused; abus·ing** **1 a** : to use wrongly : MISUSE ⟨*abuse* a privilege⟩ **b** : to use excessively ⟨*abuse* alcohol⟩ **2** : to treat cruelly : MISTREAT ⟨*abuse* a dog⟩ **3** : to attack in words : scold rudely — **abus·er** *n*

²**abuse** \ə-'byüs\ *n* **1** : a corrupt practice or custom ⟨election *abuses*⟩ **2 a** : improper or excessive use or treatment : MISUSE ⟨*abuse* of privileges⟩ ⟨drug *abuse*⟩ **b** : physical mistreatment **3** : harsh insulting language

abu·sive \ə-'byü-siv, -ziv\ *adj* : using or characterized by abuse — **abu·sive·ly** *adv* — **abu·sive·ness** *n*

abut \ə-'bət\ *vb* **abut·ted; abut·ting** : to touch along a border or with a part that sticks out — **abut·ter** *n*

abut·ment \ə-'bət-mənt\ *n* **1** : the place of abutting **2**

: something against which another thing rests its weight or pushes with force ⟨*abutments* that support a bridge⟩

abutment 2

abys·mal \ə-'biz-məl\ *adj* **1** : resembling an abyss in huge extent ⟨*abysmal* ignorance⟩ **2** : ABYSSAL — **abys·mal·ly** \-mə-lē\ *adv*

abyss \ə-'bis\ *n* : a gulf so deep or a space so great that it cannot be measured

abys·sal \ə-'bis-əl\ *adj* : of or relating to the bottom waters of the ocean depths

ac- — see AD-

aca·cia \ə-'kā-shə\ *n* **1** : GUM ARABIC **2** : any of numerous shrubs and trees of the legume family that grow in warm areas and have white or yellow flower clusters

ac·a·dem·ic \ˌak-ə-'dem-ik\ *adj* **1** : of or relating to school or college **2** : literary or general rather than technical ⟨took the *academic* course⟩ **3** : having no practical importance : THEORETICAL ⟨an *academic* question⟩ — **ac·a·dem·i·cal·ly** \-'dem-i-k(ə-)lē\ *adv*

acad·e·my \ə-'kad-ə-mē\ *n, pl* **-mies** **1 a** : ¹SCHOOL 1a; *esp* : a private high school **b** : an institution for training in special subjects or skills ⟨military *academy*⟩ **2** : an organization of people specializing in knowledge in a particular subject

acacia 2

Word History Our word *academy* comes from the Greek word *Akadēmeia*, the name of the park or grove outside of ancient Athens where the philosopher Plato taught his students. Just as schools and parks today are often named after famous persons, the *Akadēmeia* had been named in honor of a Greek hero, *Akadēmos*. [Greek *Akadēmeia*, the grove outside Athens where Plato had his school]

a cap·pel·la *also* **a ca·pel·la** \ˌäk-ə-'pel-ə\ *adv or adj* : without accompanying instrumental music ⟨sing *a cappella*⟩ [from Italian *a cappella* "in chapel style"]

ac·cede \ak-'sēd, ik-\ *vb* **ac·ced·ed; ac·ced·ing** **1** : to give consent : AGREE ⟨*accede* to a proposed plan⟩ **2** : to enter upon an office or position ⟨*acceded* to the throne in 1838⟩

ac·ce·le·ran·do \(ˌ)ä-ˌchel-ə-'rän-dō\ *adv or adj* : gradually faster — used as a direction in music

ac·cel·er·ate \ik-'sel-ə-ˌrāt, ak-\ *vb* **-at·ed; -at·ing** **1** : to bring about earlier ⟨*accelerated* our departure⟩ **2** : to move or cause to move faster — **ac·cel·er·a·tive** \-ˌrāt-iv\ *adj*

ac·cel·er·a·tion \ik-ˌsel-ə-'rā-shən, ak-\ *n* **1** : the act or process of accelerating : the state of being accelerated **2** : the rate of change of velocity with respect to time; *also* : change in velocity

acceleration of gravity : the acceleration of a freely falling body under the influence of gravity that is expressed as the rate of increase of velocity per unit of time and that amounts to a value of about 9.81 meters (32.2 feet) per second per second

ac·cel·er·a·tor \ik-'sel-ə-ˌrāt-ər, ak-\ *n* **1** : one that accelerates **2** : a device (as a pedal) in a motor vehicle used to control the speed of the motor **3** : a device that is used to give high velocities to charged particles (as electrons and protons)

ac·cel·er·om·e·ter \ik-ˌsel-ə-'räm-ət-ər, ak-\ *n* : an instrument for measuring acceleration or for detecting and measuring vibrations

¹ac·cent \'ak-ˌsent\ *n* **1** : a way of talking shared by a group (as the people of a country) **2** : greater stress or force given to a syllable of a word in speaking ⟨*before* has the *accent* on the last syllable⟩ **3** : a mark (as ´, `, or ^ accents) identifying a syllable that is stressed in speaking **4** : greater stress given to a beat in music **5** : an emphasized detail used for contrast

²ac·cent \ak-'sent, 'ak-ˌsent\ *vb* **1** : to make more noticeable : EMPHASIZE **2 a** : to say with an accent : STRESS **b** : to mark with a written or printed accent

accent mark *n* **1**

¹ACCENT 3 **2** : one of several symbols used to indicate musical stress

ac·cen·tu·ate \ik-'sen-chə-ˌwāt, ak-\ *vb* **-at·ed; -at·ing** **1** : to pronounce or mark with an accent **2**

accent mark 2

: EMPHASIZE ⟨the blue shirt *accentuates* your eyes⟩ — **ac·cen·tu·a·tion** \ik-ˌsen-chə-'wā-shən, (ˌ)ak-\ *n*

ac·cept \ik-'sept, ak-\ *vb* **1 a** : to receive or take willingly ⟨*accept* a gift⟩ ⟨*accepted* her as a member⟩ **b** : to be able or designed to take or hold (something applied or added) ⟨a surface that will not *accept* ink⟩ ⟨a computer program ready to *accept* commands⟩ **2 a** : to agree to ⟨*accept* an offer⟩ **b** : to agree to undertake (a responsibility) ⟨*accept* a job⟩ **c** : to take on an obligation to pay; *also* : to take in payment ⟨don't *accept* checks⟩ **3** : to think of as proper or normal ⟨the idea is widely *accepted*⟩ [Middle English *accepten* "receive, accept," from early French *accepter* (same meaning), derived from Latin *accipere* "receive," from *ac-, ad-* "to" and *capere* "to take" — related to CAPTURE, EXCEPT, RECEIVE] — **ac·cept·er** *or* **ac·cep·tor** \-'sep-tər\ *n*

ac·cept·able \ik-'sep-tə-bəl, ak-\ *adj* **1** : capable of or worthy of being accepted : SATISFACTORY ⟨an *acceptable* excuse⟩ **2** : barely good enough ⟨plays an *acceptable* game⟩ — **ac·cept·abil·i·ty** \ik-ˌsep-tə-'bil-ət-ē, ak-\ *n* — **ac·cept·ably** \ik-'sep-tə-blē, ak-\ *adv*

ac·cep·tance \ik-'sep-tən(t)s, ak-\ *n* **1** : the act of accepting **2** : the quality or state of being accepted or acceptable

ac·cep·ta·tion \ˌak-ˌsep-'tā-shən\ *n* : the generally understood meaning of a word or expression

¹ac·cess \'ak-ˌses\ *n* **1** : permission or power to enter, approach, or make use of ⟨*access* to secret information⟩ ⟨Internet *access*⟩ **2** : a way or means of approach ⟨a nation's *access* to the sea⟩

²access *vb* : to get at : gain access to

ac·ces·si·ble \ik-'ses-ə-bəl, ak-\ *adj* **1** : capable of being reached ⟨a resort *accessible* by train or bus⟩ **2** : capable of being used, seen, or known : OBTAINABLE ⟨*accessible* information⟩ — **ac·ces·si·bil·i·ty** \ik-ˌses-ə-'bil-ət-ē, ak-\ *n* — **ac·ces·si·bly** \-blē\ *adv*

ac·ces·sion \ik-'sesh-ən, ak-\ *n* **1** : something added : ACQUISITION **2** : increase by something added **3** : the act of agreeing ⟨*accession* to a proposal⟩ **4** : the act of coming to office or power ⟨the *accession* of a king⟩

ac·ces·so·rize \ik-'ses-ə-ˌrīz, ak-\ *vb* **-rized; -riz·ing** : to wear or decorate with accessories

¹ac·ces·so·ry \ik-'ses-(ə-)rē, ak-\ *n, pl* **-ries** **1** : something (as an object or device) that is not necessary in itself but adds to the beauty, convenience, or effectiveness of something else **2** : a person who aids another in doing wrong or in an attempt to escape justice

²accessory *adj* : aiding or helping in a secondary way : SUPPLEMENTARY

accessory fruit *n* : a fruit (as the strawberry, apple, or fig)

of which a conspicuous part consists of tissue other than that of the ripened ovary

access time *n* : the time lag between the time stored information (as in a computer) is requested and the time it is delivered

ac·ci·dent \'ak-səd-ənt, -sə-ˌdent\ *n* **1 a** : an event occurring by chance or from unknown causes **b** : ¹CHANCE 1 ⟨we met by *accident*⟩ **2** : an unintended and usually sudden and unexpected event resulting in loss or injury ⟨an automobile *accident*⟩

¹ac·ci·den·tal \ˌak-sə-'dent-ᵊl\ *adj* **1** : happening unexpectedly or by chance ⟨an *accidental* discovery of oil⟩ **2** : not happening or done on purpose ⟨an *accidental* fall⟩ — **ac·ci·den·tal·ly** \-'dent-lē, -'dent-ᵊl-ē\ *adv*

²accidental *n* : a musical note whose pitch is changed (as by a sharp or a flat) from the pitch shown in the key signature

ac·cip·i·ter \ak-'sip-ət-ər\ *n* : any of various low-flying hawks that have short wings and long tails

¹ac·claim \ə-'klām\ *vb* **1** : to welcome with applause or great praise ⟨a novel *acclaimed* by the critics⟩ **2** : to proclaim by or as if by acclamation [from Latin *acclamare*, literally "to shout at," from *ac-, ad-* "to, toward" and *clamare* "to shout" — related to CLAIM, CLAMOR] — **ac·claim·er** *n*

²acclaim *n* **1** : the act of acclaiming **2** : APPLAUSE, PRAISE

ac·cla·ma·tion \ˌak-lə-'mā-shən\ *n* **1** : a loud eager expression of approval, praise, or agreement **2** : an overwhelming positive vote by voice ⟨elected by *acclamation*⟩

ac·cli·mate \'ak-lə-ˌmāt, ə-'klī-mət, -ˌmāt\ *vb* **-mat·ed; -mat·ing** : to adapt to a new climate, environment, or situation — **ac·cli·ma·tion** \ˌak-lə-'mā-shən, ˌak-ˌlī-\ *n*

ac·cli·ma·tize \ə-'klī-mə-ˌtīz\ *vb* **-tized; -tiz·ing** : ACCLIMATE — **ac·cli·ma·ti·za·tion** \ə-ˌklī-mət-ə-'zā-shən\ *n*

ac·co·lade \'ak-ə-ˌlād\ *n* **1** : a formal salute (as a tap on the shoulder with the blade of a sword) that marks the conferring of knighthood **2** : a mark of recognition of merit : PRAISE

ac·com·mo·date \ə-'käm-ə-ˌdāt\ *vb* **-dat·ed; -dat·ing** **1** : ADAPT **2** : to bring into agreement ⟨*accommodate* the differences⟩ **3** : to do a favor for : OBLIGE 2b ⟨*accommodated* me with a ride⟩ **4** : to provide with something desired: as **a** : to provide with lodgings **b** : to make or have room for ⟨the table *accommodates* 12 comfortably⟩ **5** : to undergo visual accommodation ⟨the lens of the eye *accommodates*⟩ **synonyms** see CONTAIN — **ac·com·mo·da·tive** \-ˌdāt-iv\ *adj* — **ac·com·mo·da·tive·ness** *n*

accommodating *adj* : ready and willing to help : OBLIGING — **ac·com·mo·dat·ing·ly** *adv*

ac·com·mo·da·tion \ə-ˌkäm-ə-'dā-shən\ *n* **1 a** : something supplied that is useful and handy **b** *pl* : lodging and meals or traveling space and related services ⟨overnight *accommodations*⟩ **2** : the act of accommodating : the state of being accommodated **3** : the automatic adjustment of the eye for seeing at different distances **4** : an adjustment of differences : SETTLEMENT

ac·com·pa·ni·ment \ə-'kəmp-(ə-)nē-mənt\ *n* **1** : music played along with a solo part to enrich it **2** : an accompanying object, situation, or event

ac·com·pa·nist \ə-'kəmp-(ə-)nəst\ *n* : a musician who plays an accompaniment

ac·com·pa·ny \ə-'kəmp-(ə-)nē\ *vb* **-nied; -ny·ing** **1** : to go with or attend as a companion **2** : to perform an accompaniment to or for **3** : to occur at the same time as or along with ⟨a thunderstorm *accompanied* by high winds⟩

[Middle English *accompanien* "to accompany," from early French *acompaigner* (same meaning), from *a-* "to" and *cumpaing* "companion," from Latin *companio* "companion" — related to COMPANION, COMPANY]

synonyms ACCOMPANY, ATTEND, ESCORT mean to go along with. ACCOMPANY stresses the closeness of the relationship and stresses that the people are equals ⟨would you like to *accompany* me to the movies?⟩. ATTEND suggests waiting upon and serving someone of higher rank ⟨assistants and bodyguards *attended* the President⟩. ESCORT suggests that one is going along as a matter of protection, ceremony, or courtesy ⟨a marching band *escorted* the heroes⟩.

ac·com·plice \ə-ˈkäm-pləs, -ˈkəm-\ *n* : one associated with another in wrongdoing

ac·com·plish \ə-ˈkäm-plish, -ˈkəm-\ *vb* : to bring to a successful finish : PERFORM — **ac·com·plish·able** \-ə-bəl\ *adj*

ac·com·plished \-pisht\ *adj* **1** : shown or known to be true ⟨an *accomplished* fact⟩ **2 a** : skilled or polished through practice or training : EXPERT ⟨an *accomplished* pianist⟩ **b** : having many accomplishments

ac·com·plish·ment \ə-ˈkäm-plish-mənt, -ˈkəm-\ *n* **1** : the act of accomplishing : COMPLETION **2** : something accomplished : ACHIEVEMENT **3** : an ability, social quality, or skill gained through training or practice

¹ac·cord \ə-ˈkȯrd\ *vb* **1** : to grant as suitable or proper ⟨rights *accorded* to citizens⟩ **2** : to be in harmony : AGREE ⟨a theory that *accords* with known fact⟩

²accord *n* **1 a** : AGREEMENT 1b, HARMONY **b** : an agreement between parties ⟨reach an *accord*⟩ **2** : willingness to act or do something ⟨went of their own *accord*⟩

ac·cor·dance \ə-ˈkȯrd-ᵊn(t)s\ *n* : AGREEMENT 1b, CONFORMITY ⟨in *accordance* with a rule⟩

ac·cord·ing as \ə-ˈkȯrd-iŋ-\ *conj* **1** : in accord with the way in which **2** : depending on how or whether

ac·cord·ing·ly \ə-ˈkȯrd-iŋ-lē\ *adv* **1** : in accordance : CORRESPONDINGLY **2** : CONSEQUENTLY, SO

according to *prep* **1** : in agreement with ⟨did everything *according to* the rules⟩ **2** : as stated by ⟨*according to* the experts⟩ **3** : depending on ⟨dress *according to* the weather⟩

¹ac·cor·di·on \ə-ˈkȯrd-ē-ən\ *n* : a musical instrument that has a keyboard and a bellows and that produces tones when air is forced past metal reeds — **ac·cor·di·on·ist** \-ē-ə-nəst\ *n*

²accordion *adj* : creased to fold like an accordion ⟨*accordion* doors⟩

ac·cost \ə-ˈkȯst, -ˈkäst\ *vb* : to approach and speak to often in a challenging or aggressive way

¹accordion

¹ac·count \ə-ˈkaunt\ *n* **1** : a record of money paid out and money received **2** : a statement listing purchases and credits : BILL **3 a** : ¹VALUE 3 ⟨a man of little *account*⟩ **b** : ¹REGARD 2a ⟨held in high *account*⟩ **4** : ¹PROFIT 1, ADVANTAGE ⟨labored to no *account*⟩ **5 a** : a statement of reasons, causes, or motives ⟨gave an *account* of her actions⟩ **b** : a statement of facts ⟨*accounts* of the game⟩ **c** : a reason for an action ⟨on that *account* I must refuse⟩ **6** : a sum of money deposited in a bank [Middle English *acount, accompt* "the act or result of counting," from early French *acunte* (same meaning), from *acunter* (verb) "to add, count," from *a-* "to" and *cunter* "to count," from Latin *computare* "to count, compute" — related to COMPUTE, ¹COUNT] **synonyms** see NARRATIVE — **on account of**

: for the sake of : by reason of : BECAUSE OF — **on no account** : in no circumstances

²account *vb* **1** : to think of as ⟨*accounts* herself lucky⟩ **2** : to give an explanation ⟨have to *account* for the money I spent⟩ **3** : to be the cause ⟨illness *accounts* for so many absences⟩

ac·count·able \ə-ˈkaunt-ə-bəl\ *adj* **1** : responsible for giving an account (as of one's acts) ⟨will be held *accountable*⟩ **2** : capable of being accounted for : EXPLAINABLE — **ac·count·abil·i·ty** \-ˌkaunt-ə-ˈbil-ət-ē\ *n* — **ac·count·ably** \-ˈkaunt-ə-blē\ *adv*

ac·coun·tant \ə-ˈkaunt-ᵊnt\ *n* : a person professionally trained in accounting

ac·count·ing \ə-ˈkaunt-iŋ\ *n* **1** : the system or practice of recording the amounts of money made and spent by a person or business **2** : a statement explaining one's conduct : ACCOUNT 5a

ac·cou·tre *or* **ac·cou·ter** \ə-ˈküt-ər\ *vb* **-cou·tred** *or* **-cou·tered; -cou·tring** *or* **-cou·ter·ing** \-ˈküt-ə-riŋ, -ˈkü-triŋ\ : to provide with equipment : OUTFIT

ac·cou·tre·ment *or* **ac·cou·ter·ment** \ə-ˈkü-trə-mənt, -ˈküt-ər-mənt\ *n* : an accessory item of clothing or equipment — usually used in plural

ac·cred·it \ə-ˈkred-ət\ *vb* **1** : to send with credentials and authority to act as representative ⟨*accredit* an ambassador to France⟩ **2** : to certify as in agreement with a standard ⟨an *accredited* school⟩ **3** : to give credit to — **ac·cred·i·ta·tion** \ə-ˌkred-ə-ˈtā-shən, -ˈdā-\ *n*

ac·cre·tion \ə-ˈkrē-shən\ *n* **1** : the process of growth or enlargement; *esp* : increase or growth by addition on the outside **2** : a product or result of accretion

ac·crue \ə-ˈkrü\ *vb* **ac·crued; ac·cru·ing** **1** : to come about as a natural growth or addition ⟨benefits *accrue* to society from education⟩ **2** : to accumulate over a period of time ⟨*accrued* interest⟩ — **ac·cru·al** \-ˈkrü-əl\ *n*

ac·cu·mu·late \ə-ˈkyü-myə-ˌlāt\ *vb* **-lat·ed; -lat·ing** **1** : to gather or pile up especially little by little : AMASS ⟨*accumulate* a fortune⟩ **2** : to increase in quantity, number, or amount ⟨rubbish *accumulates* quickly⟩

ac·cu·mu·la·tion \ə-ˌkyü-myə-ˈlā-shən\ *n* **1** : a collecting together : AMASSING **2** : increase or growth by addition **3** : something accumulated : COLLECTION

ac·cu·mu·la·tor \ə-ˈkyü-m(y)ə-ˌlāt-ər\ *n* : one that accumulates; *esp* : a part (as in a computer) where numbers are totaled or stored

ac·cu·ra·cy \ˈak-yə-rə-sē\ *n, pl* **-cies** **1** : freedom from error : CORRECTNESS **2** : conformity to a standard : EXACTNESS

ac·cu·rate \ˈak-yə-rət\ *adj* **1** : free from mistakes especially as the result of care ⟨an *accurate* count⟩ **2** : agreeing exactly with truth or a standard ⟨an *accurate* copy⟩ **3** : able to give an accurate result ⟨an *accurate* gauge⟩ [from Latin *accuratus* "accurate," from *accurare* "to take care of," from *ac-, ad-* "to" and *cura* "care" — related to CURE, CURIOUS; see *Word History* at CURE] **synonyms** see CORRECT — **ac·cu·rate·ly** \-yə-rət-lē, -yərt-\ *adv* — **ac·cu·rate·ness** \-nəs\ *n*

ac·cursed \ə-ˈkərst, -ˈkər-səd\ *or* **ac·curst** \ə-ˈkərst\ *adj* **1** : being under a curse **2** : DAMNABLE 2, DETESTABLE — **ac·curs·ed·ly** \-ˈkər-səd-lē\ *adv* — **ac·curs·ed·ness** \-ˈkər-səd-nəs\ *n*

ac·cu·sa·tion \ˌak-yə-ˈzā-shən, -yü-\ *n* **1** : the act of accusing : the fact of being accused **2** : a charge of wrongdoing

ac·cu·sa·tive \ə-ˈkyü-zət-iv\ *adj* : of, relating to, or being the grammatical case that marks the direct object of a verb or the object of a preposition — **accusative** *n*

ac·cu·sa·to·ry \ə-ˈkyü-zə-ˌtōr-ē, -ˌtȯr-\ *adj* : containing or expressing accusation ⟨an *accusatory* look⟩

ac·cuse \ə-ˈkyüz\ *vb* **ac·cused; ac·cus·ing** : to charge with a fault and especially with a crime — **ac·cus·er** *n* — **ac·cus·ing·ly** \-ˈkyü-ziŋ-lē\ *adv*

ac·cused \ə-'kyüzd\ *n, pl* **accused** : one charged with wrongdoing; *esp* : the defendant in a criminal case

ac·cus·tom \ə-'kəs-təm\ *vb* : to make familiar

ac·cus·tomed \ə-'kəs-təmd\ *adj* **1** : CUSTOMARY ⟨my *accustomed* lunch hour⟩ **2** : familiar with **3** : being in the habit or custom ⟨*accustomed* to making decisions⟩

¹ace \'ās\ *n* **1** : a playing card with one large figure in its center **2** : a very small amount or degree ⟨within an *ace* of winning⟩ **3** : a point scored on a serve (as in tennis) that an opponent fails to touch **4** : a golf hole made in one stroke **5 a** : a combat pilot who has shot down at least five enemy airplanes **b** : a person who is expert at something

²ace *vb* **aced; ac·ing** **1** : to score an ace against ⟨the tennis player *aced* her opponent⟩ **2** : to earn the grade of A on (an examination)

³ace *adj* : of first or high rank or quality

acel·lu·lar \(')ā-'sel-yə-lər\ *adj* : not made up of cells

-a·ceous \'ā-shəs\ *adj suffix* : consisting of ⟨carbona*ceous*⟩ : having the nature or form of ⟨herb*aceous*⟩ [from Latin *-aceus* "consisting of"]

acet·amin·o·phen \ə-,sēt-ə-'min-ə-fən\ *n* : a crystalline compound used in medicine to relieve pain and fever

ac·e·tate \'as-ə-,tāt\ *n* **1** : a chemical compound formed by the reaction of acetic acid with another substance **2** : something made from acetate or from cellulose and acetate combined

ace·tic \ə-'sēt-ik\ *adj* : of, relating to, or producing acetic acid or vinegar

acetic acid *n* : a colorless strong-smelling liquid acid that gives the sour taste to vinegar and that is used especially in making chemical compounds (as plastics)

ac·e·tone \'as-ə-,tōn\ *n* : an easily evaporated fragrant flammable liquid compound used chiefly to dissolve or to make chemical compounds

ace·tyl·cho·line \ə-,set-'l-'kō-,lēn, -,sēt-; 'as-ə-'tēl-\ *n* : a compound released at autonomic nerve endings that functions in carrying nerve impulses

acet·y·lene \ə-'set-'l-ən, -'l-,ēn\ *n* : a compound of carbon and hydrogen that is a colorless gas used chiefly in welding and soldering and in making chemical compounds

ace·tyl·sal·i·cyl·ic acid \ə-'sēt-'l-,sal-ə-,sil-ik-\ *n* : ASPIRIN 1

¹ache \'āk\ *vb* **ached; ach·ing** **1** : to suffer a dull persistent pain **2** : to long painfully : YEARN

²ache *n* : a dull persistent pain — **achy** \'ā-kē\ *adj*

achene \ā-'kēn\ *n* : a small dry one-seeded fruit (as of the sunflower) that ripens without bursting open — **ache·ni·al** \ə-'kē-nē-əl\ *adj*

achieve \ə-'chēv\ *vb* **achieved; achiev·ing** **1** : ACCOMPLISH ⟨*achieved* our purpose⟩ **2** : to get by effort ⟨*achieve* greatness⟩ [Middle English *achieven* "achieve," from early French *achever* "to finish," from *a-* "to" and *cheef* "end, head," from Latin *caput* "head" — related to CAPITAL, CHIEF] — **achiev·able** \-'chē-və-bəl\ *adj* — **achiev·er** *n*

achieve·ment \ə-'chēv-mənt\ *n* **1** : the act of achieving **2** : something achieved

Achil·les' heel \ə-,kil-ēz-\ *n* : a special or personal weakness

Word History In Greek legend, Achilles' mother protected him from harm by dipping him in the River Styx. However, she held him by the heel while doing it. As a result this heel did not get wet and thus was not protected. Later, during the Trojan War, Achilles was killed by Paris, a Trojan prince, who shot him in the unprotected heel with an arrow. The term *Achilles' heel* has since come to refer to any weak spot or point. [named for *Achilles,* warrior in Greek legend]

Achilles tendon *n* : the strong tendon joining the muscles in the calf of the leg to the bone of the heel

ach·ro·mat·ic \,ak-rə-'mat-ik\ *adj* **1** : giving an image practically free from colors not in the object ⟨an *achromatic* lens⟩ **2** : being black, gray, or white

¹ac·id \'as-əd\ *adj* **1** : sour, bitter, or stinging to the taste : resembling vinegar in taste **2** : sharp or sour in temper : CROSS ⟨*acid* remarks⟩ **3** : of, relating to, or having the characteristics of an acid ⟨*acid* soil⟩ ⟨*acid* indigestion⟩ — **ac·id·ly** *adv* — **ac·id·ness** *n*

²acid *n* **1** : a sour substance **2** : a compound that usually dissolves in water, has a sour taste, reacts with a base to form a salt, and turns litmus paper red **3** : LSD

ac·id–fast \'as-əd-,fast\ *adj* : not easily made to lose color by acids

acid·ic \ə-'sid-ik, a-\ *adj* **1** : acid-forming **2** : ACID

acid·i·fy \ə-'sid-ə-,fī\ *vb* **-fied; -fy·ing** **1** : to make acid **2** : to change into an acid — **acid·i·fi·ca·tion** \ə-,sid-ə-fə-'kā-shən\ *n*

acid·i·ty \ə-'sid-ət-ē, a-\ *n, pl* **-ties** **1** : the quality, state, or degree of being acid **2** : the state of being extremely acid

acid precipitation *n* : precipitation (as rain or snow) with increased acidity that is caused by environmental factors

acid rain *n* : rain with increased acidity that is caused by environmental factors (as atmospheric pollutants)

ac·knowl·edge \ik-'näl-ij, ak-\ *vb* **-edged; -edg·ing** **1** : to recognize the rights or authority of **2** : to admit the truth or existence of **3** : to make known that something has been received or noticed ⟨*acknowledge* a letter⟩

synonyms ACKNOWLEDGE, ADMIT, OWN, CONFESS mean to make public something one would rather keep private. ACKNOWLEDGE suggests revealing something that has been or might be concealed ⟨the company *acknowledged* that it had been polluting the lake⟩. ADMIT stresses a demand to reveal and an unwillingness to do so ⟨why don't you *admit* that you made a mistake?⟩. OWN suggests acknowledging something of a personal nature ⟨I *own* that I can be rude sometimes⟩. CONFESS suggests an admission of weakness, failure, or guilt ⟨*confessed* involvement in the scam⟩.

ac·knowl·edged \ik-'näl-ijd, ak-\ *adj* : generally recognized or accepted ⟨the *acknowledged* leader⟩

ac·knowl·edg·ment *also* **ac·knowl·edge·ment** \ik-'näl-ij-mənt, ak-\ *n* **1 a** : the act of acknowledging **b** : an act of acknowledging some deed or achievement **2** : something given or given in return for something received

ac·me \'ak-mē\ *n* : the highest point : PEAK ⟨the *acme* of perfection⟩

ac·ne \'ak-nē\ *n* : a disorder of the skin caused by inflammation of skin glands and hair follicles and marked by pimples especially on the face

ac·o·lyte \'ak-ə-,līt\ *n* : a person who assists a member of the clergy in a service

ac·o·nite \'ak-ə-,nīt\ *n* **1** : MONKSHOOD **2** : a drug obtained from the poisonous root of the common Old World monkshood

acorn \'ā-,kȯrn, -kərn\ *n* : the roundish one-seeded thin-shelled nut of an oak tree usually having a woody cap

acorn squash *n* : an acorn-shaped winter squash with ridges on its dark green outer surface and somewhat sweet yellow to orange flesh

acous·tic \ə-'kü-stik\ *or* **acous·ti·cal** \-sti-kəl\ *adj* **1** : of or relating to the sense or organs of hearing, to

acorn squash

\ə\ abut	\au̇\ out	\i\ tip	\ȯ\ saw	\u̇\ foot
\ər\ further	\ch\ chin	\ī\ life	\ȯi\ coin	\y\ yet
\a\ mat	\e\ pet	\j\ job	\th\ thin	\yü\ few
\ā\ take	\ē\ easy	\ŋ\ sing	\th\ this	\yu̇\ cure
\ä\ cot, cart	\g\ go	\ō\ bone	\ü\ food	\zh\ vision

sound, or to the science of sounds: as **a** : deadening or absorbing sound **b** : operated by or using sound waves **2** : of, relating to, or being a musical instrument whose sound is not electronically modified ⟨*acoustic* guitar⟩ — **acous·ti·cal·ly** \-sti-k(ə-)lē\ *adv*

acous·tics \ə-'kü-stiks\ *n sing or pl* **1** : a science dealing with sound **2** *also* **acoustic** \-stik\ : the qualities in an enclosed space (as an auditorium) that make it easy or hard for a person in it to hear distinctly

ac·quaint \ə-'kwānt\ *vb* **1** : to cause to know socially ⟨became *acquainted* at school⟩ **2** : to cause to know first-hand : INFORM ⟨*acquaint* her with her duties⟩

ac·quain·tance \ə-'kwānt-ᵊn(t)s\ *n* **1** : knowledge gained by personal experience ⟨had some *acquaintance* with the subject⟩ **2** : a person one knows slightly — **ac·quain·tance·ship** \-ˌship\ *n*

ac·qui·esce \ˌak-wē-'es\ *vb* **-esced; -esc·ing** : to accept, agree, or give consent by keeping silent or by not raising objections — **ac·qui·es·cence** \-'es-ᵊn(t)s\ *n*

ac·qui·es·cent \ˌak-wē-'es-ᵊnt\ *adj* : acquiescing or tending to acquiesce — **ac·qui·es·cent·ly** *adv*

ac·quire \ə-'kwī(ə)r\ *vb* **ac·quired; ac·quir·ing** : to come to have often by one's own efforts : GAIN — **ac·quir·able** \-'kwī-rə-bəl\ *adj*

acquired *adj* **1** : gained by or as a result of effort or experience **2** : caused by environmental forces and not passed from parent to offspring in the genes ⟨*acquired* characteristics⟩

acquired immune deficiency syndrome *n* : AIDS

acquired immunity *n* : immunity that develops following exposure (as through infection or vaccination) to something that causes disease

ac·quire·ment \ə-'kwī(ə)r-mənt\ *n* **1** : the act of acquiring **2** : ACCOMPLISHMENT 3

ac·qui·si·tion \ˌak-wə-'zish-ən\ *n* **1** : the act of acquiring **2** : something acquired

ac·quis·i·tive \ə-'kwiz-ət-iv\ *adj* : having a strong wish to acquire things — **ac·quis·i·tive·ness** *n*

ac·quit \ə-'kwit\ *vb* **ac·quit·ted; ac·quit·ting** **1** : to declare innocent of a crime or wrongdoing **2** : to conduct (oneself) usually satisfactorily

ac·quit·tal \ə-'kwit-ᵊl\ *n* : the freeing (as by verdict) of a person from the charge of a crime

acre \'ā-kər\ *n* **1** *pl* : property consisting of land : ESTATE **2** : a unit of area equal to 43,560 square feet (about 4047 square meters) — see MEASURE table [Old English *æcer* "field, cultivated land"]

acre·age \'ā-k(ə-)rij\ *n* : area in acres

acre–foot *n* : the volume (as of irrigation water) that would cover one acre to a depth of one foot

ac·rid \'ak-rəd\ *adj* **1** : biting or bitter in taste or odor **2** : bitterly irritating to the feelings ⟨an *acrid* remark⟩ — **ac·rid·ly** *adv* — **ac·rid·ness** *n*

ac·ri·mo·ny \'ak-rə-ˌmō-nē\ *n, pl* **-nies** : harsh or biting sharpness especially of words, manner, or disposition — **ac·ri·mo·ni·ous** \ˌak-rə-'mō-nē-əs\ *adj* — **ac·ri·mo·ni·ous·ly** *adv* — **ac·ri·mo·ni·ous·ness** *n*

ac·ro·bat \'ak-rə-ˌbat\ *n* : a person (as a circus performer) who is very good at stunts like jumping, balancing, tumbling, and swinging from things — **ac·ro·bat·ic** \ˌak-rə-'bat-ik\ *adj* — **ac·ro·bat·i·cal·ly** \-i-k(ə-)lē\ *adv*

ac·ro·bat·ics \ˌak-rə-'bat-iks\ *n sing or pl* **1** : the art or performance of an acrobat **2** : stunts of or resembling those of an acrobat ⟨airplane *acrobatics*⟩

ac·ro·nym \'ak-rə-ˌnim\ *n* : a word (as *radar*) formed from the beginning letter or letters of each or most of the parts of a compound term

ac·ro·pho·bia \ˌak-rə-'fō-bē-ə\ *n* : fear of heights

acrop·o·lis \ə-'kräp-ə-ləs\ *n* : the upper fortified part of an ancient Greek city

¹across \ə-'krós\ *adv* **1** : from one side to the other ⟨boards sawed directly *across*⟩ **2** : to or on the opposite side ⟨got *across* in a boat⟩ **3** : so as to be understandable or successful ⟨get the message *across*⟩

²across *prep* **1** : to or on the opposite side of ⟨*across* the street⟩ **2** : so as to cross or pass at an angle ⟨lay one stick *across* another⟩

acros·tic \ə-'kròs-tik, -'kräs-\ *n* : a poem in which a set of letters (as the first letter of the lines) taken in order form a word or phrase

acryl·ic \ə-'kril-ik\ *n* **1** : ACRYLIC FIBER **2** : a paint containing an acrylic resin

acrylic fiber *n* : a quick-drying synthetic fiber used for woven and knitted cloth

acrylic resin *n* : a glassy synthetic plastic used for cast and molded parts or as coatings and adhesives

¹act \'akt\ *n* **1** : something that is done ⟨an *act* of kindness⟩ **2** : the doing of something ⟨caught in the *act*⟩ **3** : a law made by a governing body ⟨an *act* of Congress⟩ **4** **a** : one of the main divisions of a play or opera **b** : one of the parts of a variety show or circus **5** : a display of behavior that is not sincere ⟨just putting on an *act*⟩ [Middle English *act* "act, deed," from Latin *actus* "action of doing" and from Latin *actum* "something done," both from *agere* "to drive, do" — related to AGENT]

²act *vb* **1** : to perform by action especially on the stage **2** : to play the part of ⟨*act* the man of the world⟩ **3 a** : to behave in a manner suitable to ⟨*act* your age⟩ **b** : to conduct oneself ⟨*act* like a fool⟩ **4** : to take action : MOVE ⟨think before you *act*⟩ **5 a** : to perform a function : SERVE ⟨*act* as mayor⟩ **b** : to produce an effect : WORK ⟨wait for a medicine to *act*⟩

ac·tin \'ak-tən\ *n* : a protein of muscle that with myosin is active in muscular contraction

act·ing \'ak-tiŋ\ *adj* : serving temporarily or in place of another ⟨*acting* president⟩

ac·tin·i·um \ak-'tin-ē-əm\ *n* : a radioactive metallic element found especially in pitchblende — see ELEMENT table

ac·tion \'ak-shən\ *n* **1** : a legal proceeding in a court by which one demands one's right or the correction of a wrong **2** : the working of one thing on another so as to produce a change ⟨the *action* of acids on metals⟩ **3** : the process or manner of acting or functioning; *also* : such an action expressed by a verb **4 a** : a thing done : DEED **b** *pl* : BEHAVIOR, CONDUCT **5** : combat in war : BATTLE **6** : the plot of a drama or work of fiction

action figure *n* : a small-scale figure (as of a superhero) used especially as a toy

action verb *n* : a verb that expresses action ⟨"lingered" in "they lingered over dinner" and "bring" in "bring me the broom" are *action verbs*⟩ — compare LINKING VERB

ac·ti·vate \'ak-tə-ˌvāt\ *vb* **-vat·ed; -vat·ing** **1** : to make active **2** : to make (as molecules) more chemically active **3** : to make (a substance) give off radioactive particles, give off light at low temperatures, be easily affected by light, or carry an electric charge under the influence of light or other electromagnetic radiation **4** : to treat (as carbon or alumina) so as to improve the amount of adsorption **5** : to place on active military duty ⟨*activate* the reserves⟩ — **ac·ti·va·tion** \ˌak-tə-'vā-shən\ *n* — **ac·ti·va·tor** \'ak-tə-ˌvāt-ər\ *n*

activation energy *n* : the least amount of energy required to change a stable molecule into a reactive molecule

ac·tive \'ak-tiv\ *adj* **1** : producing or involving action or movement **2** : representing the subject as performing the action expressed by the verb ⟨"hits" in "she hits the ball" is an *active* verb⟩ **3** : having or requiring quick or energetic movements ⟨an *active* child⟩ ⟨*active* sports⟩ **4 a** : ready for action ⟨takes an *active* interest⟩ **b** : engaged or participating in an action or activity ⟨an *active* member⟩ **c** : erupting or likely to erupt ⟨an *active* volcano⟩ **5** : engaged in or requiring full-time service especially in the armed forces ⟨*active* duty⟩ **6** : marked by present action or use ⟨an *active* account⟩ ⟨a student's *active* vocabulary⟩ **7 a** : capable of acting or reacting ⟨*active* ingredients⟩ **b** : tending to progress or increase ⟨*active* tuberculosis⟩ — **ac·tive·ly** *adv* — **ac·tive·ness** *n*

active immunity *n* : immunity produced by the individual when exposed to an antigen — compare PASSIVE IMMUNITY

active transport *n* : the movement (as across a cell membrane) of substances from regions of lower concentration to regions of higher concentration by the use of energy

ac·tive·wear \'ak-tiv-ˌwa(ə)r, -ˌwe(ə)r\ *n* : SPORTSWEAR

ac·tiv·ist \'ak-ti-vəst\ *n* : a person who believes in forceful action (as mass demonstration) for political purposes — **ac·tiv·ism** \-ˌviz-əm\ *n*

ac·tiv·i·ty \ak-'tiv-ət-ē\ *n, pl* **-ties** **1** : the quality or state of being active **2** : forceful or energetic action **3** : a natural, normal, or assigned function: as **a** : a process that an organism carries on or participates in by virtue of being alive **b** : a similar process that involves or is capable of involving mental function **4** : an educational exercise designed to teach by firsthand experience **5** : an active force ⟨solar *activity*⟩ **6 a** : something done especially for relaxation or fun **b** : a form of organized recreation

ac·tor \'ak-tər\ *n* : one that acts; *esp* : a person who acts especially in a play or movie or on television

act out *vb* **1** : to represent in action ⟨children *act out* what they read⟩ **2** : to behave badly especially as a way of letting out painful emotions

ac·tress \'ak-trəs\ *n* : a woman or girl who acts especially in a play or movie or on television

Acts \'ak(t)s\ *or* **Acts of the Apostles** — see BIBLE table

ac·tu·al \'ak-ch(ə-w)əl, 'ak-sh(ə-w)əl\ *adj* : existing in fact and not merely as a possibility **synonyms** see REAL — **ac·tu·al·i·ty** \ak-chə-'wal-ət-ē, -shə-\ *n* — **ac·tu·al·i·za·tion** \'ak-ch(ə-w)ə-lə-'zā-shən, -sh(ə-w)ə-\ *n* — **ac·tu·al·ize** \-ˌīz\ *vb*

ac·tu·al·ly \'ak-ch(ə-w)ə-lē, 'ak-sh(ə-w)ə-lē\ *adv* : in fact or in truth : REALLY ⟨she *actually* spoke Spanish⟩ ⟨*actually*, I didn't want to go⟩

ac·tu·ary \'ak-chə-ˌwer-ē, -shə-\ *n, pl* **-ar·ies** : a person who calculates insurance premiums and dividends — **ac·tu·ar·i·al** \ˌak-chə-'wer-ē-əl\ *adj*

ac·tu·ate \'ak-chə-ˌwāt, -shə-\ *vb* **-at·ed; -at·ing** **1** : to put into action ⟨the windmill *actuates* the pump⟩ **2** : to arouse to action ⟨*actuated* by the hope of winning⟩

act up *vb* : to act in an unruly, abnormal, or annoying way

acu·ity \ə-'kyü-ət-ē\ *n* : sharpness of perception

acu·men \ə-'kyü-mən, 'ak-yə-mən\ *n* : keenness of mind : SHREWDNESS

acu·punc·ture \'ak-yə-ˌpəŋ(k)-chər\ *n* : an originally Chinese practice of inserting fine needles through the skin at specified points especially to cure disease or relieve pain [Latin *acus* "needle" and English *puncture*]

acute \ə-'kyüt\ *adj* **acut·er; acut·est** **1 a** : SEVERE 3, SHARP ⟨*acute* pain⟩ **b** : having a sudden onset and short duration ⟨*acute* disease⟩ **2** : being or forming an angle measuring less than 90 degrees ⟨an *acute* angle⟩ **3 a** : marked by keen awareness : SHREWD ⟨an *acute* observation⟩ **b** : having sharp perceptions : OBSERVANT **4** : needing speedy attention : URGENT ⟨an *acute* shortage of blood plasma⟩ **5** : felt or experienced intensely ⟨*acute* distress⟩ **synonyms** see SHARP — **acute·ly** *adv* — **acute·ness** *n*

ad \'ad\ *n* : ADVERTISEMENT 2

ad- *or* **ac-** *or* **af-** *or* **ag-** *or* **al-** *or* **ap-** *or* **as-** *or* **at-** *prefix* : to : toward — usually *ac-* before *c, k,* or *q* and *af-* before *f* and *ag-* before *g* and *al-* before *l* and *ap-* before *p* and *as-* before *s* and *at-* before *t* and *ad-* before other sounds but sometimes *ad-* even before one of the listed consonants [Latin *ad-* "to, toward"]

ad·age \'ad-ij\ *n* : an old familiar saying : PROVERB

¹ada·gio \ə-'däj-ō, -'däj-ē-ˌō, -'däzh-\ *adv or adj* : in an easy graceful manner : SLOWLY — used as a direction in music

²adagio *n* **1** : a musical composition or movement in adagio tempo **2** : a ballet duet or trio displaying difficult feats of balance, lifting, or spinning

¹ad·a·mant \'ad-ə-mənt, -ˌmant\ *n* **1** : an imaginary stone of great hardness **2** : an unbreakable or extremely hard substance [Middle English *adamant* "an imaginary stone of great hardness, diamond," from early French *adamant* (same meaning), from Latin *adamant-, adamas* "hardest metal, diamond," from Greek *adamant-, adamas* (same meaning) — related to DIAMOND; — see *Word History* at DIAMOND]

²adamant *adj* : firmly fixed or decided especially against something : UNYIELDING — **ad·a·mant·ly** *adv*

ad·a·man·tine \ˌad-ə-'man-ˌtēn, -ˌtīn\ *adj* **1** : made of or having the quality of adamant **2** : ²ADAMANT

Ad·am's apple \'ad-əmz-\ *n* : the lump in the front of the neck formed by the largest cartilage of the larynx

adapt \ə-'dapt\ *vb* : to make or become suitable; *esp* : to change so as to fit a new or specific use or situation ⟨*adapt* to life in a new school⟩ ⟨*adapt* the novel for children⟩ [from French *adapter* and Latin *adaptare*, both meaning "to adapt," from Latin *ad-* "to" and *aptus* "apt, fit" — related to APT] — **adapt·abil·i·ty** \-ˌdap-tə-'bil-ət-ē\ *n* — **adapt·able** \-'dap-tə-bəl\ *adj*

ad·ap·ta·tion \ˌad-ˌap-'tā-shən, -əp-\ *n* **1 a** : the act or process of adapting **b** : the state of being adapted **2** : adjustment to environmental conditions: as **a** : adjustment of a sense organ to the degree or quality of stimulation **b** : change in an organism or its parts that fits it better for the conditions of its environment; *also* : a structure resulting from this change **3** : something that is adapted; *esp* : a composition rewritten into a new form — **ad·ap·ta·tion·al** \-shnəl, -shən-ᵊl\ *adj* — **ad·ap·ta·tion·al·ly** \-ē\ *adv*

adapt·ed \ə-'dap-təd\ *adj* : suited by nature or design to a particular use, purpose, or situation

adapt·er *also* **adap·tor** \ə-'dap-tər\ *n* **1** : someone or something that adapts **2 a** : a device for connecting two parts (as of different diameters) of a usually larger device **b** : an attachment for adapting a device for uses not originally intended

add \'ad\ *vb* **1 a** : to join or unite to a thing so as to increase or improve it ⟨*add* a wing to the house⟩ ⟨color *adds* a creative touch⟩ **b** : to unite or combine in a single whole **c** : to include as a member of a group ⟨*add* me in⟩ **2** : to say something more ⟨*add* to her remarks⟩ **3** : to combine (numbers) into a single number that has the same total value — **add·able** *or* **add·ible** \'ad-ə-bəl\ *adj*

ad·dend \'ad-ˌend\ *n* : a number that is to be added to another

ad·den·dum \ə-'den-dəm\ *n, pl* **-den·da** \-'den-də\ : something added (as to a book)

¹ad·der \'ad-ər\ *n* **1** : a poisonous European viper; *also* : any of several related snakes **2** : any of several harmless North American snakes (as the hognose snakes)

²add·er \'ad-ər\ *n* : one that adds

ad·der's–tongue \'ad-ərz-ˌtəŋ\ *n* **1** : a fern whose spore-bearing stalk resembles a serpent's tongue **2** : DOGTOOTH VIOLET

¹ad·dict \ə-'dikt\ *vb* **1** : to devote or surrender oneself to something habitually ⟨*addicted* to detective stories⟩ **2** : to cause to

adder's-tongue 1

\ə\ abut	\aú\ out	\i\ tip	\ó\ saw	\ú\ foot
\ər\ **further**	\ch\ **chin**	\ī\ **life**	\ói\ **coin**	\y\ **yet**
\a\ **mat**	\e\ **pet**	\j\ **job**	\th\ **thin**	\yü\ **few**
\ā\ **take**	\ē\ **easy**	\ŋ\ **sing**	\th\ **this**	\yú\ **cure**
\ä\ **cot, cart**	\g\ **go**	\ō\ **bone**	\ü\ **food**	\zh\ **vision**

make a habit of using a drug ⟨nicotine is *addicting*⟩
²**ad·dict** \'ad-(ˌ)ikt\ *n* **1** : one who is addicted (as to a drug) **2** : a person devoted to something ⟨a TV *addict*⟩

ad·dic·tion \ə-'dik-shən, a-\ *n* : the quality or state of being addicted; *esp* : uncontrollable use of habit-forming drugs

ad·dic·tive \ə-'dik-tiv, a-\ *adj* : causing or characterized by addiction ⟨an *addictive* drug⟩ ⟨an *addictive* game⟩

ad·di·tion \ə-'dish-ən, a-\ *n* **1** : the result of adding : INCREASE **2** : the act, process, or operation of adding **3** : a part added (as to a building) — **in addition** : as something more : BESIDES — **in addition to** : ²BESIDES

ad·di·tion·al \ə-'dish-nəl, -ən-ᵊl\ *adj* : being an addition : EXTRA — **ad·di·tion·al·ly** \-ē\ *adv*

¹**ad·di·tive** \'ad-ət-iv\ *adj* : relating to or produced by addition — **ad·di·tive·ly** *adv*

²**additive** *n* : a substance added to another in small amounts to give or improve desirable qualities or decrease unwanted qualities ⟨a gasoline *additive*⟩ ⟨*additives* which color, flavor, or preserve food⟩

additive identity *n* : an element (as zero in the set of real numbers) of a mathematical set that leaves every element of the set unchanged when added to it

additive inverse *n* : a number that when added to a given number sums to zero ⟨the *additive inverse* of 4 is –4⟩ — compare ²OPPOSITE 3

ad·dle \'ad-ᵊl\ *vb* **ad·dled; ad·dling** \'ad-liŋ, -ᵊl-iŋ\ **1** : to make or become confused **2** : to become rotten : SPOIL ⟨*addled* eggs⟩

¹**ad·dress** \ə-'dres, a-\ *vb* **1 a** : to direct the attention of oneself ⟨*addressed* themselves to the problem⟩ **b** : to deal with ⟨prepares to *address* the problem⟩ **2 a** : to communicate directly ⟨*address* a petition to the governor⟩ **b** : to deliver a formal speech to ⟨*address* the convention⟩ **3** : to mark directions for delivery on ⟨*address* a letter⟩ **4** : to greet by a prescribed form **5** : to identify (as a computer peripheral or a piece of information) by an address or name for information transfer — **ad·dress·er** *n*

²**ad·dress** \ə-'dres, 'ad-ˌres\ *n* **1** : manner of speaking : DELIVERY **2** : a rehearsed speech **3 a** : a place where a person or organization can usually be reached **b** : the directions for delivery on mail **4 a** : a location (as in the memory of a computer) where particular information is stored **b** : a series of symbols (as numerals or letters) that identifies the location of information in a computer's memory or on the Internet or that specifies the source or destination of an e-mail message

ad·dress·able \ə-'dres-ə-bəl\ *adj* : able to be reached through an address ⟨*addressable* registers in a computer⟩

ad·dress·ee \ˌad-ˌres-'ē, ə-ˌdres-'ē\ *n* : one to whom mail is addressed

ad·duce \ə-'d(y)üs\ *vb* **ad·duced; ad·duc·ing** : to offer as example, reason, or proof

ad·duct \ə-'dəkt\ *vb* : to draw (a part of the body) toward or past a middle plane or line that divides the body or a bodily part into right and left halves

ad·duc·tor \ə-'dək-tər\ *n* : a muscle that draws a body part (as an arm or finger) toward or past a plane or a line that divides the body or a hand or foot into right and left halves

add up *vb* **1 a** : to come to a total and especially the expected total **b** : to make sense ⟨her story just doesn't *add up*⟩ **2** : to amount to a lot ⟨just a little each time, but it all *adds up*⟩

ad·e·nine \'ad-ᵊn-ēn\ *n* : one of the bases which make up the genetic code of DNA and RNA — compare CYTOSINE, GUANINE, THYMINE, URACIL

¹**ad·e·noid** \'ad-ᵊn-ˌoid, 'ad-ˌnoid\ *n* : either of two masses of tissue at the back of the pharynx that usually interfere with breathing when abnormally enlarged — usually used in plural

²**adenoid** *adj* **1** : of or relating to the adenoids **2** : relating to or affected with abnormally enlarged adenoids

ad·e·noi·dal \ˌad-ᵊn-'oid-ᵊl\ *adj* : exhibiting the signs (as a nasal voice) of one affected with abnormally enlarged adenoids : ADENOID ⟨an *adenoidal* singer⟩ — not usually used technically

aden·o·sine di·phos·phate \ə-'den-ə-ˌsēn-dī-'fäs-ˌfāt\ *n* : ADP

adenosine tri·phos·phate \-trī-'fäs-ˌfāt\ *n* : ATP

¹**ad·ept** \'ad-ˌept\ *n* : a highly skilled or well-trained individual : EXPERT

²**adept** \ə-'dept\ *adj* : very good at something **synonyms** see SKILLFUL — **adept·ly** *adv* — **adept·ness** \-'dep(t)-nəs\ *n*

ad·e·qua·cy \'ad-i-kwə-sē\ *n, pl* **-cies** : the quality or state of being adequate

ad·e·quate \'ad-i-kwət\ *adj* **1** : suitable or enough for a requirement ⟨food and water *adequate* for six people⟩ **2** : good enough ⟨your grades are barely *adequate*⟩ — **ad·e·quate·ly** *adv* — **ad·e·quate·ness** *n*

ad·here \ad-'hi(ə)r, əd-\ *vb* **ad·hered; ad·her·ing** **1** : to stay loyal (as to a cause or promise) **2** : to stick by or as if by gluing, suction, grasping, or melting **3** : to agree to observe ⟨*adhere* to the rules⟩

ad·her·ence \ad-'hir-ən(t)s, əd-\ *n* **1** : the action or quality of adhering **2** : steady or faithful attachment ⟨*adherence* to the truth⟩

¹**ad·her·ent** \ad-'hir-ənt, əd-\ *adj* : able or tending to adhere

²**adherent** *n* : a person who adheres to a leader, belief, or group

ad·he·sion \ad-'hē-zhən, əd-\ *n* **1** : steady or firm attachment; *esp* : a sticking together **2** : abnormal union of tissues following inflammation (as after surgery) **3** : the molecular attraction between surfaces of bodies in contact

¹**ad·he·sive** \ad-'hē-siv, əd-, -ziv\ *adj* : tending to adhere : prepared for adhering — **ad·he·sive·ness** *n*

²**adhesive** *n* : an adhesive substance (as glue or cement)

adhesive tape *n* : tape that is coated on one side with an adhesive and is used especially for medical purposes

adi·a·bat·ic \ˌad-ē-ə-'bat-ik, ˌā-ˌdī-ə-\ *adj* : occurring without loss or gain of heat ⟨*adiabatic* expansion of a gas⟩ — **ad·i·a·bat·i·cal·ly** \-'bat-i-k(ə-)lē\ *adv*

adieu \ə-'d(y)ü, a-\ *n, pl* **adieus** *or* **adieux** \-'d(y)üz\ : ²FAREWELL 1 — often used interjectionally [Middle English *adieu* "farewell," from early French *adieu* (same meaning), from *a Dieu*, literally "(I commit you) to God," from Latin *Deus* "God" — related to ADIOS, DEITY]

adi·os \ˌad-ē-'ōs, ˌäd-\ *interj* — used to express farewell [from Spanish *adiós* "farewell," from *a Dios*, literally "(I commit you) to God," from Latin *Deus* "God" — related to ADIEU, DEITY]

ad·i·pose \'ad-ə-ˌpōs\ *adj* : of or relating to animal fat : FATTY — **ad·i·pos·i·ty** \ˌad-ə-'päs-ət-ē\ *n*

adipose tissue *n* : tissue in which fat is stored and which has the cells swollen by droplets of fat

ad·ja·cent \ə-'jās-ᵊnt\ *adj* **1** : lying next or near : having a border or point in common ⟨a field *adjacent* to the road⟩ **2** : having a vertex or a vertex and side in common ⟨*adjacent* angles⟩ ⟨*adjacent* sides of a rectangle⟩ — **ad·ja·cent·ly** *adv*

ad·jec·tive \'aj-ik-tiv\ *n* : a word that modifies a noun by describing a quality of the thing named, indicating its quantity or extent, or specifying a thing as distinct from something else — **adjective** *adj* — **ad·jec·ti·val** \ˌaj-ik-'tī-vəl\ *adj or n* — **ad·jec·ti·val·ly** \-və-lē\ *adv*

ad·join \ə-'join, a-\ *vb* **1** : to add or attach by joining **2** : to lie next to or in contact with

ad·journ \ə-'jərn\ *vb* **1** : to bring or come to a close for a period of time ⟨Congress *adjourned*⟩ ⟨*adjourn* a meeting⟩ **2** : to move to another place ⟨let us *adjourn* to the sitting room⟩ — **ad·journ·ment** \-mənt\ *n*

ad·judge \ə-ˈjəj\ *vb* **ad·judged; ad·judg·ing 1** : to decide or rule upon as a judge : ADJUDICATE **2** : to consider or say to be : DEEM ⟨they *adjudged* the play a success⟩

ad·ju·di·cate \ə-ˈjüd-i-ˌkāt\ *vb* **-cat·ed; -cat·ing** : to decide, award, or sentence judicially ⟨*adjudicate* a claim⟩ — **ad·ju·di·ca·tion** \-ˌjüd-i-ˈkā-shən\ *n*

ad·junct \ˈaj-ˌəŋ(k)t\ *n* : ¹ACCESSORY 1

ad·jure \ə-ˈjú(ə)r\ *vb* **ad·jured; ad·jur·ing** : to command solemnly under or as if under oath — **ad·ju·ra·tion** \ˌaj-ə-ˈrā-shən\ *n*

ad·just \ə-ˈjəst\ *vb* **1** : to bring to a better state : set right ⟨*adjust* conflicts⟩ ⟨*adjust* the error⟩ **2** : to move the parts of an instrument or a piece of machinery until they fit together in the best working order ⟨*adjust* a watch⟩ ⟨*adjust* the brakes on a car⟩ **3** : to determine the amount of an insurance claim **4** : to adapt oneself to conditions ⟨had trouble *adjusting* to the new job⟩ — **ad·just·able** \-ˈjəs-tə-bəl\ *adj* — **ad·just·er** *also* **ad·jus·tor** \-ˈjəs-tər\ *n*

ad·just·ment \ə-ˈjəs(t)-mənt\ *n* **1** : the act or process of adjusting **2** : a settlement of a claim or debt **3** : the state of being adjusted **4** : a means of adjusting one part (as in a machine) in relation to another ⟨an *adjustment* for focusing a microscope⟩

ad·ju·tant \ˈaj-ət-ənt\ *n* **1** : an officer (as in the army) who assists the commanding officer in clerical work **2** : ASSISTANT

¹ad–lib \(ˈ)ad-ˈlib\ *vb* **ad–libbed; ad–lib·bing** : to improvise especially lines or a speech

²ad–lib *adj* : spoken, composed, or performed without preparation ⟨an *ad-lib* speech⟩

ad lib *adv* : without restraint or limit ⟨known for talking *ad lib*⟩

ad li·bi·tum \(ˈ)ad-ˈlib-ət-əm\ *adj* : freely as one wishes — used as a direction in music [modern Latin, "according to one's desire"]

ad·min·is·ter \ə-ˈmin-ə-stər\ *vb* **ad·min·is·tered; ad·min·is·ter·ing** \-st(ə-)riŋ\ **1** : to direct the affairs of : MANAGE ⟨*administer* a government⟩ **2** : to give out as deserved ⟨*administer* justice⟩ **3** : to give formally or ceremonially ⟨*administer* the sacraments⟩ **4** : to give as treatment ⟨*administer* a drug⟩

ad·min·is·tra·tion \əd-ˌmin-ə-ˈstrā-shən, ad-\ *n* **1** : the act or process of administering **2** : performance of supervising duties : MANAGEMENT **3** : the work involved in managing public affairs as distinguished from policy-making **4 a** : a group of persons who administer **b** *cap* : the executive branch of a government

ad·min·is·tra·tive \əd-ˈmin-ə-ˌstrāt-iv, -strət-\ *adj* : of or relating to administration ⟨an *administrative* position⟩

ad·min·is·tra·tor \əd-ˈmin-ə-ˌstrāt-ər\ *n* : a person who administers especially business, school, or government affairs

ad·min·is·tra·trix \əd-ˌmin-ə-ˈstrā-triks\ *n, pl* **-tra·tri·ces** \-ˈstrā-trə-ˌsēz\ : a woman who is an administrator

ad·mi·ra·ble \ˌad-mə-rə-bəl, -mrə-bəl\ *adj* : deserving to be admired : EXCELLENT — **ad·mi·ra·ble·ness** *n* — **ad·mi·ra·bly** \-blē\ *adv*

ad·mi·ral \ˈad-mə-rəl, -mrəl\ *n* **1** : a naval commissioned officer with a rank above that of captain; *esp* : an officer with a rank just above that of vice admiral **2** : any of several brightly colored butterflies

Word History It is a curiosity of history that *admiral*, a word meaning "naval commander," ultimately has its source in Arabic, the language of a desert people who acquired their seafaring skills largely from the Mediterranean peoples they dominated after the great expansion of Islam in the 7th century A.D. As the name for a Muslim chieftain, the Arabic word *amīr* appears as a loanword in the 9th century in Medieval Latin documents, in spellings such as *amiratus, admirandus,* and *admirallus.* These words display a variety of suffixes and an extra *d,* through confusion with the Latin verb *admirari,* "to ad-

mire." The ending *-allus* is probably from the Arabic definite article *al,* which actually belongs to the following word in phrases such as *amīr al-'alī,* "supreme commander." The specific application of *admirallus* to a commander of a fleet originated in 12th century Sicily. The usage was acquired by the Genoese and then spread to the rest of western Europe, including France and England. [Middle English *admiral* "naval commander," from early French *amiral* "commander" and Latin *admirallus* "naval commander," from Arabic *amīr-al-* "commander of the" (as in *amīr al-'alī* "supreme commander")]

¹admiralty *n* **1** : a group of officials formerly in charge of the British navy **2** : the court having authority over questions of maritime law; *also* : the system of law administered by admiralty courts

²ad·mi·ral·ty \ˈad-mə-rəl-tē, -mrəl-\ *adj* : of or relating to conduct on the sea

ad·mi·ra·tion \ˌad-mə-ˈrā-shən\ *n* **1** : an object of admiring regard **2** : a feeling of great and delighted approval

ad·mire \əd-ˈmī(ə)r\ *vb* **ad·mired; ad·mir·ing 1** : to look at with admiration ⟨*admire* the scenery⟩ **2** : to have high regard for ⟨*admired* her courage⟩ [from early French *admirer* "to marvel at," from Latin *admirari* (same meaning), from *ad-* "at" and *mirari* "to wonder" — related to MIRA-CLE] — **ad·mir·er** \-ˈmīr-ər\ *n*

ad·mis·si·ble \əd-ˈmis-ə-bəl\ *adj* : that can be or is worthy to be admitted or allowed ⟨*admissible* evidence⟩ — **ad·mis·si·bil·i·ty** \-ˌmis-ə-ˈbil-ət-ē\ *n*

ad·mis·sion \əd-ˈmish-ən, ad-\ *n* **1** : the act of admitting; *esp* : an admitting of something that has not been proved ⟨an *admission* of guilt⟩ **2** : the right or permission to enter ⟨standards of *admission* to a school⟩ **3** : the price of entrance

ad·mit \əd-ˈmit, ad-\ *vb* **ad·mit·ted; ad·mit·ting 1 a** : to allow room for : PERMIT ⟨a question that *admits* two answers⟩ **b** : to make known usually with some unwillingness ⟨*admitted* that he really didn't know⟩ ⟨*admit* a mistake⟩ **2** : to allow entry : let in ⟨*admit* a state to the Union⟩ **synonyms** see ACKNOWLEDGE

ad·mit·tance \əd-ˈmit-ən(t)s, ad-\ *n* : permission to enter : ENTRANCE

ad·mit·ted·ly \-əd-lē\ *adv* : acknowledged as true

ad·mix·ture \ad-ˈmiks-chər\ *n* **1 a** : the act of mixing **b** : the fact of being mixed **2 a** : something added by mixing **b** : a product of mixing

ad·mon·ish \ad-ˈmän-ish\ *vb* **1** : to criticize or warn gently but seriously : warn of a fault **2** : to give friendly advice or encouragement to ⟨*admonished* them to keep trying⟩ **synonyms** see REBUKE — **ad·mon·ish·ment** \-mənt\ *n*

ad·mo·ni·tion \ˌad-mə-ˈnish-ən\ *n* : a gentle or friendly criticism or warning

ad·mon·i·to·ry \ad-ˈmän-ə-ˌtōr-ē, -ˌtȯr-\ *adj* : expressing admonition : WARNING

ado \ə-ˈdü\ *n* : ¹FUSS 1, TROUBLE ⟨much *ado* about nothing⟩

ado·be \ə-ˈdō-bē\ *n* **1** : a brick or building material made of a sun-dried mixture of earth and straw **2** : a building made of adobe bricks [Spanish]

adobe 2

\ə\ abut	\aú\ out	\i\ tip	\ó\ saw	\ú\ foot
\ər\ further	\ch\ chin	\ī\ life	\ói\ coin	\y\ yet
\a\ mat	\e\ pet	\j\ job	\th\ thin	\yü\ few
\ā\ take	\ē\ easy	\ŋ\ sing	\th\ this	\yú\ cure
\ä\ cot, cart	\g\ go	\ō\ bone	\ü\ food	\zh\ vision

ad·o·les·cence \ˌad-ᵊl-'es-ᵊn(t)s\ *n* : the state or process of growing up; *also* : the period of life from puberty to maturity [Middle English *adolescence* "adolescence," from early French *adolescence* (same meaning), from Latin *adolescentia* (same meaning), from *adolescere* "to grow up" — related to ADULT] — **ad·o·les·cent** \-ᵊnt\ *adj or n*

adopt \ə-'däpt\ *vb* **1** : to take legally as one's own child ⟨*adopted* a baby girl⟩ **2** : to take as one's own ⟨*adopt* a point of view⟩ **3** : to accept formally ⟨the assembly *adopted* a constitution⟩ — **adopt·able** \ə-'däp-tə-bəl\ *adj* — **adopt·er** *n*

adop·tion \ə-'däp-shən\ *n* : the act of adopting : the state of being adopted

adop·tive \ə-'däp-tiv\ *adj* : made by or associated with adoption ⟨the *adoptive* parents⟩

ador·able \ə-'dòr-ə-bəl, -'dòr-\ *adj* **1** : deserving to be adored **2** : CHARMING, LOVELY ⟨an *adorable* child⟩ — **ador·able·ness** *n* — **ador·ably** \-blē\ *adv*

adore \ə-'dō(ə)r, -'dò(ə)r\ *vb* **adored; ador·ing 1** : ²WORSHIP 1 ⟨*adore* God⟩ **2** : to be very fond of [from early French *adourer* "to adore," from Latin *adorare* (same meaning), from *ad-* "to" and *orare* "to speak, pray" — related to ORACLE, ORATION] — **ad·o·ra·tion** \ˌad-ə-'rā-shən\ *n* — **ador·er** \ə-'dōr-ər, -'dòr-\ *n*

adorn \ə-'dòrn\ *vb* : to enhance the appearance of with ornaments

synonyms ADORN, DECORATE, EMBELLISH, BEAUTIFY mean to improve the appearance by adding something that is not essential. ADORN suggests that the thing added is beautiful in itself ⟨a gold star *adorned* the tree⟩. DECORATE suggests adding color or design to something that is plain or dull ⟨*decorated* her room with posters⟩. EMBELLISH stresses the adding of something not needed ⟨dishes *embellished* with a leaf design⟩. BEAUTIFY stresses the improvement of something plain or ugly ⟨flower boxes *beautify* the street⟩.

adorn·ment \ə-'dòrn-mənt\ *n* **1** : the action of adorning : the state of being adorned **2** : something that adorns

ADP \ˌā-ˌdē-'pē, ā-'dē-ˌpē\ *n* : a compound formed in living cells that reacts to form ATP

¹ad·re·nal \ə-'drē-nᵊl\ *adj* : of, relating to, or derived from the adrenal glands or their secretions

²adrenal *n* : ADRENAL GLAND

adrenal gland *n* : either of a pair of endocrine glands that are located near the kidney and produce the hormone epinephrine

adren·a·line \ə-'dren-ᵊl-ən\ *n* : EPINEPHRINE

adrift \ə-'drift\ *adv or adj* **1** : without power or anchor ⟨a ship *adrift* in the storm⟩ **2** : without guidance or purpose ⟨alone and *adrift* in the city⟩

adroit \ə-'dròit\ *adj* : having or showing great skill or cleverness ⟨an *adroit* leader⟩ ⟨the candidate's *adroit* use of television⟩ — **adroit·ly** *adv* — **adroit·ness** *n*

ad·sorb \ad-'sórb, -'zórb\ *vb* : to take up and hold or to become taken up by adsorption

ad·sorp·tion \-'sórp-shən, -'zòrp-\ *n* : the sticking of molecules (as of a gas or liquid) in a very thin layer to the surfaces of solid objects or liquids which the molecules come in contact with

ad·u·late \'aj-ə-ˌlāt\ *vb* **-lat·ed; -lat·ing** : to flatter or admire slavishly — **ad·u·la·tion** \ˌaj-ə-'lā-shən\ *n* — **ad·u·la·tor** \'aj-ə-ˌlāt-ər\ *n* — **ad·u·la·to·ry** \'aj-ə-lə-ˌtōr-ē, -ˌtòr-\ *adj*

¹adult \ə-'dəlt, 'ad-ˌəlt\ *adj* **1** : fully developed and mature **2** : of, relating to, or characteristic of adults [from Latin *adultus* "having grown up," from *adolescere* "to grow up" — related to ADOLESCENCE] — **adult·hood** \ə-'dəlt-ˌhùd\ *n* — **adult·ness** \ə-'dəlt-nəs, 'ad-ˌəlt-\ *n*

²adult *n* : a fully grown person, animal, or plant — **adult·like** \ə-'dəlt-ˌlīk\ *adj*

adul·ter·ant \ə-'dəl-tə-rənt\ *n* : something used to adulterate another thing

adul·ter·ate \ə-'dəl-tə-ˌrāt\ *vb* **-at·ed; -at·ing** : to make impure or weaker by adding an unnecessary or lower-grade substance; *esp* : to prepare for sale by using in whole or in part a substance that reduces value or strength [from Latin *adulterare* "to make impure," from *ad-* "to" and *alter* "other" — related to ALTER] — **adul·ter·a·tion** \ə-ˌdəl-tə-'rā-shən\ *n* — **adul·ter·a·tor** \ə-'dəl-tə-ˌrāt-ər\ *n*

adul·tery \ə-'dəl-t(ə-)rē\ *n, pl* **-ter·ies** : voluntary sexual intercourse between a married person and someone other than his or her spouse — **adul·ter·er** \-tər-ər\ *n* — **adul·ter·ess** \-t(ə-)rəs\ *n* — **adul·ter·ous** \-t(ə-)rəs\ *adj*

¹ad·vance \əd-'van(t)s\ *vb* **ad·vanced; ad·vanc·ing 1** : to move forward ⟨*advance* a few yards⟩ **2** : to help the progress of ⟨sacrifices that *advance* the cause of freedom⟩ **3** : to raise to a higher rank or position : PROMOTE ⟨was *advanced* from clerk to assistant manager⟩ **4** : to give and expect to be paid back ⟨*advance* a loan⟩ **5** : SUGGEST 1, PROPOSE ⟨*advance* a new plan⟩ — **ad·vanc·er** *n*

²advance *n* **1** : a forward movement **2** : progress in development : IMPROVEMENT ⟨recent *advances* in medicine⟩ **3** : a rise in price, value, or amount **4** : a first step or approach ⟨an unfriendly look discourages *advances*⟩ **5 a** : the giving of something in payment (as money) before goods or services are received ⟨I need an *advance* on my salary⟩ **b** : the money or goods given — **in advance** : ¹BEFORE, BEFOREHAND ⟨knew of the change two weeks *in advance*⟩ — **in advance of** : AHEAD OF

³advance *adj* **1** : made, sent, or furnished ahead of time ⟨an *advance* payment⟩ **2** : going or situated before ⟨an *advance* guard⟩ ⟨an *advance* scout⟩

ad·vanced \əd-'van(t)st\ *adj* **1** : far on in time or course ⟨a man *advanced* in years⟩ **2** : being beyond the elementary or introductory level ⟨*advanced* mathematics⟩ **3** : being far along in progress or development ⟨an *advanced* civilization⟩ ⟨a disease in an *advanced* stage⟩ **4** : having changed from a more primitive state found in an ancestor ⟨*advanced* insects like the wasps and bees⟩

ad·vance·ment \əd-'van(t)-smənt\ *n* **1** : the action of advancing : the state of being advanced **2** : a raising or being raised to a higher rank or position

ad·van·tage \əd-'vant-ij\ *n* **1** : the fact of being in a better position or condition ⟨gain the *advantage*⟩ **2** : ¹BENEFIT 1, GAIN **3** : something that helps the one it belongs to ⟨speed is an *advantage* in sports⟩ — **to advantage** : so as to give a favorable impression

ad·van·ta·geous \ˌad-ˌvan-'tā-jəs, -vən-\ *adj* : giving an advantage : HELPFUL, FAVORABLE — **ad·van·ta·geous·ly** *adv* — **ad·van·ta·geous·ness** *n*

ad·vent \'ad-ˌvent\ *n* **1** *cap* : the season beginning four Sundays before Christmas **2** : the first appearance : ARRIVAL ⟨the *advent* of spring⟩ [Middle English *advent* "Christmas season," from Latin *adventus* (same meaning), from earlier *adventus* "arrival"]

ad·ven·ti·tious \ˌad-(ˌ)ven-'tish-əs, -vən-\ *adj* **1** : coming from an outside source and not an essential part : ACCIDENTAL **2** : appearing in other than the usual or normal place ⟨*adventitious* roots⟩ — **ad·ven·ti·tious·ly** *adv* — **ad·ven·ti·tious·ness** *n*

¹ad·ven·ture \əd-'ven-chər\ *n* **1** : an action involving unknown risks or dangers **2** : the encountering of risks ⟨the spirit of *adventure*⟩ **3** : an unusual or exciting experience ⟨the field trip was an *adventure*⟩

²adventure *vb* **-ven·tured; -ven·tur·ing** \-'vench-(ə-)riŋ\ **1** : ²RISK 1, VENTURE **2** : to venture upon ⟨explorers *adventuring* the wilderness⟩

ad·ven·tur·er \əd-'vench-(ə-)rər\ *n* **1** : a person who looks for adventures **2** : a person who tries to become wealthy or powerful by trickery

ad·ven·ture·some \əd-'ven-chər-səm\ *adj* : ADVENTUROUS

ad·ven·tur·ous \əd-'vench-(ə-)rəs\ *adj* **1** : ready to take risks or to deal with the new and unknown ⟨*adventurous* explorers⟩ **2** : having unknown dangers and risks ⟨an *adventurous* voyage⟩ — **ad·ven·tur·ous·ly** *adv* — **ad·ven·tur·ous·ness** *n*

synonyms ADVENTUROUS, VENTURESOME, DARING mean exposing oneself to more danger than one has to. ADVENTUROUS suggests a willingness to accept risks but does not rule out showing good sense ⟨*adventurous* campers backpacking in the mountains⟩. VENTURESOME suggests a lively eagerness for dangerous undertakings ⟨*venturesome* deep-sea explorers⟩. DARING stresses lack of fear and even boldness in looking for danger ⟨racing-car drivers are often very *daring*⟩.

ad·verb \'ad-ˌvərb\ *n* : a word used to modify a verb, an adjective, another adverb, a preposition, a phrase, a clause, or a sentence and often used to show degree, manner, place, or time — **adverb** *adj* — **ad·ver·bi·al** \ad-'vər-bē-əl\ *adj or n* — **ad·ver·bi·al·ly** \-bē-ə-lē\ *adv*

¹**ad·ver·sary** \'ad-və(r)-ˌser-ē\ *n, pl* **-sar·ies** : someone or something that struggles with, opposes, or resists : ENEMY, OPPONENT

²**adversary** *adj* : involving two persons or two sides who oppose each other ⟨our *adversary* system of justice⟩

ad·verse \ad-'vərs, 'ad-ˌvərs\ *adj* **1** : acting in an opposite direction ⟨*adverse* winds⟩ **2** : opposed to one's interests ⟨*adverse* testimony⟩; *esp* : not friendly or favorable ⟨*adverse* criticism⟩ **3** : causing harm : HARMFUL ⟨*adverse* effects of a drug⟩ — **ad·verse·ly** *adv* — **ad·verse·ness** *n*

ad·ver·si·ty \ad-'vər-sət-ē\ *n, pl* **-ties** : an instance or condition of serious or continued misfortune

ad·vert \ad-'vərt\ *vb* : to make a reference : REFER ⟨*advert* to a previous remark⟩

ad·ver·tise \'ad-vər-ˌtīz\ *vb* **-tised; -tis·ing 1** : to announce publicly especially by a printed notice or a broadcast ⟨*advertise* a sale⟩ **2** : to call public attention to especially by pointing out desirable qualities so as to create a desire to buy or to do business with ⟨*advertise* a cereal⟩ ⟨*advertise* a store⟩ **3** : to give a public notice or advertisement ⟨*advertise* for a lost dog⟩ — **ad·ver·tis·er** *n*

ad·ver·tise·ment \ˌad-vər-'tīz-mənt, əd-'vərt-əz-\ *n* **1** : the act or process of advertising **2** : a public notice; *esp* : one published or broadcast

ad·ver·tis·ing \'ad-vər-ˌtī-ziŋ\ *n* **1** : the action of calling something to the attention of the public especially by paid announcements **2** : published or broadcast advertisements **3** : the business of preparing advertisements

ad·vice \əd-'vīs\ *n* : an opinion or suggestion offered about a decision or course of conduct : COUNSEL

ad·vis·able \əd-'vī-zə-bəl\ *adj* : reasonable or proper under the circumstances : WISE, PRUDENT — **ad·vis·abil·i·ty** \-ˌvī-zə-'bil-ət-ē\ *n* — **ad·vis·ably** \-'vī-zə-blē\ *adv*

ad·vise \əd-'vīz\ *vb* **ad·vised; ad·vis·ing 1 a** : to give advice to : COUNSEL ⟨*advised* them to save their money⟩ **b** : RECOMMEND 3 ⟨*advised* caution⟩ **2** : to give information or notice to : INFORM 1 ⟨were *advised* of bad flying conditions⟩ **3** : to talk over a problem or decision : CONSULT ⟨*advised* with her parents⟩ — **ad·vis·er** *or* **ad·vi·sor** \-'vī-zər\ *n*

ad·vised \əd-'vīzd\ *adj* : thought about : CONSIDERED ⟨an ill-*advised* plan⟩ — **ad·vis·ed·ly** \-'vī-zəd-lē\ *adv*

ad·vise·ment \əd-'vīz-mənt\ *n* : careful consideration ⟨take a matter under *advisement*⟩

ad·vi·so·ry \əd-'vīz-(ə-)rē\ *adj* **1** : having the power or right to advise ⟨an *advisory* committee⟩ **2** : giving or containing advice ⟨an *advisory* opinion⟩

ad·vo·ca·cy \'ad-və-kə-sē\ *n* : the act or process of advocating : SUPPORT

¹**ad·vo·cate** \'ad-və-kət, -ˌkāt\ *n* **1** : a person who argues for the cause of another especially in a court of law **2** : a person who argues for, recommends, or supports a cause or policy ⟨an *advocate* of civil rights⟩ [Middle English *advocat* "one that pleads a case for another (in court)," from early French *advocat* (same meaning), from Latin *advoca-*

tus (same meaning), derived from *advocare* "to call to one's aid, summon," from *ad-* "to, toward, near" and *vocare* "to call" — related to PROVOKE, REVOKE, VOCATION]

²**ad·vo·cate** \'ad-və-ˌkāt\ *vb* **-cat·ed; -cat·ing** : to speak in favor of : argue for

adze *also* **adz** \'adz\ *n* : a cutting tool that has a thin arched blade set at right angles to the handle and is used chiefly for shaping wood

ae·des \ā-'ēd-ēz\ *n, pl* **aëdes** : any of a genus of mosquitoes including carriers of disease (as yellow fever)

ae·gis \'ē-jəs\ *n* **1** : PROTECTION 1a, DEFENSE ⟨under the *aegis* of the law⟩ **2** : PATRONAGE 1, SPONSORSHIP ⟨under the *aegis* of the museum⟩

adze

aeolian *variant of* EOLIAN

ae·on *or* **eon** \'ē-ən, 'ē-ˌän\ *n.* **1** : a very long period of time : AGE **2 a** *usu* eon : a very large division of geologic time usually longer than an era **b** : a unit of geologic time equal to one billion years

aer- *or* **aero-** *combining form* **1** : air : atmosphere ⟨*aer*ate⟩ ⟨*aer*obic⟩ **2** : gas ⟨*aero*sol⟩ **3** : aviation ⟨*aero*nautics⟩ [from Greek *aer-, aero-* "air"]

aer·ate \'a(-ə)r-ˌāt, 'e(-ə)r-\ *vb* **aer·at·ed; aer·at·ing 1** : to expose to or supply or fill to the limit with air ⟨*aerate* the soil⟩ **2** : to supply (blood) with oxygen by respiration **3** : to combine or fill with gas — **aer·a·tion** \ˌa(-ə)r-'ā-shən, ˌe(-ə)r-\ *n* — **aer·a·tor** \'a(-ə)r-ˌāt-ər, 'e(-ə)r-\ *n*

¹**ae·ri·al** \'ar-ē-əl, 'er-\ *adj* **1 a** : of, relating to, or occurring in the air or atmosphere ⟨an *aerial* display on a trapeze⟩ **b** : living or growing in the air rather than on the ground or in water **c** : running on cables or rails that are raised above the ground ⟨an *aerial* railway⟩ **2 a** : of or relating to aircraft **b** : designed for use in, taken from, or operating from aircraft ⟨*aerial* photograph⟩ — **aer·i·al·ly** \-ē-ə-lē\ *adv*

²**aerial** *n* **1** : ANTENNA 2 **2** : FORWARD PASS

aerial root *n* : a root (as for clinging to a wall) that does not enter the soil

aer·ie \'a(ə)r-ē, 'e(ə)r-, 'i(ə)r-\ *n* **1** : the nest of a bird on a cliff or a mountaintop **2** : a dwelling placed high up

aer·o·bat·ics \ˌar-ə-'bat-iks, ˌer-\ *n sing or pl* : spectacular flying feats and maneuvers — **aer·o·bat·ic** \-ik\ *adj*

aer·o·bic \ˌa(-ə)r-'ō-bik, ˌe(-ə)r-\ *adj* **1** : living, active, or occurring only in the presence of oxygen **2** : of, relating to, or caused by aerobic organisms (as bacteria) — **aer·o·bi·cal·ly** \-bi-k(ə-)lē\ *adv*

aer·o·bics \ˌa(-ə)r-'ō-biks, ˌe(-ə)r-\ *n sing or pl* : a system of exercises intended to improve the body's ability to take in and use oxygen

aero·drome \'ar-ə-ˌdrōm, 'er-\ *n, British* : AIRPORT, AIRFIELD

aero·dy·nam·ics \ˌar-ō-dī-'nam-iks, ˌer-\ *n* : a science that deals with the motion of fluids (as air) that are gases and with the forces acting on bodies exposed to them — **aero·dy·nam·ic** \-ik\ *adj*

aero·naut \'ar-ə-ˌnȯt, 'er-, -nät\ *n* : a person who operates or travels in an airship or a balloon

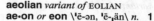

A aerial root

\ə\ abut	\au̇\ out	\i\ tip	\o̊\ saw	\u̇\ foot
\ər\ further	\ch\ chin	\ī\ life	\o̊i\ coin	\y\ yet
\a\ mat	\e\ pet	\j\ job	\th\ thin	\yü\ few
\ā\ take	\ē\ easy	\ŋ\ sing	\th\ this	\yu̇\ cure
\ä\ cot, cart	\g\ go	\ō\ bone	\ü\ food	\zh\ vision

aero·nau·tics \,ar-ə-'nòt-iks, ,er-\ *n* **1** : a science dealing with the operation of aircraft **2** : the art or science of flight — **aero·nau·ti·cal** \-'nòt-i-kəl\ *adj*

aero·plane \'ar-ə-,plān, 'er-\ *chiefly British variant of* AIRPLANE

aero·sol \'ar-ə-,säl, 'er-, -,sòl\ *n* : a mixture of fine solid or liquid particles and gas ⟨smoke and fog are *aerosols*⟩

¹aero·space \'ar-ō-,spās, 'er-\ *n* **1** : the earth's atmosphere and the space beyond **2** : a science dealing with aerospace

²aerospace *adj* : of or relating to aerospace, to the vehicles used in aerospace or their manufacture, or to travel in aerospace ⟨*aerospace* medicine⟩

aes·thet·ic *or* **es·thet·ic** \es-'thet-ik, is-\ *adj* : of or relating to beauty or what is beautiful — **aes·thet·i·cal·ly** \-i-k(ə)-lē\ *adv*

aes·thet·ics *also* **es·thet·ics** \es-'thet-iks, is-\ *n* : a branch of philosophy that studies and explains the principles and forms of beauty especially in art and literature

aestivate, aestivation *variant of* ESTIVATE, ESTIVATION

af- — see AD-

¹afar \ə-'fär\ *adv* : from, to, or at a great distance

²afar *n* : a great distance ⟨a voice from *afar*⟩

af·fa·ble \'af-ə-bəl\ *adj* : being at ease and pleasant especially in conversation ⟨an *affable* host⟩ **synonyms** *see* GRACIOUS — **af·fa·bil·i·ty** \,af-ə-'bil-ət-ē\ *n* — **af·fa·bly** \'af-ə-blē\ *adv*

af·fair \ə-'fa(ə)r, -'fe(ə)r\ *n* **1 a** *pl* : commercial, professional, public, or personal business ⟨government *affairs*⟩ ⟨arranged my *affairs* before leaving⟩ **b** : ²CONCERN 1, MATTER ⟨not your *affair* at all⟩ **2 a** : EVENT 1b, ACTIVITY ⟨a social *affair*⟩ **b** : PRODUCT 2, THING ⟨the house was a two-story *affair*⟩ **3** : a brief romantic relationship

¹af·fect \ə-'fekt, a-\ *vb* **1** : to show a liking for : FANCY ⟨*affect* flashy clothes⟩ **2** : FEIGN 1, PRETEND ⟨*affect* indifference⟩

²affect *vb* : to produce an effect upon: as **a** : to produce a significant influence upon or change in ⟨paralysis *affected* his limbs⟩ **b** : to act upon (as a person or a person's feelings) so as to cause a response ⟨the criticism *affected* her deeply⟩

af·fec·ta·tion \,af-,ek-'tā-shən\ *n* : an unnatural form of behavior usually intended to impress others ⟨the accent was an *affectation*⟩

af·fect·ed \ə-'fek-təd, a-\ *adj* : not natural or genuine — **af·fect·ed·ly** *adv* — **af·fect·ed·ness** *n*

af·fect·ing \ə-'fek-tiŋ, a-\ *adj* : causing a feeling of pity, sympathy, or sorrow — **af·fect·ing·ly** \-tiŋ-lē\ *adv*

¹af·fec·tion \ə-'fek-shən\ *n* : a quality or feeling of liking and caring for another

²affection *n* : DISEASE, DISORDER ⟨an *affection* of the brain⟩

af·fec·tion·ate \ə-'fek-sh(ə-)nət\ *adj* : feeling or showing a great liking for a person or thing : LOVING — **af·fec·tion·ate·ly** *adv*

af·fer·ent \'af-ə-rənt, 'af-,er-ənt\ *adj* : bearing or conducting inward; *esp* : conveying impulses toward the central nervous system — **af·fer·ent·ly** *adv*

af·fi·ance \ə-'fī-ən(t)s\ *vb* **-anced; -anc·ing** : to promise in marriage

af·fi·da·vit \,af-ə-'dā-vət\ *n* : a sworn statement in writing

¹af·fil·i·ate \ə-'fil-ē-,āt\ *vb* **-at·ed; -at·ing** : to connect closely often as a member, branch, or associate — **af·fil·i·a·tion** \-,fil-ē-'ā-shən\ *n*

²af·fil·i·ate \ə-'fil-ē-ət\ *n* : an affiliated person or organization

af·fin·i·ty \ə-'fin-ət-ē\ *n, pl* **-ties** **1** : relationship by marriage **2 a** : a feeling of closeness or sympathy because of shared interests **b** : ATTRACTION; *esp* : an attractive force between substances or particles that causes them to enter into and remain in chemical combination

af·firm \ə-'fərm\ *vb* : to state positively or with confidence

synonyms *see* ASSERT — **af·fir·ma·tion** \,af-ər-'mā-shən\ *n*

¹af·fir·ma·tive \ə-'fər-mət-iv\ *adj* **1** : declaring that the fact is so ⟨gave an *affirmative* answer⟩ **2** : being positive or helpful ⟨take an *affirmative* approach⟩ — **af·fir·ma·tive·ly** *adv*

²affirmative *n* **1** : an expression (as the word *yes*) of agreement **2** : the affirmative side in a debate or vote

affirmative action *n* : an active effort to improve the educational and employment opportunities of members of minority groups and women

¹af·fix \ə-'fiks, a-\ *vb* **1** : to attach physically : FASTEN ⟨*affix* a stamp to a letter⟩ **2** : to attach in any way : ADD ⟨*affix* a signature to a document⟩

²af·fix \'af-,iks\ *n* : a letter or a group of letters attached to the beginning or end of a word that serves to produce a derivative word or an inflectional form

af·flict \ə-'flikt\ *vb* : to cause suffering or unhappiness to

af·flic·tion \ə-'flik-shən\ *n* **1** : the state of being afflicted **2** : something that causes pain or unhappiness

af·flu·ence \'af-,lü-ən(t)s *also* a-'flü-, ə-'flü-\ *n* : the state of having much wealth or property

af·flu·ent \'af-,lü-ənt *also* a-'flü-, ə-'flü-\ *adj* : having plenty of money and the things money can buy [Middle English *affluent* "abundant," derived from Latin *ad-* "to" and *fluere* "to flow" — related to FLUID] — **af·flu·ent·ly** *adv*

af·ford \ə-'förd, -'fòrd\ *vb* **1** : to be able to do or to bear without serious harm ⟨you can't *afford* to waste your strength⟩ **2** : to be able to pay for ⟨unable to *afford* a new car⟩ **3** : to supply one with : PROVIDE, FURNISH ⟨tennis *affords* good exercise⟩ — **af·ford·able** \-'förd-ə-bəl, -'förd-\ *adj*

af·fray \ə-'frā\ *n* : a noisy quarrel or fight

af·fright \ə-'frīt\ *vb, archaic* : FRIGHTEN 1, ALARM

¹af·front \ə-'frənt\ *vb* : to insult openly : OFFEND

²affront *n* : a deliberately insulting or disrespectful act or utterance

Af·ghan \'af-,gan\ *n* **1** : a person born or living in Afghanistan **2** *not cap* : a blanket or shawl made of knitted or crocheted colored wool — **Afghan** *or* **Af·ghani** \af-'gan-ē, -'gän-\ *adj*

Afghan hound *n* : any of a breed of tall swift hunting dogs originating in Afghanistan with a coat of long silky hair and a long silky bunch of hair on the head

Afghan hound

afi·cio·na·do \ə-,fish-(ē-)ə-'näd-ō, -,fis-ē-\ *n, pl* **-dos** : a person who really likes and appreciates something ⟨an *aficionado* of Mexican food⟩ ⟨science fiction *aficionados*⟩ [Spanish, derived from Latin *affectio* "affection"]

afield \ə-'fēld\ *adv* **1** : to, in, or on the field **2** : away from home **3** : out of a regular, planned, or proper course : ASTRAY

afire \ə-'fī(ə)r\ *adj or adv* : being on fire

aflame \ə-'flām\ *adj or adv* : AFIRE

afloat \ə-'flōt\ *adj or adv* **1 a** : carried on or as if on the water **b** : being at sea **2** : circulating about : RUMORED ⟨there was a story *afloat*⟩

aflut·ter \ə-'flət-ər\ *adj* **1** : flapping quickly **2** : nervously excited

afoot \ə-'fùt\ *adv or adj* **1** : on foot ⟨travels *afoot*⟩ **2** : in the process of development : UNDER WAY ⟨a plan was *afoot* to seize power⟩

afore \ə-'fō(ə)r, -'fò(ə)r\ *adv or conj or prep, chiefly dialect* : BEFORE

afore·men·tioned \-,men-chənd\ *adj* : mentioned before

afore·said \-ˌsed\ *adj* : said or named before

afore·thought \-ˌthȯt\ *adj* : thought of or planned beforehand : PREMEDITATED ⟨with malice *aforethought*⟩

afoul of \ə-ˈfaú-ləv\ *prep* **1** : in or into collision or entanglement with ⟨one ship ran *afoul of* the other⟩ **2** : in or into conflict with ⟨they fell *afoul of* the law⟩

afraid \ə-ˈfrād, *Southern also* -ˈfre(ə)d\ *adj* **1** : filled with fear or dread ⟨*afraid* of snakes⟩ **2** : filled with concern or regret ⟨*afraid* she might be late⟩ **3** : having a dislike for something ⟨not *afraid* to work hard⟩ [Middle English *affraied* "filled with fear," from *affraien* "to frighten," from early French *affraier, effreer* "to frighten" — related to ¹FRAY]

afresh \ə-ˈfresh\ *adv* : from a new start : AGAIN

Af·ri·can \ˈaf-ri-kən\ *n* **1** : a person born or living in Africa **2** : a person of African ancestry — **African** *adj*

African–American *n* : an American having African and especially black African ancestors — **African–American** *adj*

African elephant *n* : ELEPHANT a

African sleeping sickness *n* : SLEEPING SICKNESS 1

African violet *n* : a tropical African plant widely grown as a houseplant for its velvety fleshy leaves and showy purple, pink, or white flowers

Af·ri·kaans \ˌaf-ri-ˈkän(t)s, -ˈkänz\ *n* : a language developed from 17th century Dutch and used in the Republic of South Africa

Af·ri·ka·ner \ˌaf-ri-ˈkän-ər\ *n* : a person born in South Africa whose native language is Afrikaans and whose ancestors were from Europe

Af·ro \ˈaf-rō\ *n* : a hairdo of tight curls in a full evenly rounded shape — **Af·roed** \-rōd\ *adj*

Af·ro–Amer·i·can \ˌaf-rō-ə-ˈmer-ə-kən\ *n* : AFRICAN-AMERICAN — **Afro–American** *adj*

Afro

aft \ˈaft\ *adv* : near, toward, or in the stern of a ship or the tail of an aircraft

¹af·ter \ˈaf-tər\ *adv* : following in time or place : LATER, BEHIND [Old English *æfter* "behind, later"]

²after *prep* **1 a** : behind in time or place ⟨following *after* us⟩ ⟨*after* dinner⟩ **b** : below in rank or order ⟨the highest mountain *after* Mount Everest⟩ **2** : for the reason of catching, seizing, or getting ⟨ran *after* the ball⟩ ⟨go *after* gold⟩ **3 a** : with the name of or a name derived from that of ⟨named *after* his father⟩ **b** : in imitation of ⟨patterned *after* a Gothic cathedral⟩

³after *conj* : later than the time when ⟨opened the door *after* she knocked⟩

⁴after *adj* **1** : later in time ⟨in *after* years⟩ **2** : located toward the stern of a ship or tail of an aircraft

after all *adv* : in spite of what was indicated or expected ⟨decided to go *after all*⟩ ⟨it rained *after all*⟩

af·ter·birth \ˈaf-tər-ˌbərth\ *n* : the placenta and membranes of the fetus that are expelled after childbirth

af·ter·burn·er \-ˌbər-nər\ *n* : a burner attached to the tail pipe of a turbojet engine for forcing fuel into the hot exhaust gases and burning it to provide extra forward push

af·ter·deck \-ˌdek\ *n* : the rear half of the deck of a ship

af·ter·ef·fect \-ə-ˌfekt\ *n* : an effect that arises after the first or immediate effect has decreased or disappeared ⟨a medicine with no noticeable *aftereffects*⟩

af·ter·glow \-ˌglō\ *n* **1** : a glow remaining (as in the sky after sunsets) where a light has disappeared **2** : a pleasant feeling that lingers after something is done, experienced, or achieved ⟨the *afterglow* of success⟩

af·ter·guard \-ˌgärd\ *n* : the sailors stationed on the poop or after part of a ship

af·ter·im·age \-ˌim-ij\ *n* : a usually visual sensation continuing after the stimulus causing it has ended

af·ter·life \-ˌlīf\ *n* **1** : an existence after death **2** : a later period in one's life

af·ter·math \ˈaf-tər-ˌmath\ *n* **1** : ²RESULT 1, CONSEQUENCE ⟨felt tired as an *aftermath* of the race⟩ **2** : the period immediately following a usually destructive event ⟨the *aftermath* of war⟩

  Word History The second part of *aftermath* comes from the Old English word *mæth,* meaning "the result of a mowing or harvesting," that is, a crop. This word was derived from the Old English verb *māwan,* which survives today as our modern English *mow.* During a good growing season in England, a second and sometimes a third crop of hay could be grown after the first mowing. When this crop was cut, it was the aftermath. Since the 17th century, the meaning of *aftermath* has broadened to include all kinds of results, not just those of a second mowing. [Old English *mæth* "mowing," from *māwan* "to mow"]

af·ter·noon \ˌaf-tər-ˈnün\ *n* : the part of day between noon and sunset — **afternoon** *adj*

af·ter–shave \ˈaf-tər-ˌshāv\ *n* : a lotion for use on the face after shaving

af·ter·taste \-ˌtāst\ *n* : a sensation (as of flavor) continuing after the stimulus causing it has ended

af·ter·thought \-ˌthȯt\ *n* **1** : a later thought about something one has done or said **2** : something not thought of originally

af·ter·ward \ˈaf-tə(r)-wərd\ *or* **af·ter·wards** \-wərdz\ *adv* : at a later time

ag- — see AD-

again \ə-ˈgen, -ˈgin, -ˈgān\ *adv* **1** : in return ⟨bring us word *again*⟩ **2** : another time : ANEW ⟨come see us *again*⟩ **3** : in addition ⟨half as much *again*⟩ **4** : on the other hand ⟨I may, and *again* I may not⟩ **5** : MOREOVER, FURTHER ⟨*again,* there is another matter to consider⟩ [Old English *ongēan* "opposite, back"]

against \ə-ˈgen(t)st, -ˈgin(t)st, -ˈgān(t)st\ *prep* **1 a** : opposed to ⟨a campaign *against* disease⟩ ⟨play *against* each other⟩ **b** : contrary to ⟨*against* the law⟩ **2** : ⁴OPPOSITE ⟨over *against* the park⟩ **3 a** : in preparation for ⟨storing food *against* the winter⟩ **b** : as a protection from ⟨a shield *against* aggression⟩ **4** : in or into contact with ⟨ran *against* a tree⟩ ⟨leaning *against* the wall⟩ **5** : in a direction opposite to ⟨*against* the wind⟩ **6** : before the background of ⟨green trees *against* the blue sky⟩

agape \ə-ˈgāp *also* ə-ˈgap\ *adj* : having the mouth open in wonder or surprise ⟨the crowd stood *agape* at the speaker⟩

agar \ˈäg-ər\ *also* **agar–agar** \ˈäg-ə-ˈräg-ər\ *n* **1** : a jelly-like substance obtained from a red alga and used especially in culture media or to give firmness to foods **2** : a culture medium containing agar

ag·ate \ˈag-ət\ *n* **1** : a smooth-looking quartz having its colors arranged in stripes or forms that look like clouds or moss **2** : a playing marble of agate or glass

aga·ve \ə-ˈgäv-ē\ *n* : any of a genus of plants (as the century plant) that have spiny-edged leaves and flowers in tall branched clusters and include some cultivated for fiber or for ornament

¹age \ˈāj\ *n* **1 a** : the time of life when a person attains some right or capacity ⟨the voting *age* is 18⟩; *esp* : MAJORITY 1 ⟨come of *age*⟩ **b** : the time from birth to a specified date ⟨a child six years of *age*⟩ **c** : normal lifetime **d** : the later part of life ⟨youth and *age*⟩ **2** : a period of time associated with a particular person or thing ⟨machine *age*⟩

\ə\ abut	\aú\ out	\i\ tip	\ȯ\ saw	\ú\ foot
\ər\ further	\ch\ chin	\ī\ life	\ȯi\ coin	\y\ yet
\a\ mat	\e\ pet	\j\ job	\th\ thin	\yü\ few
\ā\ take	\ē\ easy	\ŋ\ sing	\th\ this	\yú\ cure
\ä\ cot, cart	\g\ go	\ō\ bone	\ü\ food	\zh\ vision

⟨*Age* of Discovery⟩ **3** : a long period of time ⟨did it *ages* ago⟩ **synonyms** see PERIOD

²**age** *vb* **aged; ag·ing** *or* **age·ing 1** : to become or cause to become old or old in appearance ⟨his troubles *aged* him⟩ **2** : to become or cause to become mellow or mature : RIPEN ⟨letting cheese *age*⟩

-age \ij\ *n suffix* **1** : total amount : collection ⟨mile*age*⟩ **2 a** : action : process ⟨cover*age*⟩ **b** : result of ⟨break*age*⟩ **c** : rate of ⟨dos*age*⟩ **3** : house or place of ⟨orphan*age*⟩ **4** : state : status ⟨bond*age*⟩ **5** : fee : charge ⟨post*age*⟩ [Middle English *-age* "collection," from early French *-age* (same meaning), from Latin *-aticum,* suffix of mass and abstract nouns]

aged *adj* **1** \'ā-jəd\ : very old ⟨an *aged* oak⟩ **2** \'ājd\ : having reached a specified age ⟨a child *aged* ten⟩ — **ag·ed·ness** \'ā-jəd-nəs\ *n*

age·ism \'ā-(ˌ)jiz-əm\ *n* : prejudice or discrimination against people of a particular age and especially against the elderly — **age·ist** \-jist\ *adj*

age·less \'āj-ləs\ *adj* **1** : not growing old or showing the effects of age ⟨an *ageless* face⟩ **2** : ETERNAL 1, TIMELESS ⟨an *ageless* story⟩ — **age·less·ly** *adv* — **age·less·ness** *n*

agen·cy \'ā-jən-sē\ *n, pl* **-cies 1** : the office or function of an agent **2** : a person or thing through which power is used or something is achieved : MEANS **3** : an establishment doing business for another ⟨an insurance *agency*⟩ **4** : a part of a government that manages projects in a certain area ⟨a health *agency*⟩

agen·da \ə-'jen-də\ *n* : a list of items of business to be considered (as at a meeting)

agent \'ā-jənt\ *n* **1 a** : something that produces an effect ⟨a cleansing *agent*⟩ **b** : a chemically, physically, or biologically active substance **2** : a person who acts or does business for another ⟨government *agents*⟩ ⟨a real estate *agent*⟩ [Middle English *agent* "one that produces an effect," derived from Latin *agere* "to drive, act, do" — related to ACT, AGILE]

Age of Fishes : the Devonian period

Age of Mammals : the Cenozoic era

Age of Reptiles : the Mesozoic era

age–old \'a-'jōld\ *adj* : having existed for ages : ANCIENT ⟨an *age-old* story⟩

ag·er·a·tum \ˌaj-ə-'rāt-əm\ *n* : any of a large genus of tropical American herbs related to the daisies and often cultivated for their small showy heads of blue or white flowers

Ag·ge·us \a-'gē-əs\ *n* : HAGGAI

¹**ag·glom·er·ate** \ə-'gläm-ə-ˌrāt\ *vb* **-at·ed; -at·ing** : to gather into a ball, mass, or cluster

²**ag·glom·er·ate** \ə-'gläm-ə-rət\ *n* **1** : a jumbled mass or collection **2** : a rock composed of volcanic pieces of various sizes

ag·glom·er·a·tion \ə-ˌgläm-ə-'rā-shən\ *n* **1** : the action or process of collecting in a mass **2** : a heap or cluster of dissimilar elements — **ag·glom·er·a·tive** \ə-'gläm-ə-ˌrāt-iv\ *adj*

ag·glu·ti·nate \ə-'glüt-ᵊn-ˌāt\ *vb* **-nat·ed; -nat·ing 1** : to cause to stick : FASTEN **2** : to cause to clump or experience agglutination **3** : to unite into a group or gather into a mass

ag·glu·ti·na·tion \ə-ˌglüt-ᵊn-'ā-shən\ *n* **1** : the action or process of agglutinating **2** : a mass or group formed by the union of separate elements **3** : a reaction in which particles (as red blood cells or bacteria) suspended in a liquid collect into clumps usually as a response to a specific antibody — **ag·glu·ti·na·tive** \-'glüt-ᵊn-ˌāt-iv, -ət-\ *adj*

ag·glu·ti·nin \ə-'glüt-ᵊn-ən\ *n* : an antibody causing agglutination

ag·gran·dize \ə-'gran-ˌdīz *also* 'ag-rən-\ *vb* **-dized; -diz·ing** : to make great or greater (as in power, wealth, or reputation) — **ag·gran·dize·ment** \ə-'gran-dəz-mənt, -ˌdīz-*also* ˌag-rən-'dīz-mənt\ *n* — **ag·gran·diz·er** *n*

ag·gra·vate \'ag-rə-ˌvāt\ *vb* **-vat·ed; -vat·ing 1** : to make more serious or severe ⟨*aggravate* an injury⟩ **2** : to make angry by bothering again and again [from Latin *aggravare* "to make heavier," from *ad-* "to" and *gravare* "to burden," from *gravis* "heavy" — related to ³GRAVE, GRAVITY, GRIEVE]

ag·gra·va·tion \ˌag-rə-'vā-shən\ *n* **1** : the act or result of aggravating **2** : something that aggravates

¹**ag·gre·gate** \'ag-ri-gət\ *adj* **1** : formed by the collection of units or particles into one mass or sum ⟨*aggregate* expenses⟩ **2** : clustered in a dense mass or head ⟨an *aggregate* flower⟩ [Middle English *aggregat* "made up of a collection," derived from Latin *aggregare* "to cause to join together," from *ag-, ad-* "to, toward" and *greg-, grex* "flock, herd" — related to CONGREGATE, SEGREGATE]

²**ag·gre·gate** \'ag-ri-ˌgāt\ *vb* **-gat·ed; -gat·ing 1** : to collect or gather into a mass or whole **2** : to amount to as a whole : TOTAL

³**ag·gre·gate** \'ag-ri-gət\ *n* **1** : a collection or sum of units or parts **2 a** : a hard material (as sand or gravel) used especially in making concrete **b** : a clustered mass of individual soil particles considered the basic structural unit of soil

aggregate fruit *n* : a compound fruit (as a raspberry) made up of the several separate ripened ovaries of a single flower

ag·gre·ga·tion \ˌag-ri-'gā-shən\ *n* **1** : the collecting of units or parts into a mass or whole **2** : a group, body, or mass composed of many distinct parts

ag·gres·sion \ə-'gresh-ən\ *n* **1** : an attack made without reasonable cause **2** : the practice of making attacks **3** : hostile or destructive behavior or outlook [derived from Latin *aggredi* "to attack," from *ad-* "to" and *gradi* "to step, go"]

ag·gres·sive \ə-'gres-iv\ *adj* **1 a** : showing readiness to attack ⟨an *aggressive* dog⟩ **b** : practicing aggression ⟨an *aggressive* nation⟩ **2** : being forceful in getting things done ⟨an *aggressive* sales campaign⟩ **3** : growing, developing, or spreading rapidly ⟨*aggressive* weeds⟩ — **ag·gres·sive·ly** *adv* — **ag·gres·sive·ness** *n*

ag·gres·sor \ə-'gres-ər\ *n* : a person or country that attacks without reasonable cause

ag·grieved \ə-'grēvd\ *adj* **1** : troubled or distressed in spirit **2** : having a cause for complaint; *esp* : suffering from injury or loss

aghast \ə-'gast\ *adj* : struck with terror, amazement, or horror

ag·ile \'aj-əl, -ˌīl\ *adj* **1** : able to move quickly and easily : NIMBLE ⟨an *agile* gymnast⟩ **2** : mentally quick ⟨an *agile* thinker⟩ [Latin *agilis* "nimble, agile," from *agere* "to drive, act, do" — related to ACT, AGENT] — **ag·ile·ly** \-ə(l)-lē, -ˌī(l)-lē\ *adv* — **agil·i·ty** \ə-'jil-ət-ē\ *n*

aging *present participle of* AGE

ag·i·tate \'aj-ə-ˌtāt\ *vb* **-tat·ed; -tat·ing 1** : to move with an irregular, rapid, or violent action ⟨water *agitated* by wind⟩ **2** : to stir up : EXCITE, DISTURB ⟨*agitated* by bad news⟩ **3** : to try to stir up public feeling ⟨*agitate* for equal rights⟩ — **ag·i·tat·ed·ly** \-ˌtāt-əd-lē\ *adv* — **ag·i·ta·tion** \ˌaj-ə-'tā-shən\ *n*

ag·i·ta·tor \'aj-ə-ˌtāt-ər\ *n* **1** : a person who stirs up public feeling **2** : a device for stirring or shaking

aglit·ter \ə-'glit-ər\ *adj* : glittering by reflecting light

aglow \ə-'glō\ *adj* : glowing with warmth or excitement

ag·nos·tic \ag-'näs-tik, əg-\ *n* : a person who believes that whether God exists is not known and probably cannot be known [from Greek *agnōstos* "unknown," from *a-* "not" and *gnōstos* "known"] — **agnostic** *adj* — **ag·nos·ti·cism** \-'näs-tə-ˌsiz-əm\ *n*

ago \ə-'gō\ *adj or adv* : earlier than the present time ⟨many years *ago*⟩

agog \ə-'gäg\ *adj* : full of interest or excitement ⟨kids all *agog* over new toys⟩